LAW AND ECONOMICS
AND
THE ECONOMICS OF LEGAL REGULATION

INTERNATIONAL STUDIES IN ECONOMICS AND ECONOMETRICS

Volume 13

1. Harder T: Introduction to Mathematical Models in Market and Opinion Research With Practical Applications, Computing Procedures, and Estimates of Computing Requirements. Translated from the German by P.H. Friedlander and E.H. Friedlander. 1969.
2. Heesterman ARG: Forecasting Models for National Economic Planning. 1972.
3. Heesterman ARG: Allocation Models and their Use in Economic Planning. 1971.
4. Durdağ M: Some Problems of Development Financing. A Case Study of the Turkish First Five-Year Plan, 1963–1967. 1973.
5. Blin JM: Patterns and Configurations in Economic Science. A Study of Social Decision Processes. 1973.
6. Merkies AHQM: Selection of Models by Forecasting Intervals. Translated from the Dutch by M. van Holten-De Wolff. 1973.
7. Bos HC, Sanders M and Secchi C: Private Foreign Investment in Developing Countries. A Quantitative Study on the Evaluation of its Macro-Economic Impact. 1974.
8. Frisch R: Economic Planning Studies Selected and Introduced by Frank Long. Preface by Jan Tinbergen. 1976.
9. Gupta KL: Foreign Capital, Savings and Growth. An International Cross-section Study. 1983.
10 Bochove CA van: Imports and Economic Growth. 1982.
11. Bjerkholt O, Offerdal E (eds.): Macroeconomic Prospects for a Small Oil Exporting Country. 1985.
12. Weiserbs D (ed.): Industrial Investment in Europe: Economic Theory and Measurement. 1985.
13. Graf von der Schulenburg J-M, Skogh G (eds.): Law and Economics & The Economics of Legal Regulation. 1986.

Law and Economics and The Economics of Legal Regulation

edited by

J.-Matthias Graf von der Schulenburg
(Wissenschaftszentrum Berlin)

Göran Skogh
(University of Lund)

1986 **KLUWER ACADEMIC PUBLISHERS**
DORDRECHT / BOSTON / LANCASTER

Distributors

for the United States and Canada: Kluwer Academic Publishers, P.O. Box 358, Accord Station, Hingham, MA 02018-0358, USA
for the UK and Ireland: Kluwer Academic Publishers, MTP Press Limited, Falcon House, Queen Square, Lancaster LA1 1RN, UK
for all other countries: Kluwer Academic Publishers Group, Distribution Center, P.O. Box 322, 3300 AH Dordrecht, The Netherlands

Book-information

Selected papers of a Conference of the International Institute of Management Wissenschaftszentrum Berlin

Library of Congress Cataloging in Publication Data

Law and economics and the economics of legal regulation.

(International studies in economics and econometrics ; 13)
"Selected papers of a conference of the International Institute of Management Wissenschaftszentrum Berlin."
Includes index.
Contents: Law and economics and the economics of legal regulation / Göran Skogh -- Efficiency, equity, and inalienability / Susan Rose-Ackerman -- Negotiated settlement / Gordon Tullock -- [etc.]
1. Law--Congresses. 2. Economics--Congresses.
3. Industrial laws and legislation--Congresses.
I. Schulenburg, Johann-Matthias, Graf von der.
II. Skogh, Göran, 1943- . III. International Institute of Management. IV. Series: International studies in economics and econometrics ; v. 13.
K487.E3L385 1986 343'.07 86-16302

ISBN-13:978-94-010-8476-5 e-ISBN-13: 978-94-009-4442-8
DOI: 10.1007/978-94-009-4442-8

Copyright

CONTENTS

ACKNOWLEDGEMENT

On June 24–26, 1985 the International Institute of Management of the Wissenschaftszentrum Berlin organized a conference on "Law and Economics of Legal Regulation". This conference was held in connection with the Annual Meeting of the European Association of Law and Economics. At the conference forty papers were presented focusing on the principles of the economics of law, antitrust regulations, economic aspects of public decision processes, the theory of property rights, health economics, and regulations to protect the environment. Employing an anonymous referee-process, eleven papers were selected for publication in this volume.

The selection resulted from the idea of offering high-quality papers, presented at the conference, to a larger audience. The papers document the latest developments in the research on law and economics and will enhance further research in this field.

We would like to thank the participants and contributors and regret that we can not include more of the interesting papers presented at the conference. Special thanks are due to Meinolf Dierkes, President of the Wissenschaftszentrum Berlin, and Manfred Fleischer, International Institute of Management, for their support. We are also very grateful to those who have served as referees.

J.-Matthias v.d. Schulenburg
Berlin

Göran Skogh
Lund

LIST OF CONTRIBUTORS

Peter H. Aranson is Professor of Economics at Emory University. He received his PhD in Political Science from the University of Rochester (1972). His research encompasses related issues in the fields of Public Choice and Law and Economics. He serves as co-editor of Public Choice and formerly served as editor of the Supreme Court Economic Review. He is a member of the Editorial Board of the Journal of Politics. His publications include "American Government: Strategy and Choice", "Judicial Control of the Political Branches: Public Purposes and Public Law", The Cato Journal (Winter 1985), and "A Theory of Legislative Delegation", Cornell Law Review (November 1982) (with E. Gellhorn and G.O. Robinson).

John Ashworth is Lecturer in Economics, University of Durham, England since 1977.

Roger Van den Bergh is Doctor of Law at the University of Antwerp (1982). His doctoral research focused on "Buying Power and Price Discrimination". He is Professor of Business Law at the Antwerp Business School (Handelshogeschool) and Assistant Professor at the Law School of the University of Antwerp (U.I.A.). He has published several books and articles on Belgian and European Competition Law. His current research is in the area of the economics of Belgian law.

Hugh S.E. Gravelle is Reader in Economics at Queen Mary College, University of London. He has published papers on public enterprise, health economics, uncertainty and the economics of law. His current research interests include the pricing of court services, unemployment and suicide and the evaluation of breast cancer screening.

David H. Haddock is Associate Professor of Economics at Emory University, Atlanta, and a Research Professor at the Emory University Law and Economics Center. He is a specialist in both the economic analysis of law and industrial organization. Since receiving a PhD in 1980 from the University of Chicago, he has published articles examining delivered pricing systems, negligence standards in torts, securities regulation, punitive damages, and property rights. Before moving to Emory, he worked at UCLA and Ohio State University. During the 1984–85 academic year, he was a Research Fellow in Civil Liability at the Yale Law School, where much of the work on the paper included here was completed.

Michael Hutter is Assistant Professor of Economics at the University of Munich. He holds an M.A. degree from the University of Washington (Seattle) and received his doctorate from the University of Munich. He has published in the areas of law and economics, history of economic thought, competition theory, health economics and economics of the arts.

Susan M. Jaffer studied economics and accountancy at the University of Melbourne, and has worked as a chartered accountant. From 1983/5 she was Research Officer at the Institute for Fiscal Studies, London, where her research concerned issues in the economics of regulation. She is now an econometrician researcher in the London Office of National Economic Research Associates.

John A. Kay is Director at the Institute for Fiscal Studies, London, and a Fellow of St. John's College, Oxford. He taught economics at Oxford University before taking up his present appointment. He is joint author of the British Tax System, now in its fourth edition and of Concentration in Modern Industry and the reform of Social Security. He has published work on industrial economics and fiscal policy.

Jonathan R. Macey is Visiting Professor of Law at the University of Virginia Law School and Associate Professor of Law at Emory University School of Law where he is also Senior Academic Member of the Law and Economic Center. He received his A.B. in 1977 from Harvard University and his J.D. in 1982 from Yale Law School. He has published articles in the fields of corporate law, banking regulation, law and economics, and the economics of regulation.

Ivy Papps is Lecturer in the Economics of the Middle East, Department of Economics, University of Durham, England since 1975.

Susan Rose-Ackerman is Professor of Law and Political Economy at Columbia University and Director of Columbia Law School's Center for Law and Economic Studies. She is co-author of "The Uncertain Search for Environmental Policy" (1974), the author of "Corruption: A Study in Political Economy" (1978), and a writer of numerous articles in professional journals. Her current work involves the relationship between administrative law and social science.

J.-Matthias Graf v.d. Schulenburg is currently on leave from the University of Munich and Research Fellow at the International Institute of Management of the Wissenschaftszentrum Berlin. He holds a master's degree in economics from the University of Göttingen and received his doctorate from the University of Munich. In 1981–82 he was a Visiting Fellow at the Woodrow Wilson School of International and Public Affairs at Princeton University. His publications are in the fields of risk and insurance, health economics and international monetary theory.

Göran Skogh is Associate Professor at the University of Lund and President of the European Association of Law and Economics. His dissertation "Straffrätt och Samhällsekonomi" (Penal law and Economics), Lund Economic Studies, was published in 1973. He edited "Law and Economics: Report from a symposium in Sweden", Societatis Juridicae Lundensis, no 28, 1977. After that he has published work on the economics of crime, liability, regulation and insurance.

David J. Storey is Principal Research Associate at the Centre for Urban and Regional Development Studies, University of Newcastle upon Tyne, England.

Gordon Tullock graduated from the University of Chicago Law School in 1947. He then spent ten years in the Diplomatic Service, specializing on China. Since 1958 he has held various academic appointments. Currently he is Harris Distinguished University Professor at George Mason University. He is a past-president of the Southern Economic Society and of the Public Choice Society. He is author of numerous books and articles, and Editor of Public Choice.

PART ONE

INTRODUCTION

LAW AND ECONOMICS AND THE ECONOMICS OF LEGAL REGULATION

Göran Skogh

The application of economic theory to law has undergone rapid development. The *Law and Economics* literature currently covers most aspects of the legal system, e.g. *property, contract, tort, legal procedure, criminal law, public law* and *regulation.*[1] Most of the research has been American or British. However, the importance of the subject has become more widely recognized and today there is also a great interest in Law and Economics in continental Europe.[2]

The expansion of Law and Economics research into many different fields has led to a remarkable increase in the understanding of the way in which the law determines the use of scarce resources, and the way in which scarce resources influence the legal structure. However, the science is still in its infancy. After the seminal work of Ronald Coase (1960), Guido Calabresi (1961), Garry Becker (1968), James Buchanan (1974), Richard Posner (1977) and others, research has now turned into a phase of clarification and empirical testing. This volume contains eleven such contributions.

The selection is from a set of papers presented at the conference on "Law and Economics and the Economics of Legal Regulation" arranged by the International Institute of Management, Wissenschasftszentrum Berlin, 24–26 June 1984. The conference was attended by 80 participants and 40 papers were presented. This is an indication of the interest in Law and Economics and in the ongoing research. Some chapters extend the field of research, while others survey the theories, point out shortcomings and suggest improvements. Several tests established theories with the aid of quantitative or qualitative data.

The book is divided into three parts. Section I contains the introduction. Section II contains Chapters 2 to 6, which are devoted to the general economic analysis of law. Section III contains Chapters 7 to 11, which cover applications of the Economics of Regulation.

The first contribution by Susan Rose-Ackerman is entitled "Efficiency, Equity and Inalienability". She argues that the theory of property rights, that emphasizes the importance of a clear, well-defined set of tradeable rights, has not generally gone on to raise the more subtle and complex question of whether entitlements should be limited by inalienability rules that restrict transferability, ownership or use. Property is, however, a "bundle of rights" that might be extended or restricted by law. For instance, property owners have to accept certain forms of trespass, and some uses of the property may be excluded e.g. by community zoning. Some property may be freely used, but not allowed to sell etc. Susan Rose-Ackerman develops a classification of entitlements designed to illuminate the wide range of property relationships found in the modern welfare state — from prohibitions on the sale of parts of the body to historical preservation statutes, mineral leases and restrictions on the sale of endangered species. The analysis examines possible normative rationales for these restrictions. Economically-based rationales related to problems of externality control, imperfect information, "prisoner's dilemmas" and administrative costs are emphasized. The paper moves beyond these concerns, however, to show how some restrictions on property rights can serve redistributive goals while other restrictions may impose unfair costs.

The subsequent two chapters analyse economic models of common law procedure and out of court settlements. Legal disputes are frequently settled by negotiations between the parties rather than by a trial. According to the theory developed by Rubin (1977) and others, the parties will normally not go to court except when their expectations about the probable outcome differs. If expectations are the same, it always pays to settle. Costly court procedures are thereby avoided. In Chapter 3, Gordon Tullock analyses the negotiation procedure as part of an elaborate bargaining game in which the threat is a part. Contrary to earlier studies he argues that the extremely costly nature of American litigation procedures provides an extensive bargaining range. It is sensible to invest resources in attempting to obtain as much of the bargaining range as possible yourself. The investment of such resources in the United States makes the negotiated settlements nearly as expensive as actual trials. Hence, reforms that lower the high costs of legal proceedings in the United States are desirable.

Recent studies of the common law process have sought to explain its tendency to adopt allocatively efficient, or inefficient, rules to govern decisions in cases involving property, contract and tort law. In Chapter 4, Peter Aranson surveys this literature. He finds a surprising variety and abundance of models, using related but sometimes contradictory assumptions, resulting in few general propositions about common law efficiency. The essay reviews three general critisisms of these models: The absence of general findings, which derives from the model variety itself; the problem of decentralized information and preference revelation; and the difficulties that common law courts face in setting efficiency-seeking boundaries between their own domain and that of legislation.

In Chapter 5, Hugh Gravelle models default risks and the optimal pricing of court enforcement services. All contracts in which the performance of the contacting parties is sequential embody default risk. Using the example of debt contracts, the chapter models the implications of court supplied remedies which enable the creditor to partially recover the loan from the defaulting debtor. Default risk is endogenous and the debtor-creditor contract may be inefficient if the creditor cannot monitor the actions of the debtor and is unable to commit to a particular extent to which changes in the price at which court enforcement services are sold to the creditor can alleviate the inefficiencies resulting from the debtor's moral hazard. In general, the price will diverge positively or negatively from marginal cost depending on (a) whether the consistent (creditable) choice of enforcement is too large or too small compared with the case in which commitment is possible and (b) the effect of post default enforcement on the debtor's price default behaviour. It is also shown that, by contrast with the usual public firm results, direct controls on the quantity, as well as the price, of the publicly supplied service (enforcement) can raise welfare.

In Chapter 6, Michael Hutter presents a theory of institutional change based on the assumption that transaction costs represent costs of communication. Two propositions about the production of institutional changes which are valuable to economic actions are developed; one of them predicts the emergence of specialized "conversation circles" to process information needed for specific projects. The other one predicts that production occcurs by establishing a type of relationship between the the economy and its dialogue system which can be characterized as "therapeutic interaction". The validity of the propositions is demonstrated by a number of historical changes in the pharmaceutical patent law of the Federal Republic of Germany, the U.S. and the Republic of Italy. The chain of action leading to a particular case of legal change — the U.S. Supreme Court decision on the patentability of micro-organisms (DiamonD v. Chakrabarty) — is discussed in detail.

The second part of the book deals with the "Economics of Regulation". This approach diverges essentially from economic text-books where regulation is explained as a result of "market-failures". According to the market-failure theory, Government corrects for e.g. monopolies or externalities to make the economy more efficient, and to redistribute income in accordance with social-welfare goals. In opposition to this "public interest" theory, writers like George Stigler (1971), Richard Posner (1974) and Sam Peltzman (1976) have argued that regulation is a result of the demand for regulation by rent-seeking groups that invest resources to obtain protection of their business from public authorities. Politicians and the administration "supply" regulation for votes, taxes or other forms of payment. The theory suggest that small single-issue oriented groups will be the most effective in gaining transfers at the expense of the counter-parties or the general public.

The first study in the Economics of Regulation section, Chapter 7, is written by J.-Matthias Graf von der Schulenburg and concerns regulatory measures to enforce high quality production of self-employed professionals. The market for services of self-employed professionals, such as doctors, dentists and lawyers, is characterized by a high degree of consumer uncertainty as to the service quality. Governmental regulations, such as quality standards, barriers to entry for new suppliers and regulations of the professional education, are imposed on those markets to ensure high quality. In addition, the prices of the services are often regulated by fee-schedules. After a short review of the economic literature on markets, where consumers are uncertain about the product quality, a model of a dynamic market process is developed to analyse the quality control mechanisms in markets for services of self-employed professions. The model takes into consideration the specific characteristics of markets of self-employed professionals where new (young) suppliers enter the market and other suppliers retire and leave the market. The model focuses on the quality decision of new supplier entering the market with a given market structure. The most interesting result derived from the model is that the higher the relative number of low quality suppliers, the higher is the probability that a new supplier will decide for low quality as well. Therefore, a high quality policy should try to keep the percentage of high quality producers above a critical level so that a new supplier who enters the market also opts for high quality. It is argued that price regulations for self-employed professionals are a sufficient means of ensuring high quality production, and that entry barriers hinder and increase the costs of a quality enforcing policy.

The essay "Controlling insider trading in Europe and America: The Economics of the Politics" by David Haddock and Jonathan Macey follows in Chapter 8. The United States has some of the world's toughest restrictions on "insider trading", which is trading in a firm's shares by employees (and others closely related to the firm) when they know something about the firm's future prospects that the rest of the population does not know. The effectiveness of the US restrictions is limited by the ability of some insiders to use foreign intermedaries to mask their activities. The US has pressed European governments to modify their own laws in ways that would facilitate the enforcement of U.S. restrictions.

The writers argue that not all non-insider stockholders are the beneficiaries of the ban on insider trading. The stockholders best able to capitalize on new information, given the ban of insider trading, are "market professionals", in other words brokers, specialists, analysts and others who work on or closely with the stock exchanges. Recent legal rulings have reduced the risk to the professionals. Permitting market professionals to trade on information that is not generally known, while forbidding insiders to do so increases shareholders' salary obligations to the insiders with no offsetting benefit to them.

In Chapter 9 a study on 'The Regulation of Shop Opening Hours in the United Kingdom" is presented. In common with Britain, most European countries restrict the hours during which shops may open. In Britain these restrictions relate to evening and Sunday trading. The chapter describes the social and economic pressures which led to the introduction of these rules and more recent moves to reform them. It analyses the likely effect of deregulation on costs and prices, using an extensive data base of cost structures in UK retailing and survey data on the demand for extended opening. It is concluded that the likely long term effect of deregulation would be a reduction in both costs and prices.

Belgian policy towards the retailing trade is studied in Chapter 10. The legal rules with respect to the retailing trade offer a rich source of empirical material for testing hypotheses derived from the economic theory of regulation. The chapter supports the view that economic regulation is a product supplied to interest groups, rather than an expression of the "public interest". One example is licensing requirements that protect the income of established retailers. Public interest arguments, advanced in favour of these regulations (such as quality improvement and consumer information) cannot justify the existing legal situation. In addition to entry barriers created through licensing and other protective regulations (prohibition of sales at loss prices and comparative advertising) can be explained by cartelization agreements.

Chapter 11 examines an EEC Directive controlling discharges of mercury to the aquatic environment and analyses the efficiency of the environmental policy-making process of the Community. The conclusion from data derived from the UK Chlor-alkali industry is that the commission failed to obtain correct information about the determinants of discharges and, perhaps as a result, produced a Directive which was inefficient in the sense that marginal abatement costs differ across plants, and ineffective in that it has had very little impact on total discharges of mercury from the UK industry to British waterways.

NOTES

1. For a survey of the "New Law and Economics", see Veljanovski (1982). An introductory text-book is "Readings in the Economics of Law and Regulation" by A. Ogus and C. Veljanovski (1984). The most classic in the field is "Economic Analysis of Law" by R. Posner (1977).
2. The European Association for Law and Economics (EALE) was founded in 1984 in Lund, Sweden. The EALE organises meetings and distributes information to researchers working in the field. Persons interested in information from the organisation are welcome to write to EALE, The Department of Economics, University of Lund, Box 5137, S-220 05 Lund, Sweden.

REFERENCES

Becker, G., "Crime and Punishment. An Economic Approach". *The Journal of Political Economy*, 76, 1968, 169–217.

Buchanan, J., *The Limit of Liberty. Between Anarchy and Leviathan.* The University of Chicago Press, 1975

Calabresi, G. "Some Thoughts on Risk Distribution and the Law of Torts". *Yale Law Journal*, 70, 1961, 499–553.

Coase, R., "The Problem of Social Costs", *The Journal of Law and Economics*, 3, 1960, 1–44.

Ogus, A. and Veljanovski, C. *Readings in the Economics of Law and Regulation*, Clarendon Press, Oxford, 1984.

Peltzman, S., "Towards a More General Theory of Regulation", *The Journal of Law and Economics*, 19, 1976, 211–240.

Posner, R., *Economic Analysis of Law*, 2nd edition, 1977.

Posner, R., "Theories of Econmic Regulation", *Bell Journal of Economics*, 5, 1974, 335–358.

Rubin, P.H., "Why is the Common Law Efficient?", *Journal of Legal Studies*, 6, 1977, 51–64.

Stigler, G., "The Theory of Economic Regulation", *Bell Journal of Economics*, 2, 1971, 3–21.

Veljanovski, C., *The New Law and Economics. A Research Review.* Center for Socio-Legal Studies, Oxford, 1982.

PART TWO

LAW AND ECONOMICS

EFFICIENCY, EQUITY AND INALIENABILITY

Susan Rose-Ackerman

1. INTRODUCTION

Property to the lawyer is a "bundle of rights". Yet in writing on the law and economics of property rights only a few of the many possible "bundles" have been analyzed with any thoroughness. Recent work on the economics of property rights emphasizes the importance of a clear, well-defined set of rights to facilitate trading and accountability.[1] This research emphasizes the importance of assigning rights to valuable resources to particular owners, but it has not generally gone on to raise more subtle and complex questions about whether entitlements should ever be limited by inalienability rules which restrict the entitlement's transferability, ownership and use.

The most important steps in the direction of a richer theory of property rights came from Guido Calabresi and Douglas Melamed on the one hand, and Charles Reich (1964, 1965) on the other. Calabresi and Melamed emphasize the distinction between property rules and liability rules. Under a property rule, property can be sold, donated, or discarded, but only if the owner is willing to give up the entitlement and the recipient is willing to accept it. Under a liability rule, others may take your entitlement by, for example, destroying it in an accident, but they must then compensate you at a rate determined by a governmental body. Because Calabresi and Melamed's treatment of inalienability is colored by this emphasis on quid pro quo transfers, they discuss only one kind of inalienability – where ownership is legal but sales are not permitted – and they fail to discuss the economic rationales for even this form of restriction.

Reich's work is notable for its attempt to expand the concept of property to cover government benefits amd subsidies. Reich used the language of "property rights" in order to establish the validity of certain claims under the U.S. Constitution but he did not analyze the peculiarities of this "new property". Instead he wished to demonstrate the similarities between subsidies and other more conventional forms of property rather than emphasize the differences. Nevertheless, by labeling food stamps and rental apartments in public housing as "entitlements", he helped lay the groundwork for a broader conception of property rights which could include legal relationships governing things as diverse as kidneys, wild game, mineral leases and babies.

This paper builds on the pioneering work of Calabresi and Melamed and Reich by developing efficiency and equity rationales for restrictions on the transferability, ownership and use of property. I demonstrate that inalienability rules can be second-best responses to various kinds of market failures and point out both how some restrictions on property rights serve redistributive goals and how other restrictions may impose unfair costs.

The efficiency rationales for inalienability rules are second-best responses to market failures that arise because of externalities, imperfections in information, or difficulties of coordination. The straightforward reponses of internalizing the externality through fees or taxes, of subsidizing the provision of information, and of facilitating joint action may, for one reason or another, be costly. In such cases, the alternative of restricting market trades becomes a realistic possibility. Instead of correcting the market failure through policies that rely on price incentives and market processes, inalienability rules address the difficulty with a set of prohibited or required actions that make market incentives less, rather than more, important. I consider each of the three types of market failure in turn.

Externalities figure prominently in discussions of market failure and provide the most commonly recognized rationale for inalienability rules. Production and consumption externalities occur when the profits of firms or the satisfaction levels of individuals are affected by transactions in which they are not directly involved. These third parties would be willing to pay to obtain the benefits or to avoid the harms imposed on them, but because they are not part of the transaction, benefits are too low and costs are too high. For example, in the absence of regulation, a factory may create water pollution as part of its production process because it need not account for the harm caused by pollution. Economists generally seek to control externalities by creating market-like incentives through tax and subsidy schemes that encourage firms and individuals to respond to marginal shifts in costs and benefits.[2] Economic analysts have also recognized that other alternatives that involve the definition or rearrangement of property rights may be equally satisfactory. Thus, externality problems may be solved by "internalizing" them or by providing "separate facilities" solutions. Under the former, a single individual is given title to both the property causing the externality and the property affected by it. So long as this does not create monopoly power, the new owner will have an incentive to behave efficiently.[3] Under the latter, property relations are rearranged so that externality producers are separated from those who would suffer from the externality.[4]

Unfortunately, optimality may be difficult to achieve in a world with high transaction costs. Even a tort law system that places liability on the person who can most efficiently reduce the harm[5] may not be effective in all situations, and taxes and subsidies may be difficult to implement because of political opposition or inadequate information.[6] In the second-best world faced by regulators, there will be room for direct regulation of behavior.

Markets also frequently work poorly because information is imperfect and asymmetrical. This kind of market failure provides a second, and less widely recognized, rationale for inalienability rules in particular contexts. First, consider information asymmetries. If buyers are unaware of product defects, then high quality sellers cannot command higher prices than low quality sellers, and there may be a general deterioration in quality. A second information problem arises when two products look alike but one can be legally possessed while the other cannot. Buyers can then expect suppliers fraudulently to claim that their illegal products actually fall into the legal category.

Finally, difficulties of coordination may cause resources to be allocated inefficiently. This problem is closely related to the more pervasive problem of externalities, but because it has several distinctive features, I consider it as a separate category. The coordination problem arises most clearly in the case of pure public goods – urban parkland, for example – consumed in common by a large group. No one has an incentive to provide the efficient amount of this good because the supplier bears all the costs and receives only a fraction of the benefits. Closely analogous to this case is the "prisoner's dilemma": all would benefit from coordinated action, but in the absence of coercion, independent action is inefficient.

More narrowly focused coordination problems arise in controlling the opportunistic behavior of a person who purports to act on behalf of another. An inalienability rule may mitigate these problems when the law that directly controls the parties' relationship is inadequate.

The imposition of restrictions on alienability will, of course, generally have distributive as well as efficiency consequences. While analysts primarily concerned with efficiency may view a policy's redistributive impact as an unwelcome side effect, sometimes the distributive effects of a rule will be its primary justification. Because restrictions on transferability, ownership, and use single out a particular type of good or service for special treatment, these restrictions usually cannot be justified on broad redistributive grounds. Rather, the distributive case for inalienability is more narrowly focused. If policymakers wish to benefit a particular sort of person but cannot easily identify these people ex ante, they may be able to impose restrictions on the entitlement that are less onerous for the worthy group than for others who are nominally eligible.

Restraints on alienation also may have redistributive effects incidental to the primary justification for the policy. Restrictions justified on efficiency grounds frequently impose costs on a small concentrated group. Therefore, policymakers must decide whether to compensate these losers. In some cases, the appropriate response to redistributive effects will be straightforward. Where policymakers believe that the affected group deserves to bear the costs of the policy, there should be no compensation. The group might, for example, be composed of people earning monopoly profits. Although economic discussions of monopoly power commonly stress the inefficiencies of markets with a single seller, a basic distributive principle generally seems to lurk behind these analyses. The principle is this: except as a reward for risk-taking, no one is entitled to profits that exceed the competitive rate of return because of market imperfections. Economic rents or earnings above this level can be confiscated by the state for redistribution to others.[7] Compensation is also not justified if the owners accepted the risk of the restriction at the time of purchase. This expectation will have been reflected in the original purchase price, and it would be redundant to compensate the owners further.[8] Conversely, compensation will be appropriate where there is no principled reason for the group to bear the costs of the policy and where doing so would not undermine the effectiveness of the restriction.

Fundamental policy conflicts arise, however, when a group does not deserve to bear the costs of the restraint but where compensation would undermine the purpose of the restriction. For example, compensating blood donors for the fact that they cannot sell their blood would convert the process into something similar to a market trade and would undermine the use of a policy of obtaining blood only from voluntary, unpaid donors to assure high quality blood supplies. If the distributive costs are believed to be high in such situations, policymakers should consider alternatives to inalienability rules.

These issues are first addressed in Section 2 in the context of rules that restrict the transferability of entitlements. Then in Section 3 I examine rules that limit ownership and use and go on in Section 4 to consider restrictions that may require certain actions as a condition for retaining a property right. Throughout the analysis I point first to market failures that may jusitfy the use of inalienability rules and then discuss the most important distributive consequences.

2. RESTRICTIONS ON TRANSFERABILITY

2.1. Modified inalienability rules

Under what I shall call a modified inalienability rule sales of a good are prohibited but gifts are permitted. Modified inalienability provides a useful starting point because of the range of possible rationales for permitting gifts while outlawing sales. The most important efficiency justifications are: (1) conservation and supply management; (2) the regulation of close substitutes; and (3) the assurance of high quality output. I argue that each of the efficiency claims has merit in a restrictive range of circumstances but that using modified inalienability to achieve distributive goals is unjustified except to prevent monopoly gains.

2.1.1. Conservation and supply management

The law may sometimes prohibit payment of suppliers because of the very responsiveness of supply to price that is the hallmark of a properly functioning market. The problem is an inefficiency caused by the market itself. If market trades are permitted, supply will be larger than under a modified inalienability rule. Suppose, however, that high levels of supply impose external costs on society, which are not reflected in market price. Outlawing sales is then a possible way to improve the allocation of resources. Two examples will illustrate this point: population control and the conservation of wild animals and primitive cultures.

Those concerned with the social costs of overpopulation may wish to restrict the freedom of individuals to decide how many children to bring into the world. They may not only support family planning, subsidized abortions, and birth control but also oppose a legalized market in adoptions. They may want to prohibit the sale of babies for fear that women will produce children for profit, thus exacerbating the problem of overpopulation. As Robert Pritchard notes, however, the prohibition has resulted in shortages of newborn children available for adoption, thereby "leaving many couples deprived of the privileges and joys of child rearing".[9] Thus he raises the issue of concentrated costs to justify using the market even in this context. The difficulty with this argument is that even with a legal adoption market some people will be unable to adopt children because the price will be too high. All adoption policies have distributive consequences for both parents and children. It is not at all obvious, for example, that children themselves would generally be worse off if the sale of newborn infants were permitted. So long as an adoption market is not ruled out ex ante on moral grounds, the issues are largely empirical: How responsive is supply to price? What would be the impact on children and on prospective parents? How would the costs and benefits be distributed?

Consider next the conservation of wild animals. Conservation objectives may be furthered by preventing the commercial exploitation of endangered species through laws that permit the use of the resource for fun (or survival), but not for profit. The best American example is the regulation of wild fish and game resources. It would not violate public policy with respect to fish and game if a hunter, while on a vacation trip, happened to be lucky, shot more pheasants than he could use, and sold a few to friends. If sales were permitted, however, other people might decide to take up hunting because of the profitable opportunities available. Thus, a number of states have rules against sales.[10] These laws facilitate conservation by discouraging the entry of profit seeking hunters or fisherman.

A similar problem arises when the state wishes to preserve a group's way of life. Once again, a modified inalienability rule can help accomplish this aim. Recent U.S. laws and treaties preserve the right of Eskimos and other Alaskan natives to hunt certain kinds of game in spite of more stringent controls on the general public.[11] These native groups are, however, sometimes prohibited from selling their catch.[12] Without such a prohibition, outsiders and profit-motivated tribal leaders might invest in the tribe's activities and in the process both destroy tribal life and undermine the conservationist aims of the general prohibitions.

2.1.2. Regulating close substitutes

Sometimes a free market has no adverse effects on the production and distribution of a good but instead complicates some other public policy. For example, if it is difficult for buyers and law enforcement officials to distinguish between a forbidden good and a close substitute, preventing sale of the substitute can aid enforcement of a law against possession or transfer of the forbidden good, To illustrate, consider the use of modified inalienability rules in the Endangered Species Act and the Migratory Bird Treaties. Since there is apparently no reliable way to date stuffed animals, fur, feathers,[13] and most other animal products, enforcement is simplified if the law prohibits all sales of a species, not just the sale of animals killed after the law's effective date.[14]

When a modified inalienability rule makes the administration of a law inexpensive and convenient, there is a strong argument for compensating those who find that their possessions have unexpectedly fallen in value. Otherwise the state would not need to take into account the full costs of its policy, and a group that is unlucky enough to own a close substitute for the regulated product bears a disproportionate share of the cost. The case of Andrus v. Allard[15] provides an example. The statutes at issue prohibited the killing of eagles after a certain date. To ease the administration of the statutes, the Secretary of the Interior issued regulations prohibiting the sale of eagles killed before that date. The effect of the prohibition was to reduce the value of Indian artifacts made of "old" eagles by changing the owners' legal entitlement from a pure property rule to a modified inalienability rule. The owners challenged the statutes on the grounds that they constituted an unconstitutional "taking" of property requiring payment of compensation.[16]

The Supreme Court accepted the administrative convenience rationale behind the Interior Department regulations and rejected the owners' compensation claims on the ground that no "taking" had occurred. The government had not "physical[ly] inva[ded]" the owners' property, and had prevented only "one means of disposing of the artifacts".[17] The Court, however, never directly faced the important issue of whether the payment of compensation would undermine the reasons for promulgating the rule in the first place. In particular, in setting up a compensation scheme, the Interior Department would have faced the problem of distinguishing between legitimate holders of "old" eagle feathers and those making dishonest claims. In fact, however, a number of alternatives were open to the Interior Department that would have provided some form of compensation without undermining the legislative purpose. Before the protective law took effect, for example, holders of eagles and eagle feathers could have been required to obtain licenses certifying the legality of their holdings. Sales would then have been legal only if owners had licenses. Alternatively, the government might have stood ready to purchase all specimens presented to it by a certain date, or licenses holders could have retained possession but been paid compensation.

2.1.3. Quality control

In an influential book on human blood, Richard Titmuss (1971) argues for modified inalienability on quality control grounds. The argument, developed further by Kenneth Arrow (1972), views modified inalienability as a response to the general problems created by markets with imperfect information. If it is difficult for hospitals to judge whether blood contains the damaging hepatitis virus, while individuals know their own health history, then ideally one would design a collection system that gives contributors an incentive to reveal any past cases of hepatitis.[18] On the one hand, if people are paid for their blood, they may try to hide damaging information. On the other hand, if they are induced to donate their blood for altruistic reasons, those who have had hepatitis presumably will not make contributions. Of course, there may well be other systems of property rights – such as sale followed by liability for damages,[19] labelling by source,[20] or more careful selection of donors[21] – that respond to the quality control problem. But a purely voluntary system is, at the very least, a method worthy of serious consideration.[22]

The argument for modified inalienability, however, is not without weaknesses. First of all, the quality control benefits of gift giving operate only on the supply side of the market. Thus, once the blood has been collected, there is no quality control argument against selling the blood to patients.[23] One cannot contend that paying customers are generally less likely to make effective use of blood transfusions than are other users. Such a dual system may not be feasible, however. Quite simply, gifts may not be forthcoming if donors know that the collection agency is selling their gifts[24] and do not consider the collection agency to be a worthwhile charity.[25] Second, even if the blood is of high quality, the supply of donations may be insufficient to meet the demand. This problem can be mitigated by paying donors' expenses,[26] insuring them against future medical complications,[27] or providing other forms of compensation that lower the cost of donating without permitting individuals to profit financially from their blood.[28] Since such expedients may not always be effective, however, undersupply may continue to be a serious potential problem.

Moreover, even if a system of voluntary blood donations proves workable, the Titmuss proposal should not be unthinkingly generalized. Blood is a very special commodity. Once a person gives or sells some blood, more is produced "automatically" so long as the person has not sold or given away so much as to injure his health. The quality of the blood produced is not affected by the price at which it can be sold, and the quantity inside people's veins is always sufficient to meet the demand. Thus, the only quality control problem is the proper selection of suppliers. Furthermore, with the exception of a few people with rare blood types, there is no monopoly power problem.[29] Suppose, in contrast, that the market for used cars were outlawed and the Salvation Army encouraged people to donate cars for distribution to the needy. Since cars do not spontaneously regenerate themselves in the garages of the altruistic, it appears unlikely that many high quality cars will be given away.

Yet automobiles are like blood in that individual owners know more about the quality of their cars than the buyers or donees can easily find out.[30] Even if a purely voluntary system would induce people with "lemons" to throw them away rather than donate them, the overall quantity and quality of used cars would be low.[31] As another example, suppose that the military only wanted patriotic fighters to join the armed forces but had no good way to test for patriotism. It might try accordingly to establish a volunteer army that paid only subsistence wages. This plan would be unlikely, however, to attract more than a few super-patriots, and most volunteers might instead be unemployed people with very low skill levels.

2.1.4. Blood, body parts, and fairness

Many people oppose the sale of blood to patients on the ground that it is unfair to allocate a basic necessity of life on the basis of ability to pay. In a competitive market, this argument seems difficult to sustain for two reasons. First, the distributive arguments against sales may not be strong enough to overcome the inefficiency of nonmarket transactions. Making free a good that actually has an opportunity cost will produce excess demand, since the value of the good to marginal consumers will exceed its marginal cost. If, in addition, suppliers are not reimbursed, quantity will be inefficiently low. Second, there do not seem to be any strong distributive reasons for treating the goods in question differently from close substitutes. Artificial limbs are for sale, but not real kidneys. On purely distributive grounds it seems unfair to treat people whose problem requires a mechanical or chemical solution differently from those who need living tissue. In the field of health, such distinctions seem particularly problematic, since most people are covered by public or private health insurance.[32]

If the market is not competitive, however, the distributive arguments against sales may have more merit. The monopoly power issue arises most clearly in the provision of human tissue. Because overall supply is not affected by market structure, monopoly power only affects the distribution of benefits between donor and donee. Thus, if tissue typing shows that your kidney is the best one to transplant into your cousin, a bilateral monopoly situation is created[33] and if sales are permitted, you might hold out for a large payment in return for saving your cousin's life. Similarly, some types of rare antibodies are only available from a few people and are extremely valuable in the production of certain drugs.[34] In such contexts, an entirely unregulated market could have undesirable distributive consequences if people exercise their monopoly over scarce bodily tissues and antibodies at the expense of the sick. Prohibiting sales is not, however, the only response to the problem. One could instead imitate the policy followed in more conventional cases of monopoly power by permitting sales but regulating prices so that they reflect the marginal costs and risks borne by the donor.[35]

2.2. Modified property rules

Consider next the converse of a modified inalienability rule under which sales at market prices are permitted but gifts are outlawed. In contrast to modified inalienability rules, such modified property rules are relatively uncommon and apply to particular situations rather than types of goods and services. Under such rules, property may be sold at market prices but cannot be given away. Most commonly, modified property rules have been imposed on people who are either insolvent or about to die. In both cases, these rules solve problems that arise because someone with an interest in the property has no legal claim until some event, i.e., bankruptcy or death, occurs. These difficulties are examples of the agency-principal problems familiar to economic analysts in contexts as different as shareholder control of corporate managers and the relationship between insurance companies and their customers.[36] The restriction on gifts substitutes for laws that directly control the relationship between the parties. The modified property rule is a second-best way of recognizing the property interests of creditors, heirs, and tax collectors in situations where the nominal owner may choose to overlook their claims.

Consider bankruptcy law first. Gifts made before a declaration of bankruptcy are condemned as "fraudulent conveyances", but sales of assets are legal so long as "reasonably equivalent value" is received.[37] Without this restriction on gifts, a person who became insolvent could simply give away all his assets to family and friends, go bankrupt, and then accept reciprocal gifts from them afterwards. This practice would introduce an element of risk into the making of loans that would serve no productive purpose. Ex ante the volume of loans would be inefficiently low and interest rates inefficiently high to take account of this possibility of hiding assets from creditors.

In contrast, prohibitions on gifts made close to the time of death can be justified mainly on distributive grounds. Originally, such rules protected heirs against pressure applied by clerics and doctors to dying relatives.[38] At present, in the United States the laws of most states and the federal government do not prevent gifts made close to the time of death. However, a weak form of modified property rule remains the legal standard for death related transactions: certain gifts made within three years of death are treated as part of one's estate for tax purposes. The purpose of this rule is to protect the government against the tax avoidance activities of dying individuals and their heirs.[39]

3. LIMITS ON OWNERSHIP AND USE

Restrictions on ownership and use will sometimes be effective second-best substitutes for more flexible, incentive-based systems of externality control. In this section, I consider a wide range of such restrictions, from limits on who may drive automobiles to controls on the use of historic buildings and undeveloped land. In practice, of course, externality control is not a central reason for many existing limitations. Instead, they are based on paternalistic motives or are blatantly designed to create monopoly rents. My purpose is not to justify such restrictions but rather to indicate the narrow range of cases where economic efficiency may be furthered by limiting who may use or own a product and what may be done with it.

3.1. Restrictions on ownership

Ownership restrictions work in conjunction with the tort law system to prevent conduct dangerous to third parties.[40] They prevent groups of people, e.g., people under sixteen or those with diabetes, from owning certain goods or engaging in certain activities, e.g., purchasing liquor, driving a car, or obtaining a pilot's license. Inalienability rules of this kind are second-best methods of control because they treat all members of a group alike. These restrictions thus are likely to be both over- and underinclusive. In contrast, a tort law system, requiring compensation ex post, can be sensitive to individual differences in behavior but may be costly and time-consuming to implement. In practice, we have a mixed system which combines ex ante restrictions with ex post liability. Tort law emphasizes those practices that are inherently most difficult to measure ex ante. For example, while tests of driving ability, knowledge of traffic laws, and color blindness determine who will obtain a driver's license, the possibility of a tort suit after an accident is likely to deter people from driving carelessly.

The use of statistical evidence to sort out applicants is efficacious if the measuring rod is directly related to behavior. Proxies are often used, however, because of measurement difficulties. Simple criteria such as age can often be understood as substitutes for more complex criteria such as health status or ability where problems of measurement ex ante and of attributing causation ex post are likely to be serious. Thus, if there is a strong statistical relationship between the age of an automobile driver and the probability of being in an accident, the state can forbid people below a certain age from driving cars instead of designing a costly individualized test to sort out the careful children. Costs are imposed on careful children by this method of accident prevention, but they must be balanced against the costs of more discriminating tests.[41]

There are limits to this method, however. We seem to be reluctant to use statistical patterns to distinguish between people on the basis of demographic criteria beyond their control. Thus we do not allow white women to drive at an earlier age than males and blacks, even though the statistical evidence shows that white women are safer drivers.[42] Age, however, is less suspect than race or gender since all people age at the same rate and is, therefore, frequently used as a basis for distributing benefits and burdens. Furthermore, even though a demographic characteristic is something over which an individual has no control, it may still be used to distinguish between people if the causal link is well established and close to being deterministic. Thus, diabetics may be prevented from obtaining commercial pilots' licenses or driving trucks with hazardous cargoes, and color-blind people may be unable to obtain drivers' licenses.[43]

Ideally, people should be compensated for unfair burdens resulting from the use of statistical regularities instead of individual behavior. Compensation is impossible, however, for just the reason that statistical evidence is used initially to limit ownership and use: individual distinctions are costly or impossible to make.

Even though I have treated ownership restrictions as a second-best response to controlling externalities, I have idealized their role. In practice, such restrictions frequently are designed to give some profession or occupation monopoly power. It is, for example, very difficult to argue that most professional licensure laws are primarily concerned with quality control.[44] Simple restrictions on the number of market participants also are generally explicit grants of monopoly power to a limited group. While limits on the number of taxicabs in a city may reduce traffic congestion, they also benefit license holders;[45] restrictions on the number of bank offices in a state do not even have a limited market failure rationale. Thus, while a combination of externality control and administrative convenience may justify some restrictions, the possibility of such a justification should not create a presumption in favor of these regulations.

3.2. Required use

Some entitlement regulations require a small set of actions while permitting a wide range of other uses. As a condition for retaining ownership, the law may mandate actions that produce positive externalities. These regulations substitute for market-oriented systems that pay a subsidy set equal to the external benefits such actions produce.[46]

Two examples are especially interesting: historical preservation and preservation of the habitats of endangered species. In the United States historical preservation statutes typically require that owners preserve at least the facades of certain buildings. Permission is required for any alterations to the affected portions of the building and demolitions are permitted only under very restricted conditions. For example, the New York City Landmarks Preservation Law emphasizes the protection and preservation of external arhitectural features and internal features, such as building lobbies or auditoriums, that are open to the public, and it only rarely allows demolition.[47] Similarly, the Endangered Species Act may require landowners to avoid destroying the habitat of an endangered species.[48] Both of these policies can be justified by the external benefits of maintaining the affected property in its original form.

Two problems militate against regulatory statutes that require preservation. First, they may lead to too much or too little preservation because the government's criterion of value will not always equal the opportunity costs of foregone development. Second, in the absence of countervailing subsidies, the cost of preservation is borne by those who own the property at the time the law is promulgated, unless, of course, the law actually increases property values.[49] But both the problem of inefficient preservation and the problem of concentrated costs can be avoided by a law that pays owners a bounty to preserve their land or buildings. This system could be more efficient than outright prohibitions if the bounty were set equal to the external benefits of preservation. Historical buildings would be torn down and habitats destroyed only if their external benefits were too low to justify their preservation given the land's alternative uses.[50] Although in practice quantifying these benefits is very difficult, attempts to do so will frequently be preferable to required use regulations when the effect of the latter is to impose all the costs on the producer of the social benefits.

3.3. Limits on use

Conversely, other laws forbid certain activities in an attempt to limit negative externalities. For example, land use zoning laws may prevent owners from using their land for certain things such as a store or a factory but may permit apartment buildings so long as maximum density requirements are met and sewer and water lines are provided.[51] Zoning laws do not require development as a condition of ownership; rather, their economic function is to control the externalities of development if it occurs.

Here too, the regulations are second-best substitutes for a policy that balances the benefits and cost of development in individual cases.[52] They also have some of the same undesirable distributive costs as laws requiring certain actions. Once again, those who own the land at the time the zoning law is passed bear the cost along with those who would have benefited if the property had been put to its most profitable use. The purchase of development rights by government is a noncoercive alternative to zoning that forces the state to take into account the costs of restricting land use. In a few jurisdictions this policy has been applied to farmland.[53]

4. COERCED USE

I use the term "coerced use" to apply to situations in which all permitted activities are also required. When the government sells, leases, or gives property to private individuals, the state may impose restrictions in an attempt to control the use of the property. If the property is sold to the highest bidder, the regulations will adversely affect government revenues if they require owners to restrict their pursuit of profitable opportunities. How, then, can it be in the public interest to impose such controls? While some such restrictions have little to recommend them on normative grounds, others can be justified by appeals to efficiency and distributive justice. I discuss four rationales in turn: agency-principal problems that arise from the nature of the contractual situation, avoidance of a "prisoner's dilemma", the entitlement holders' poor information and inability to fend for themselves, and the distribution of scarce benefits to the worthy. Three applications are stressed: United States leasing programs for natural resources, the Homesteading Acts of nineteenth century America, and government transfers to the needy.

4.1. Contracting problems: mineral leases

In the United States, the federal government sells (or gives away) leases that permit private individuals and firms to exploit natural resources on federal lands and on the continental shelf. Most of these leases – e.g., for coal and oil – provide that holders forfeit their claims if they do not actually extract the resource.[54] A leaseholder who does not wish to exploit the resource, however, can assign or sublease to someone else.[55]

Coercive conditions will further efficiency only if they help correct agency-principal problems in the basic lease. Under most federal leases, leaseholders must pay a royalty of x percent on sales proceeds.[56] Agency-principal problems arise because one hundred dollars of sales is only worth (1-x) hundred dollars to the lessee. Shifting all the costs to the lessee, but not all of the marginal gains, gives him too little incentive to prospect and exploit the resource. The royalty is inefficient ex post but may be desirable ex ante as a way of sharing the risks of exploitation between the government and the private firm. If such risk sharing is deemed desirable, then a "due diligence" requirement will help correct the inefficiency created by the royalty scheme.[57]

Arguments in favor of restrictive clauses are more difficult to make, however, where the lease is granted in return for a fixed payment. Such provisions may be justifiable where market imperfections such as monopoly power or systematically biased information discourage current production.[58] Absent market imperfections, however, due diligence requirements in such leases encourage excess exploration in the present, controlled only by the government's decision on the quantity of leases to make available each year.

4.2. "Prisoner's Dilemmas"

It is difficult to be a pioneer in an empty land. Life is easier with neighbors who can help in emergencies, share farm equipment, and assist in capital projects such as construction. Furthermore, as more people settle in a given area, more specialized tradesmen, such as blacksmiths and carpenters, will move in, and villages will be built. Since it is easier to develop one's land once others are nearby, everyone has an incentive to wait for everyone else. Speculators with no interest in farming may purchase some land and hold it for resale. In some markets, speculators can serve a useful economic function, but here they can exacerbate the "prisoner's dilemma".[59] Everyone is better off if all settle than if no one settles, but if others settle, then it is best for each person to wait until others have overcome the initial hardships.

One way around the dilemma is to impose a conditionally coercive entitlement rule that imposes conditions on those who wish to become landowners. The original Homesteading Acts in nineteenth century America, for example, gave people land for a nominal fee after they certified that they had worked the land for five years.[60] The land could not be sold or given away to private individuals during that period. If a homesteader did not complete his term of resident farming, the land was forfeited to the state. The people attracted to the territory by this program both made future economic development easier and aided the political ambitions of the original residents who sought to move their territories toward statehood. Thus, the entitlement rule was conditionally coercive, and hence more restrictive than the transferable mineral leases discussed above.[61]

At present, the prisoner's dilemma may well provide an important justification for subsidized housing programs with coercive conditions. Poorly maintained housing affects the value of neighboring property with the net result that no one may find it worthwhile to incur maintenance expenses. If all could be induced to upgrade their property, all would benefit. Subsidies could be provided to landlords and homeowners on the condition that they fix up their property. However, if property owners can sell their upgraded assets to the highest bidder, a subsidy program of this kind is not conditionally coercive. Conditional coercion arises when the government wishes not merely to improve neighbourhood quality but also to make it possible for the former residents to remain in the newly upgraded housing. Thus, landlords may be forbidden to evict tenants and tenants may be eligible for subsidy only if they live in apartments that fulfill housing code standards.[62] Similarly, urban homesteading programs, which are quite self-consciously modeled after the homesteading programs for nineteenth century farmers, encourage low and moderate income people to fix up old housing and impose resale restrictions to ensure that the rehabilitated building continues to provide housing for families with low and moderate incomes.[63]

The prisoner's dilemma rationale is less clearly applicable to natural resource leases, but it may be valid in particular cases. Latecomers may have lower costs than early entrants because those who first develop the resource bear higher costs than later developers. Roads must be built to extract timber from inaccessible areas, and oil exploration by one firm in one area may provide information to owners or leaseholders of neighboring areas. In such situations, due diligence clauses can overcome the incentive to hold back and let others move first.

4.3. Poor information and paternalism

Following Charles Reich, many commentators view government transfer programs as creating a kind of "new property".[64] If so, the new property rights are often conditionally coercive. In general, people cannot sell or give away their benefits to others, and for some benefits, such as public housing, people forfeit their claim to a service by not using it. Even the right to receive straight cash grants through a welfare program with no restrictions on use is not a pure property right. An eligible person can give the payments she receives to anyone but cannot transfer the right to receive these payments. In-kind programs providing such benefits as housing, food, or day care also frequently restrict both the use and transferability of the benefit itself. Such coercion is justified as a way of overcoming the market failure caused by poor information and shopping opportunities.[65] or from a paternalistic concern for poor children and their families.[66] Social benefit programs can induce people to consume food, housing, health care, or education by making these services relatively inexpensive and prohibiting transfers.

A similar argument can be used to justify the Homesteading Acts. Those who wished to encourage the development of western lands could well have believed that homesteaders, if left to themselves, would have had an inefficiently short time horizon. Conditional coercion encouraged homesteaders to endure the hard initial years by subsidizing fixed costs in a way that gave them an incentive to remain on the land. Eventually, their skills improved, and the risks of farming fell. Here, too, the efficiency rationale based on imperfect information merges into a kind of paternalism.

4.4. Distribution to the "worthy"

Suppose that for some reason the free market allocation of a scarce public benefit is unacceptable. Assume further that the number of qualified individuals using some clear standard such as income, employment status, or family composition exceeds the supply available. Thus, program administrators face a distributive problem that may be solved in a number of ways, including first-come-first-served queues, the approval of applications, under-the-table payoffs, or a lottery. Alternatively, restrictions may be imposed that are less onerous for those who most deserve to receive the benefit. If determining worthiness through tests and application approval is costly and unreliable, the restrictions are a substitute sorting device. Such requirements may be particularly desirable if they also serve a productive purpose, as did the rural and urban homesteading laws.

Consider first the Homesteading Acts. Central to the homesteading program was the idea that a newly available resource (e.g., land in the western United States suitable for farming) should not go to those who already had capital but to those without other wealth.[67] This, however, was only an argument for giving the land to the poor in the first instance, not for requiring them to work on the property. To justify coercive conditions and restrictions on transfer we must add a second factor: in practice, the number of valuable sites was less than the number of landless people so long as the state took into account both the scale economies of production and the transaction costs of assembling a farm from a multitude of small entitlements. Thus, there needed to be some method to assign sites other than willingness to pay since market sales could defeat the redistributive purpose. In this context, homesteading emerges as a plausible choice. It is a more efficient allocation mechanism than a first-come-first-served queue since the time expended is not wasted waiting in line but is used in productive activities. Seen in this light, a conditionally coercive rule can use willingness to work to determine who among the poor can best develop the resource. Of course, this policy also means that the very poor with no farming skills do not benefit from the program. It represents a compromise between accomplishing redistributive goals and assuring the efficient development of resources.

A similar rationale underlies many social welfare programs. When the number of needy people exceeds the supply of subsidized goods, it seems prudent to ration the scarce supply only to those people who will actually use the in-kind benefit themselves. Selling subsidized apartments to the highest bidders would undermine the redistributive purposes of the program. Since the price is not set to clear the market, demand will exceed supply even when transferability is restricted. Therefore, costly conditions may be added, such as willingness to perform maintenance chores in the building or to spend time fixing up the premises. The analogy to the Homesteading Acts is particularly close for redistributive programs that also have economic development or growth as a secondary goal. The restrictions on use and transferability in these programs can both accomplish redistributive objectives when demand exceeds supply at the subsidized price and encourage neighborhood preservation in much the same way as the Homesteading Acts induced people to endure the hardships of farming on the frontier.

Once again, however, this mix of efficiency and distributive rationales cannot be extended indefinitely. For example, it cannot be used to justify the coercive conditions in federal mineral leasing programs. Most leases are sold to high bidders, not given to those deemed especially worthy independent of their willingness to pay. Noncompetitive leases that are given to the "first" qualified applicant have distributive consequences, but not ones that make sense on normative grounds.[68] Furthermore, given the specialized skills needed to exploit mineral resources, it seems unlikely that these programs should be designed to serve a redistributive purpose.

5. CONCLUSIONS

The classification of entitlements developed here encompasses a broad range of property relations and permits an analysis of a variety of economic rationales including problems of imperfect information and foresight, as well as administrative costs and externalities. I have also attempted to incorporate distributive arguments that may justify some types of inalienability or provide justifications for compensation. My aim is not to rationalize all existing restrictions, but to isolate plausible arguments for some.

I have shown how restrictions on the transferability, ownership, and use of property can be justified under a range of different assumptions about the structure of the world and the cost of alternatives. I have also tried to show the limited applicability of some kinds of inalienability rules. Easy generalizations are frequently invalid. While an argument can be made for relying on blood donations, it cannot be generalized to products like used cars, even though they share similar informational characteristics. Federal homesteading laws and federal mineral leases may appear similar in form but have very different rationales. The sale of both blood and "old" eagles might be permitted if certain institutional arrangements are not too costly to establish.

In this paper alienability is frequently justified not as an ideal policy but as a second-best response to the messiness and complexity of the world. It is generally possible to conceive of an alternative policy that would be superior if transaction costs were lower. Thus, if the argument against the sale of blood rests primarily on quality control grounds, a cheap and effective test for contamination would undermine the argument. This reliance on imperfect information and transaction costs to justify inalienability rules should not be seen as a weakness of the analysis, however. Instead, it is a way to rescue the concept of inalienability from its simplistic rejection by market-oriented economists or its overly enthusiastic embrace by paternalistic moralists.

NOTES

1. See, e.g., Anderson and Hill (1975), Demsetz (1967), Furubotn and Pejovich (1972), North (1978).
2. Musgrave & Musgrave, 692–715 (1976). For applications to environmental pollution, see Dorfman & Dorfman (1977); Freeman, Haveman & Knesse (1973).

3. See Sweeney, Tollison & Willett (1974) pp. 186–88.
4. See Mishan (1967).
5. See Calabresi (1970).
6. For a discussion of some of the problems with pricing policies, see Rose-Ackerman (1973); Rose-Ackerman (1977).
7. Without this principle, antitrust laws and statutes that regulate public utilities would require the state to compensate monopolists for their loss of monopoly power. See Rose-Ackerman (1982) (applying this argument in the context of competition between nonprofit and for-profit firms).
8. See Blume & Rubinfeld, (1984); Wittman (1984).
9. Prichard (1984) p. 342. But cf. Landes & Posner (1978) (defending a market for adopted children).
10. See, e.g., Me. Rev. Stat. Ann. tit. 12, §§ 7452(9) (A), 7456(5), 7457(s), 7615 (1964 & Supp. 1984–85); N.Y. Envtl. Conserv. Law §§ 11–0536, –1319(2), –1705(10), –1729 (McKinney 1984 & Supp. 1984–85).
11. Eskimos are explicitly exempted from some provisions of both the Endangered Species Act of 1973, 16 U.S.C. § 1539(e) (1982), and the Marine Mammal Protection Act of 1973, 16 U.S.C.§ 1371(b) (1982). See generally Coggins & Modrcin (1979) (exploring the conflict between Indian rights and federal wildlife law).
12. Under both the Endangered Species Act and the Marine Mammal Protection Act, Alaskan natives may hunt endangered or threatened species if these are used "primarily" for subsistence or are made into "authentic native articles of handicrafts and clothing". 16 U.S.C. §§ 1317(b), 1539(e) (1982).
13. See Andrus v. Allard, 444 U.S. 51, 58 (1979).
14. In United States v. Richards, 583 F.2d 491 (10th Cir. 1978). In Delbay Pharmaceuticals v. Department of Commerce, 409 F.Supp. 637 (D.D.C. 1976), brought under the Endangered Species Act, the Commerce Department seized Delbay's inventory of imported spermaceti. Delbay argued that it should be able to sell its spermaceti because it was imported before the law went into effect. In rejecting Delbay's claim, the court emphasized administrative difficulties: "A total ban is easier to enforce than a partial ban. If there were a continued market in this country for spermaceti, it might encourage the illegal taking of sperm whales to supply this market". Id. at 642.

    Similarly, in Andrus v. Allard, 444 U.S. 51 (1979), the Supreme Court upheld a prohibition on the sale of eagles and products made of eagle feathers even though the eagles were killed before the law went into effect. Gift giving, however, was expressly permitted by the Court. See id. at 66.
15. 444 U.S. 51 (1979).
16. Id.
17. Id. at 65. In addition to possession and transportation of their property, the owners could also "donate or devise the protected birds" and could "exhibit the artifacts for an admissions charge". Id. at 66.
18. New tests do permit better screening for hepatitis A and B, but existing procedures are still not effective for Non-A, Non-B hepatitis. "Non-A, Non-B Hepatitis" (1984). Recent concern about the transmission of AIDS through blood transfusion has raised similar issues even in the context of donated blood. However, a reliable test does now seem to be available. "Results of AIDS Tests" (1985).
19. See Kessel (1974).
20. Food and Drug Administration regulations require blood to be labeled "paid donor" or "volunteer". Scott (1981).
21. See Cooper & Culyer (1968); Sapolsky & Finkelstein (1977).

22. United States law on this subject varies. The *Uniform Anatomical Gift Act* (UAGA), 8A U.L.A. 15 (1983), which has been adopted by all fifty states and the District of Columbia, treats only gifts from dead bodies; it does not resolve the legal status of sales from either the living or the dead. Stason (1968). Cf. "Retailing Human Organs Under the Uniform Commercial Code" (1983) which advocates amendments to the UAGA to permit the sale of organs.
23. See Cooper & Culyer (1968); cf. Calabresi & Bobbitt (1978).
24. See Titmuss (1971) p. 151.
25. This problem is not unsolvable. One could, for example, imagine churches or day care centers raising money by selling donated blood just as they now sell donated food, clothing, and household goods. Blood banks could merge with charities or give their proceeds to federated fundraising organizations.
26. See Council of Europe (1978). Article 9 states that "[n]o substance may be offered for profit. However, loss of earnings and any expenses caused by the removal or preceding examination may be refunded". Council of Europe, (1979) favors outlawing sales of human tissue but authorizes payment for shipping expenses.
27. See, e.g., "California's Response to the Problem of Procuring Human Remains for Transplantation", *California Law Review* (1969).
28. Compensation may take the form of promises to supply blood in the future if donors or their families need it, or to make gifts in the donors' names to charities of their choice. Titmuss, (1971) pp. 78–88.
29. Cf. United States v. Garber, 607 F.2d 92 (5th Cir. 1979).
30. The problem of low quality used cars forcing good ones out of the marketplace is analyzed in Akerlof (1970).
31. Cf. Rottenberg (1971).
32. Even if a persuasive argument can be made against selling the entitlement to users, it may still be possible to obtain some of the benefits of market transactions by having the state purchase the good or service from suppliers for free distribution to the public based on nonmarket criteria. For proposals along these lines dealing with the supply of human tissue, see Brams (1977); Dukeminier (1970); Sanders & Dukeminier (1968); "Compulsory Removal of Cadaver Organs" (1969); "The Sale of Human Body Parts" (1974).
33. See, e.g., Strunk v. Strunk, 445 S.W.2d 145 (Ky. 1969); McFall v. Shimp, 10 Pa. D & C.3d 90 (1978).
34. See, e.g., United States v. Garber, 607 F.2d 92 (5th Cir. 1979).
35. Of course, other personal attributes that give people monopoly rents are not so regulated. One problem with taxing the returns to beauty, strength, and intelligence, however, is that individuals should be given an incentive to develop their natural gifts. In contrast, although people can be compensated for the time, trouble, and risk of organ removal, they cannot affect their tissue type.
36. See, e.g., Ross (1973) p. 134; Shavell (1979).
37. 11 U.S.C. § 548(a) (1982). See generally Hanna & MacLachlan, (1957) pp. 204–22, 233–55 (discussing the Uniform Fraudulent Conveyance Act and providing excerpts from the leading cases).
38. In Louisiana, for example, gifts to either doctors or "ministers of religious worship" cannot be made by a sick person who dies of his illness. The person may, however, pay for services rendered. La. Civ. Code Ann. art. 1489 (West 1952). In Georgia, no one with a spouse or child may devise more than one-third of her estate to charitable or religious institutions if the will is executed within 90 days of the person's death. Ga. Code Ann. § 53-2-10 (1982). Similarly, old treatises on gifts note that a gift to

one's "spiritual adviser" will be regarded with suspicion by courts especially if made *mortis causa*. See, e.g., Thornton (1893, p. 456).

39. In recent years the consolidation of the gift and estate tax systems in the United States has mooted the problem of determining intent. Yet, since the federal government taxes gifts differently from sales, it becomes important to define a sale. Within three years of death, the IRS will scrutinize sales to be sure that "adequate consideration" in money or money's worth has been received. If the IRS is not satisfied, the balance will be taxed as if it were a gift. See Englebrecht, Moore & Fowler, (1981).
40. See generally Calabresi (1978).
41. Another factor is whether the tests will in fact screen effectively. In the United States, some states attempt to screen out more careful younger drivers by requiring that 16 and 17 year-olds complete driver education courses before obtaining licenses. See, e.g., Cal. Veh. Code § 12057 (West 1971). At 18, anyone who passes the state test can obtain a license. See, e.g., id. § 12512. Robertson and Zador (1978) argue, however, that such statutes achieve precisely the opposite result: increasing the number of 16 and 17 year-old drivers increases the automobile accident death rate.
42. See Underwood (1979 pp. 1434–1442). In the United States the most prominent suspect criteria are race, sex, and national origin.
43. Because of a concern for accident risks, the U.S. Federal Highway Administration prohibits diabetics on insulin from driving trucks in intercity or interstate commerce, Hricko, 1981, p.130. New York City taxi drivers are similarly restricted. N.Y. City Admin. Code, ch. 65, § 2305 (1975).
44. Cf. Stigler (1971).
45. Given the casual short-term nature of individual taxi rides, state regulation of some aspects of quality appears justified. N.Y. City Admin. Code, ch. 65, §§ 2301–2319 (1975). Although some restrictions on the ownership and use of taxicabs appear justified on efficiency grounds, limitations on entry, which are less easy to justify, accompany them. See Kitch, Isaacson & Kaster (1971).
46. See generally, "Bank Charter, . . ." (1962).
47. N.Y. City Admin. Code, ch. 8-A. §§ 207-1.0(g), (m), (n), −5.0(a), −6.0, −10.0 (1976).
48. A recent court of appeals decision can be read to support this view even though it dealt with the State of Hawaii rather than private landowners. See Palila v. Hawaii Dep't of Land & Natural Resources, 639 F.2d 495 (9th Cir. 1981); "*Palila vs. Hawaii Department of Land and Natural Resources*: A New Interpretation of 'Taking' . . ." (1983) which argues for a broad reading of the Palila case).
49. Listokin (1982) summarizes recent research, including evidence on both increases and decreases in property values under historical preservation statutes. Rose (1984) p. 142 argues in favor of compensation.
50. See Wittman (1984) p. 75.
51. See generally Roberts (1982).
52. Because zoning is a local government function, however, it can itself produce external costs. Large lot zoning in the suburbs combined with selective zoning for industry contributes to the clustering of dirty industry and poor, minority families in central cities or old industrial towns while some suburbs maintain themselves as wealthy enclaves. Neither efficiency nor fairness supports this kind of narrowly focused residential zoning. See Mills (1979).
53. For example, the Suffolk County government in New York State will purchase farmers' "development rights" up to the limit of its budget. The value of these rights

is the difference between the value of the property for its highest and best use and its value for agricultural purposes. See Roberts (1982) p.76. Less ambitious programs are in effect in Connecticut, Massachusetts, New Hampshire, and New Jersey. Id. at 83–87.

54. See Federal Land Policy and Management Act of 1976, § 302, 43 U.S.C. § 1732 (1982); Outer Continental Shelf Lands Act, ch. 345, 67 Stat. 462, § 6(10), 43 U.S.C. § 1337(b) (2) (B) (1982); Mineral Leasing Act of 1920, ch. 85, 41 Stat. 437, § 7, 30 U.S.C. §207 (1982); Kalter & Tyner, 51 (Kalter & Vogely eds. 1976); Nelson, 7 Reg. 34 (Jan.-Feb. 1983). The Federal Coal Leasing Amendments Act of 1975, Pub. L. No. 94–377, 90 Stat. 1083 (1976) (codified in scattered sections of 30 U.S.C. (1982), requires development of future coal leases within 10 years, id. § 6, at 1087 (codified at 30 U.S.C. § 207 (1982), but does not cover leases issued before 1976 unless the lessees consent. Id. § 5(b) (5), at 1086 (codified at 30 U.S.C. § 202a(5) (1982).
55. The sublease must be approved by the Secretary of the Interior. 30 U.S.C. § 187 (1982). At least for oil and gas leases, assignments or subleases can be disapproved "only for lack of qualification of the assignee or sublessee or for lack of sufficient bond". 30 U.S.C. § 187a (1982).
56. Low royalties of 8% to 12.5% are common. The royalty can be reduced if the lessee demonstrates that lease stipulations make development of a tract uneconomical. Kalter & Tyner (1976) pp. 56–57.
57. Private oil and gas leases also frequently contain profit-sharing provisions combined with clauses requiring the lessee to explore for resources and to exploit them if found. For summaries of the current state of the law in this area, see "The Implied Covenant to Reasonably Develop" (1983) and "Oil and Gas" (1983).
58. Nelson (1983) pp. 36–38. The Department of Interior, however, apparently has not enforced these provisions vigorously. Council on Economic Priorities, (1974) p. 28.
59. The prisoner's dilemma game between individuals A and B has the following form where B's net returns are listed first in each box.

		A	
		Develop Now	Develop Later
B	Develop Now	10, 10	6, 12
	Develop Later	12, 6	7, 7

If both develop now, they share the social overhead costs and maximize total benefits. If both wait, they also share costs and lose the profits of early development. If A develops later while B develops now, B must bear all the startup costs and cannot prevent some of the benefits of this investment from accruing to A.
60. See Act of May 20, 1862, ch. 75, 12 Stat. 392; Gates (1968) pp. 393–99.
61. See Gates (1968) pp. 393–99. Eventually, the conditionally coercive features of the Homesteading Acts were weakened by the addition of a commutation clause. Homesteaders could purchase their claim outright after a residence of fourteen months. Act of Mar. 3, 1981, ch. 561, § 6, 26 Stat. 1095, 1098; Hughes (1906) p. 351; Shannon (1945) pp. 51–75.

62. See, e.g., U.S. Housing Act of 1937, § 8, 42 U.S.C. § 1437f(a) (1976).
63. See Department of Housing Preservation and Development, The City of New York, Urban Homesteading, Request for Proposals, Dec. 9, 1983, at 4 (unpublished).
64. See Reich (1964, 1965).
65. Barlow v. Collins, 397 U.S. 159 (1970), illustrates a situation in which program beneficiaries, in this case tenant farmers, argued for restrictions on the transferability of their entitlements.
66. See generally Rose-Ackerman (1983) (discussing the rationales for in-kind programs).
67. See, e.g., Seymour v. Sanders, 21 F. Cas. 1133, 1135 (C.C.D. Minn. 1874) (No. 12,690) reprinted in Lewis (1879 p. 219).
68. 26 U.S.C. § 226(c) (1982); 43 C.F.R. §§ 3111.1-.7 (1984). Council on Economic Priorities (1974) pp. 22–28, describes the allocation of coal leases prior to the 1976 law and claims that the prices paid, even when rent and royalty payments are considered, were far below the discounted present value of the mineral resources.

REFERENCES

Akerlof, George A., "The Market for 'Lemons': Quality Uncertainty and the Market Mechanism", *Quarterly Journal of Economics*, August 1970, 84, 488–500.

Anderson, Terry L. and Hill, P.J., "The Evolution of Property Rights: A Study of the American West", *Journal of Law and Economics*, April 1975, 18, 163–179.

Arrow, Kenneth, "Gifts and Exchanges", *Philosophy and Public Affairs*, Summer 1972, 1, 343–362.

Blume, Lawrence and Rubinfeld, Daniel L., "Compensation for Takings: An Economic Analysis", *California Law Review*, July 1984, 72, 569–628.

Brams, Marvin, "Transplantable Human Organs: Should Their Sale be Authorized by State Statutes?", *American Journal of Law and Medicine*, Summer 1977, 3, 183–195.

Calabresi, Guido, *The Costs of Accidents*, New Haven: Yale University Press, 1970.

———, "Torts – The Law of the Mixed Society", *Texas Law Review*, February 1978, 56, 519–534.

———, and Bobbitt, Philip, *Tragic Choices*, New York: Norton, 1978.

———, and Melamed, A. Douglas, "Property Rules, Liability Rules, and Inalienability: One View of the Cathedral", *Harvard Law Review*, April 1972, 85, 1089–1128.

Coggins, George Cameron and Modrcin, William, "Native American Indians and Federal Wildlife Law", *Stanford Law Review*, February 1979, 31, 375–423.

Cooper, Michael and Culyer, Anthony, *The Price of Blood*, London: Institute of Economic Affairs, 1968.

Demsetz, Harold, "Toward a Theory of Property Rights", *American Economic Review* (Papers and Proceedings) May 1967, 57, 347–359.

Dorfman, Robert and Dorfman, Nancy, *Economics of the Environment*. 2d ed., New York: Norton, 1977.

Dukeminier, Jesse, Jr., "Supplying Organs for Transplantation", *Michigan Law Review*, April 1970, 68, 811–866.

Englebrecht, Ted D.; Moore, Michael L. and Fowler, Anna C., *Federal Taxation of Estates, Gifts and Trusts*, Englewood Cliffs, N.J.: Prentice-Hall, 1981.

Freeman, A. Myrick; Haveman, Robert and Kneese, Allan, *The Economics of Environmental Policy*, New York: John Wiley & Sons, 1973.

Furubotn, Eirik and Pejovich, Svetozar, "Property Rights and Economic Theory: A Survey of Recent Literature", *Journal of Economic Literature*, December 1972, 10, 1137–1162.

Gates, Paul W., *History of Public Land Law Development*, Written for the Public Land Law Review Commission, Washington, D.C., 1968.

Hanna, John and MacLachlan, James Angell, *Cases & Materials on Creditors' Rights and Corporate Reorganization*, Fifth Edition, Brooklyn, N.Y.: Foundation Press, 1957.

Hricko, Andrew, "Drivers of Hazardous Cargoes – Legal Aspects of a Maximum Age and Increased Physical Requirements", *Federation of Insurance Counselors*, 1981, 31, 126–134.

Hughes, Hugh J., "The Abuse of the Homestead Law", *The American Lawyer*, August 1906, 14, 350–352.

Kalter, Robert J. and Tyner, Wallace E., "Disposal Policy for Energy Resources in the Public Domain", in R.J. Kalter and W.A. Vogely, eds., *Energy Supply and Government Policy*, Ithaca, N.Y.: Cornell University Press, 1976, ch. 3.

Kessel, Reuben, "Transfused Blood, Serum Hepatitis, and the Coase Theorem", *Journal of Law & Economics* October 1974, 17, 265–290.

Kitch, Edmund; Isaacson, Marc and Kasper, Daniel, "The Regulation of Taxicabs in Chicago", *Journal of Law and Economics*, October 1971, 14, 285–350.

Landes, Elizabeth M. and Posner, Richard, "The Economics of the Baby Shortage", *Journal of Legal Studies*, June 1978, 7, 323–348.

Lewis, J. Vance, *A Collection of Leading Cases on the Public Land Laws of the United States*, Washington: J.V. Lewis, 1879.

Listokin, David et el., *Landmarks Preservation and the Property Tax: Assessing Landmark Buildings for Real Taxation Purposes*, New Brunswick, N.J.: Center for Urban Policy Research, Rutgers University; New York: New York Landmarks Conservancy, 1982.

Mills, Edwin, "Economic Analysis of Urban Land Use Controls", in P. Mieskowski and M. Straszheim, eds., *Current Issues in Urban Economics*, Baltimore: Johns Hopkins University Press, 1979, pp. 511–541.

Mishan, Ezra H., *The Costs of Economic Growth*, London: Staples, 1967.

Musgrave, Robert and Musgrave, Peggy, *Public Finance in Theory and Practice*, Second Edition, New York: McGraw-Hill, 1976.

Nelson, Robert, "Undue Diligence: The Mine-It-Or-Lose-It Rule for Federal Coal", *Regulation*, January/February 1983, 7, 34–38.

North, Douglas, "Structure and Performance: The Task of Economic History", *Journal of Economic Literature*, September 1978, 16, 963–978.

Prichard, J. Robert S., "A Market for Babies?", *University of Toronto Law Journal*, 1984, 34, 341–357.

Reich, Charles A., "Individual Rights and Social Welfare: The Emerging Legal Issues", *Yale Law Journal*, June 1965, 74, 1245–1257.

———, "The New Property", *Yale Law Journal*, April 1964, 73, 733–787.

Roberts, Ernest F., *The Law and the Preservation of Agricultural Land*, Ithaca, N.Y.: Northeast Regional Center for Rural Development, 1982.

Robertson, Leon and Zador, Paul, "Driver Education and Fatal Crash Involvement of Teenaged Drivers", *American Journal of Public Health*, October 1978, 68, 959–965.

Rose, Joseph, "Landmarks Preservation in New York", *Public Interest*, Winter 1984, 74, 132–145.

Rose-Ackerman, Susan, "Effluent Charges: A Critique", *Canadian Journal of Economics*, November 1973, 6, 512–527.

———, "Inalienability and the Theory of Property Rights", *Columbia Law Review*, June 1985, 85, 931–969.

———, "Market Models for Pollution Controls", *Public Policy*, Summer 1977, 25, 383–406.

———, "Social Services and the Market", *Columbia Law Review*, October 1983, 83, 1405–1439.

———, "Unfair Competition and Corporate Income Taxation", *Stanford Law Review*, May 1982, 34, 1017–1039.

Ross, Steven, "The Economic Theory of Agency: The Principal's Problem", *Americam Economics Review* (Papers and Proceedings) May 1973, 63, 134–139.

Rottenberg, Simon, "The Production and Exchange of Used Body Parts", in *Toward Liberty: Essays in Honor of Ludwig von Mises*, Vol. II, Menlo Park, Cal.: Institute for Humane Studies, 1971, 322–333.

Sanders, David and Dukeminier, Jesse, Jr., "Medical Advance & Legal Lag: Hemodialysis and Kidney Transplantation", *UCLA Law Review*, February 1968, 15, 357–413.

Sapolsky, Harvey and Finkelstein, N., "Blood Policy Revisited – A New Look at the 'Gift Relationship'", *The Public Interest*, Winter 1977, 46, 15–27.

Scott, Russell, *The Body as Property*, New York: Viking Press, 1981.

Shannon, Frederick A., *The Farmers' Last Frontier*, New York: Holt, Rinehart and Winston, 1945.

Shavell, Steven, "Risk Sharing and Incentives in the Principal and Agent Relationship", *Bell Journal of Economics*, Spring 1979, 10, 55–73.

Stason, E. Blythe, "The Uniform Anatomical Gift Act", *The Business Lawyer*, July 1968, 23, 919–929.

Stigler, George, "The Theory of Economic Regulation", *Bell Journal of Economics and Management Science*, Spring 1971, 2, 3–21.

Sweeney, Richard James; Tollison, Robert D. and Willett, Thomas D., "Market Failure, the Common-Pool Problem and Ocean Resource Exploitation", *Journal of Law and Economics*, April 1974, 17, 179–192.

Thornton, W.W., *A Treatise on the Law Relating to Gifts and Advancements*, Philadelphia: T. & J.W. Johnson, 1893.

Titmuss, Richard M., *The Gift Relationship*, New York: Vintage Books, 1971.

Underwood, Barbara D., "Law and the Crystal Ball: Predicting Behavior with Statistical Inference and Individualized Judgment", *Yale Law Journal*, June 1979, 88, 1408–1448.

Wittman, Donald, "Liability for Harm or Restitution for Benefit?", *Journal of Legal Studies*, January 1984, 13, 57–80.

"Bank Charter, Branching, Holding Company and Merger Laws: Competition Frustrated", *Yale Law Journal*, January 1962, 71, 502–536.

"California's Response to the Problem of Procuring Human Remains for Transplantation", *California Law Review*, May 1969, 57, 671–693.

"Compulsory Removal of Cadaver Organs", *Columbia Law Review*, April 1969, 69, 693–705.

Council on Economic Priorities, *Leased and Lost: A Study of Public and Indian Coal Leasing in the West*, Economic Priorities Report 5, No. 2, 1974.

Council of Europe, Committee of Ministers, *Harmonisation of Legislations of Member States Relating to Removal, Grafting and Transplantation of Human Substances*, Resolution (78)28, adopted 11 May 1978 and explanatory memorandum 29.

Council of Europe, Committee of Ministers, *International Exchange and Transportation of Human Substances*, Recommendation R(79)5, adopted 14 March 1979 and explanatory memorandum.

"The Implied Covenant to Reasonably Develop: Should Hard-Mineral Applications Follow Oil and Gas Precedent?", *Houston Law Review*, May 1983, 20, 883–898.
"Non-A, Non-B Hepatitis", *The Lancet*, November 10, 1984, 2, 1077–1078.
"Oil and Gas: Preservation of Leaseholds Following Well Failure", *Oklahoma Law Review*, Winter 1983, 36, 151–164.
"*Palila vs. Hawaii Department of Law and Natural Resources*: A New Interpretation of 'Taking' Under the Endangered Species Act of 1973", *Idaho Law Review*, Winter 1983, 19, 157–176.
"Results of AIDS Tests", *New York Times*, March 26, 1985.
"Retailing Human Organs Under the Uniform Commercial Code", *John Marshall Law Review*, Spring 1983, 16, 393–417.

NEGOTIATED SETTLEMENT

Gordon Tullock

In a legal dispute between two parties the ultimate recourse, is of course, a legal trial. Far more commonly however, the matter is settled without going to court. If the legal situation is clear, one side or the other will probably simply accept the situation. Where there is doubt, either of law or of fact, more often than not, there is some kind of a compromise. Sometimes this compromise is directly negotiated by the parties without the intervention of attorneys, and sometimes lawyers take the leading role in the settlement. If attorneys do the bulk of the work, but there is no trial, the procedure is referred to as an out of court settlement. Only in the exceptional case, does the matter actually go to trial.

In a way the trial is an outcome of the failure of the negotiation process. In the first stage, before the lawyers have been brought in, the parties implicitly threaten each other with high legal expenses and in the second their lawyers threaten to actually go to court. Only if the bargaining process fails to settle the matter is there a trial.

In the American Law and Economics field there is what I might call an orthodox position on this matter. "Because litigation is costly, both parties can gain if they agree to settle. The plaintiff forms a minimum 'ask' equal to his expected net gain from further litigation . . . similarly, the defendent forms a maximum offer equal to his total expected payout. If the offer exceeds the 'ask' for some amount within this bargaining range, there could be a settlement. If the 'ask' . . . exceeds the offer, litigation continues." (Danzon, June 1980). It is the thesis of this paper that this standard theoretical proposition is deeply misleading.[1]

Before turning to the theoretical problem, however, it is necessary to discuss briefly the cost of litigation in the United States since it is this cost which in my opinion, makes the above theory completely inadequate. I should say that I am unpopular in American Law Schools because I am in favor of adopting the European system of civil procedure partly in order to reduce costs. (Tullock, 1980) Thus, I am now discussing a legal system with which I have relatively little sympathy, one of the major reasons for this lack of sympathy is its extreme expense.

Data on the actual cost of American Legal Proceedings are generally poor.[2] The Rand Foundation however, has been engaging in a lot of rather tedious research in this area and has developed reasonably reliable figures. As a summary, Danzon and Lillard say, ". . . in most . . . forms of tort litigation, total litigation costs for the plaintiff and defendant together roughly equal compensation received by plaintiffs." (Danzon and Lillard) Other research by the Rand Foundation indicates that the total governmental courts cost, i.e., cost of courts etc., is about twenty percent of the amount awarded. Thus the total social cost of a law suit in which, say, $10,000, is awarded is about $12,000.[3] Note that with these costs, it would be almost inevitable that the two parties would reach an out of court settlement if the theory given above were correct. It would be almost impossible for the plaintiff and defendant to be so far apart in their evaluations of the likely outcome that they chose to go to court. To take an extreme case, assume that there is a suit for $10,000 and that each party assumes that their legal cost will be $5,000. If the plaintiff were absolutely certain he would win, and the defendant were also absolutely certain of victory, a payment of $5,000 from the defendant to the plaintiff would still leave each of them in exactly the same situation that they would anticipate from a trial. If the state were to offer each of them $500 in order to avoid the $2,000 cost to the state, we would have a clear cut pareto optimal move.

Even if we assume that the cost is somewhat lower, and I shall assume for reasons of illustration in the rest of this paper that they are only one third of the award rather than one half,[4] the plaintiff would have to think that he had better than a 5 out of 6 chance of winning and the defendant that he had more than a 5 out of 6 chance of winning before the bargaining range would be eliminated. Clearly once again, such gigantic errors in estimate are rare.

In the United States, once lawyers have been hired, settling cases out of court is almost as expensive as trying them. For example, Kakalik, Ebener, Felstiner, and Shanley, (1983) show that legal expenses of the plaintiff for claims that actually go to trial are forty seven percent of the amount at issue, whereas if they are settled out of court, the amount is forty one percent. For defendants, in such cases (mainly insurance companies who may want reputations as tough fighters) the percentages are fifty three percent for the trial and forty percent for out of court settlement. Thus the threat to start legal proceedings is an extremely potent one. There is no data on how many "cases" are settled before lawyers are called in, but the number must be large.

I don't want to argue that these costs are perfectly accurate. They are, however, the best data we now have. Further, a number of different studies show roughly the same thing.[5] When I was in law school, I was told that I should normally charge one third of whatever is issue for the trial and one quarter if I settled the case out of trial. These numbers obviously were conservative compared to present practice. But why are the out of court settlement costs so high? Further, if out of court settlement costs are so high, why don't the parties settle the matter themselves without hiring lawyers?

In essence, the negotiations go through two stages, before and after the attorneys have been brought in. In the early stage each of the parties has very little in the way of sunk cost but is threatening the other party with quite large costs if the other party does not agree with his proposal. Presumably, most of the disputes are settled in this area, but we have no real data on it.

Eventually, one or the other party has his lawyer write a letter.[6] The other party then either gives in (not uncommon) or hires his own lawyer and the high expenses begin. Up to this point, the high legal costs have been potential rather than actual expenditures. With the two lawyers working the legal costs cease to be merely potential and become real. Indeed, as the work proceeds, they gradually become sunk costs with the result that the potential cost steadily shrinks.

Let us look a little bit at the theory. Suppose that I am claiming $30,000 from you. Both you and I think that if we hire lawyers and go to trial, I have a 50/50 chance of winning, but our legal costs would be about $10,000. For the purpose of this example assume that when we do hire lawyers, they will agree with both of these estimates.[7] We both know that if we go to trial it will cost us $10,000 in legal fees. Thus, my estimate of the present discounted value of the case is $5,000. Your estimate of the present value is minus $25,000. If we followed Dr. Danzon's advice, you should be willing to pay $24,000 to avoid this expectancy of $25,000. I on the other hand, should be willing to take $6,000. At first glance, this appears to give us a wonderful bargaining range.

The problem with this is that if you would be willing to pay the $24,000 I would be a fool to accept less, and if I would be willing to take $6,000, you would be a fool to pay more. We are in a typical bargaining situation, in which both of us gain by not going through the trial, but where the question of how that gain should be divided among us is something for which there is no A priori solution. Either of us should be willing to invest resources in increasing the share of that $20,000 bargaining range which we receive.[8]

Note that the high trial cost means that both of us can make quite sizeable errors in our own favor in estimating the odds on success in the trial and still have a bargaining range.[9] Suppose, for example that the plaintiff thinks he has a two out of three chance of winning and the defendant makes a similar error in his own favor. This is surely a large difference, but it leaves the plaintiff with an expectancy, after legal costs, of $10,000 and the defendant with an expectancy of minus $20,000. The bargaining range is shorter than in our previous example, but still quite sizeable.

But why run any legal expenses at all? Why not settle without calling in the attorneys? It is, of course, true that the parties are more likely to make mistakes in their estimates of the outcome than experienced attorneys. As in the monopsony-monopoly case, if repeated dealings are expected, it is likely that the parties will take that into account. This may account for the fact that most law suits take place between parties who have not sued each other in the recent past and who will not sue one another again. If continuous dealings are expected, a wholesaler and one of his retailers, for example, most disputes will be settled cheaply and informally.

We are here partially paralyzed by the fact that in spite of a great deal of serious research, there is really no good theory of bargaining. In the particular case of legal proceedings however, we do have some reasonably good empirical data simply from observing what happens. Let us stick currently with our fifty-fifty case, i.e., one in which each party thinks he has about a fifty percent chance of winning.

This of course means about fifty percent granted they both have equally good or bad representation. If the two parties chose to try the case on their own, without lawyers,[10] each would have a fifty-fifty chance and if both had very highly skilled attorneys they would still have a fifty-fifty chance. If one of them chose to handle the case himself and the other had a highly skilled attorney however, the odds would be drastically changed. This is of course, the reason that it is possible for the lawyers on both sides of a case to feel that they have earned their fee. (Truibek, Sarat, Felstiner, Kritzer, and Grossman 1983) Indeed, in the United States, where most parties actually ask for more than they expect they'll get, and defendants frequently counter claim, it is not impossible that the plaintiff might make $40,000 if he had an attorney and the defendant did not. While if the defendant had an attorney and the plaintiff did not, the plaintiff might get a payment of $5,000 to $10,000 on his counter claim, while paying nothing on the plaintiff's claim.

What actually happens is that each party begins preparation for actually going to trial. This is partly because they may have to go to trial and hence should be prepared, and partly because of its threat potential.

The party who simply negotiated and did not engage in pre-trial discovery, interogation, etc., would be at a great disadvantage compared to his opponent who did. Indeed, the settlement would certainly go badly against him. Thus, this elaborate pre-trial work is not only true preparation for the trial, it is a very important part of the bargaining process.

This work has two effects. The first is that it, of course, increases the party's knowledge of the case. Note, under American procedure, under which each of the parties are permitted to question the other party's witnesses and examine any evidence that the other party proposes to present before the trial begins, this information is not only of the world in general, but very specifically of the case available to your opponent. It is possible that this improvement of information might make one party or the other decide that he had drastically over estimated his chance of success with the result that he drops out. It is, however, just as likely that a given party on examining in detail his opponents witness and evidence will come to the conclusion that his case is stronger than he thought it was as that he will come to the conclusion that it is weaker. Thus, the improved information is not in and of itself a guarantee that there will be settlement.

There is however, another aspect here. This procedure is costly, further, it is, in the United States, very much more costly than the trial itself. Thus, if we assume once again, our paradigm case, the total bargaining range falls as the pre-trial preparation goes on. Suppose each party has spent \$5,000 on a pre-trial preparation and still has \$5,000 in estimated cost left. Under these circumstances, the discounted value of continuing with the case, recognizing sunk costs as sunk costs, is \$10,000 for the plaintiff and minus \$20,000 for the defendant. The bargaining range has shortened. The plaintiff certainly will not ask for more than \$19,000 now, although he might conceivably have asked for \$24,000 before.

By the time the two parties are ready to go to trial, it is likely that they have already expended at least three-quarters of the total amount planned,[11] Indeed, the trial itself, may consume as little as \$2,000 to \$2,500 from each party. Thus, when they are ready to go to trial, their bargaining range is down to, let us say, the present discounted value of \$13,000 for defendant and a minus \$17,000 for the plaintiff. By now, the profits from investing resources in bargaining has shrunk greatly, and of course, there is a risk which can be avoided by negotiated settlement.

We have not quite finished here. In the United States it is not at all unusual for cases to be settled after the trial has begun. Indeed, it is not unknown for a case to be tried all the way to the point where the jury retires to consider their verdict and then be settled at that point. In this last case, of course, the only bargaining ranges that remain would come either from a disagreement from the two parties as to the odds, or the fact that they are risk averse and hence would be willing to pay at least something to eliminate the remaining risk.

We thus have an explanation for the extremely high costs of actually settling a case out of court in the United States. The existance of a highly costly procedure means that even if the parties have no difference in their estimate of the probabilities of outcome, they are willing to invest large amounts of money in attempting to get for themselves the bulk of that bargaining range. This procedure is not only costly in itself, it drives up the cost of out of court settlement. Lawyers and professional witnesses[12] are almost the sole gainers from this procedure.

Suppose that we had a low cost method of trying cases. Let us assume that it has the same or better "accuracy" than the current American system. Under these circumstance not only would the trials be cheaper, but the pre-trial preparation would be less expensive. Once again, take a case of $30,000 in which the plaintiff and attorney both think that there is a 50/50 chance of victory. Just for ease of calculating, let us assume that the costs of litigation will be only $1,000 for each side. The plaintiff should be willing to take any amount above $14,000 and the defendant to pay any amount under $16,000 so the bargaining range is quite short. Thus, settlements are rather likely although it also should be said that the total cost is low enough so that this might offset that factor.

As mentioned above, I am a proponent of the continental legal procedure. There are so far as I know no data on European court proceedings to put beside those of the Rand Corporation. It would be most desirable to develop such data. The simple fact that the total legal establishment, including lawyers is so much smaller in Europe, is evidence that litigation costs are sharply lower, and this must include preparation for trial as well as trial.[13]

So far we have assumed that the odds are roughly even. There is another aspect of American legal theory which I think is not yet orthodox, but is showing signs of becoming orthodox, which claims that litigated cases are almost always more or less even. This work was started by Priest and Klein (1984). It was criticized by Wittman (1985) and defended again by Priest (January 1985). From the standpoint of a student coming new to the area Priest's response to Wittman, is a better way of getting an introduction to the subject than reading the first two articles. The result of going over the same reasoning a second time and defending it against criticism has made Priest's exposition much clearer. Essentially, the argument is that errors in judging the odds are more likely in even cases.

Before turning to my reasons for disagreeing with this line of reasoning, I'd like to point out that all of these authorities are agreed that there is one particular type of case in which the likelihood of success is not 50/50. This is the case in which it is fairly clear who should win, but the absolute amount of damages is at issue. In these cases, statistics as to win and loss are of little or no importance. One would have to have statistics on who thought how much would be paid and then as to how much actually was paid in order to be able to tell whether this was roughly a 50/50 case.

Further, and this again is a point with which all three of these authors are fully familiar, these two kinds of cases can be mixed in the data. Suppose for example, we have a number of lawsuits between people injured in automobile accidents and the insurance companies holding policies on the appropriate cars. In some case, the insurance company argues that it simply is not responsible for the accident because of, let us say, contributory neglegence on the part of the plaintiff. In others, the insurance company, although making a pro-forma argument of this sort, is actually simply trying to get a fairly low damage settlement. Current statistics would mix these two together with the result that we would probably find the plaintiffs won more often than defendants in such cases. This would be essentially erroneous data, but data which would be difficult to correct.

All of this, to repeat, is fully known and taken account of by Priest, Klein and Wittman. Priest and Klein in essence, argue that the only cases that go to trial are those which are more or less evenly balanced and Wittman doubts this. In both cases, the argument is partially theoretical and partially empirical. It seems to me that empirical evidence here is pretty much pointless. A case goes to trial because the defendant and plaintiff have not been able to reach an out of court adjustment. There doesn't seem A Priori, any reason why a failure to make an agreement would be more likely when the defendant has a stronger case than when the plaintiff has a stronger case, or vice versa. If the failures are about evenly divided between those cases which might have been stronger for the plaintiff, and those cases where defendant is stronger than plaintiff, then the roughly 50/50 break would be observed.[14] This doesn't tell us anything about how close the cases were in reality. Suppose that we are in European courts, and that my previous guess of $1,000 of the cost of European proceeding is accurate. The plaintiff who thought he had about a one in five chance of winning, might well bring a case because the $6,000 which a one in five represents, minus a $1,000 lawyers fee, is still a positive number. He might fail to make a deal with the defendant who offered only $2500, so that the case goes to trial, although the average over many such cases would be five out of six decisions for defendant.

This however, would be offset by those cases in which defendants who thought they had only a one in five chance of winning refused to settle for $27,500 demanded by plaintiff and who lost five out of six cases. The two sets of cases, when added together, would give you a 50/50 break between plaintiffs and defendants, although none of these cases are even remotely close to a 50/50 probability of success.

In the above example, I've had to turn to the European procedure, which I assume is quite cheap, rather than the extremely expensive American procedure. Under the American procedure, there is indeed, some reason to believe that only reasonably balanced cases will be brought to trial. Suppose, once again, we are using my paradigm case for $30,000, and that the defense lawyer and the plaintiff's lawyer both think that the plaintiff has a one in five chance of success. Clearly, such a low chance of success is not enough to pay these very high legal costs. Under the circumstances, the defendants lawyer may simply refuse to make any settlement at all, and the plaintiffs lawyer may abandon the case.[15]

Thus, in those cases, tried in the American courts, it seems highly likely that there will actually be no litigation unless both lawyers evaluate the chance of success highly enough so that they will pay the cost of the proceedings. Note that this is to some extent dependent on the stage of the proceedings. Suppose for example, the lawyer for the plaintiff begins on the assumption that he has a 50/50 chance of winning. About half way through the pre-trial discovery, however, he uncovers evidence which leads him to lower the estimate of success to one in four. Since there is already $5,000 sunk and $5,000 is the esitmate of the remaining costs, he should continue the litigation. $5,000 is less than $7,500 which is the present value of the one quarter chance of the $30,000.

If the defendants attorney also changes his estimate to the same degree and in the same amount, he would lower the net cost of the case to his client to $12,500 which is of course, the one fourth chance of paying out $30,000 plus the $5,000 in legal expenses still to be incurred. There is still a very sizeable bargaining range, and resources invested to obtain that bargaining range are still sensible.

If however, the plaintiff and defendants attorneys had reached the same estimate of the odds before the preparation of the case began, it is likely that the defendants attorney would have informed his client that the plaintiff's attorney was not actually serious and the plaintiff's attorney would have informed his client that proceeding with the lawsuit would be unwise. Thus, there would be no formal settlement, simply a dropping of the case by the plaintiff. Here it should be pointed out that lower costs would lead to cases being taken to trial where with higher costs, the odds would be too high on one side or the other. The one in four chance of winning $30,000 minus a rather low legal cost, might still be a positive number.

But in any event, in the United States, these high court costs mean that the threat to litigate or the threat to defend is only credible when the case is reasonably likely to be successful. Exactly how likely depends on the measure of the cost to be run. Further, some attorney's, as a matter of policy, charge as high a fee for getting the other side to abandon their case before any serious work has been done, as if they had put a lot of work in on the case. When you hire such an attorney you, to some extent, hire his reputation as a tough litigator and pay for that reputation[16] even if he doesn't do very much except write a nasty letter to your opponent. In these cases, out of court settlement, which takes the excellence of the attorney into account, is not impossible. Of course, the excellence of an attorney on one side is frequently counter-balanced by an equally excellent and equally tough attorney on the other side.[17] These high litigation costs then tend to drive American litigation somewhat towards the evenly balanced cases.

Note that this argument is totally different from arguing that people are more likely to make errors in judging evenly balanced cases. The latter statement of psychology may indeed be true, but it is more or less irrelevant. The high cost of litigation in the United States eleminates very early cases in which one party or the other has very little chance of success, because these cases have a negative present value. Once one gets over this barrier however, these high costs both offer a motive for reaching settlement, i.e., to avoid the cost and make the settlement hard by driving the minimum cost that the plaintiff is willing to accept and the maximum amount which the defendant is willing to pay, far far apart and hence provide a wide bargaining range for expensive investment of resources. The end product is what we do observe, i.e., a cost of settlement which is nearly as high as the cost of actually going to trial.

This explanation offers a possible solution to a problem which has always mystified me.[18] Many american suits are switched to arbitral tribunals after the dispute arises. The reasons why parties would choose the cheaper (and probably more accurate) arbitral procedure when they enter into contracts is, of course, obvious. Once a dispute has arisen, however, one party or the other presumably has the weaker case, and hence would benefit from a lengthy and expensive proceeding. Why does he give up the threat potential of a regular case?

Looked at as a bargaining manoeuvre, however, the offer of arbitration has many advantages. Neither party is likely to admit that they fear a speedy and economical decision. Thus the refusal of arbitration is likely to damage the bargaining position of the side who so refuses. It is more or less a confession that their case is weak. Hence an offer of arbitration may be made, and accepted, as part of the bargaining process.

So far, I have pretty much completely ignored risk aversion and it is now time to take it up. Cases occasionally occur in the United States in which the jury has retired to reach its verdict and one of the attorney's approaches the other and suggests a settlement. We now have no further costs involved in litigation and both parties are as well informed about what is going to happen as it is possible to be without telepathically polling the jurors. Further, not much time can be spent in negotiations.

Under these circumstances, it is clearly to the benefit of both parties to eliminate the risk of the next few hours by properly discounting the outcome. Although it does happen in the United States, it isn't terribly common.

There are two possible reasons. The first of these, which I would say is the orthodox explanation,[19] is that the plaintiff thinks his chances are better than the defendant does and the difference is greater than their mutual risk aversion. I cannot disprove this, but there is an alternative explanation which is at least as good.

The alternative explanation is simply that the person who offers a settlement at a reasonable rate, almost immediately puts himself in a bad position for bargaining. Once again, take our paradigm case, and assume that the plaintiffs attorney approaches the defendants attorney and offers to settle for \$15,000. The defence attorney may feel just as the plaintiffs attorney does, that there is a 50/50 chance for the jury going either way, and yet say, "No, we won't give you more than \$10,000." He is investing resources in this case, the willingness to bear risk, in an effort to improve his bargaining position. If the plaintiff is truely risk averse, then he surely should be willing to pay something for reduction in the risk. I.e., accept \$14,000 or perhaps \$13,000. It is worth the defendants lawyers time to try and get a good bargain.

Note, we are back in the previous situation. If both parties are risk averse,[20] there is a bargaining range. Suppose for example, each of them would be willing to pay \$2,000 to get rid of the risk. That means that the plaintiff would be willing to accept a settlement of \$13,000 and the defendant pay \$17,000. Both attorney's know that any sign of haste or uncertainty on their part is likely to toughen the negotiating stance of the other. Both know that the other will be somewhat better off because of risk aversion if he makes a settlement which is somewhat more unfavorable to him than \$15,000. The outcome is clearly uncertain and in practice, this particular type of settlement is quite rare in the United States.

Obviously the reason this kind of settlement is rare is not that risk aversion is unknown among American plaintiffs or defendants, its just that the existence of risk aversion, even in this very pure situation both provides an incentive for a settlement and provides a bargaining range. Investment of resources to gain for yourself, as much as possible of that bargaining range, is obviously sensible. That this means that the risk is necessarily born rather than relieved in most cases is unfortunate.

Nevertheless, this particular piece of empirical data, that is that kind of settlement is rare (although not unknown), is evidence that in general, the possibility of making profits out of investing resources in bargaining, tends to dominate the arguments for settlement based on risk aversion.

If we look at settlements before the trial, they are certainly much commoner than settlements after trial, and before decison. This implies that bargaining costs, in general, do not dominate the total cost of the proceedings. The extremely high cost of settlements in the United States however, indicates that the difference is a narrow one. The two parties could after all, settle quickly at the beginning without having all of those costs. The individual who suggested it however, would alm ost certainly be giving almost the whole of the bargaining range to his opponent. Further, he is advertising that he is easy to beat down by threats of lawsuits. Under the circumstances, it is not surprising that the average case consists of very expensive preparation for trial and then a settlement.

NOTES

1. The above quotation does not mention risk aversion. This is not because the orthodoxy ignores risk aversion, but because it is normally brought in only after formal discussion of the bargaining range. I will follow this precedent, and leave risk aversion to the later part of my article.
2. As far as I know there isn't any on the costs of European proceedings, but there are far fewer lawyers per capita than in the United States. Empirical research on this matter would certainly be desirable.
3. *Costs of the Civil Justice System*, J.S. Kakalikand R.L. Ross, Rand/R-2985-ICJ. The referee feels that I have misread the Rand studies, and that the parties' costs are only about half my estimates. The studies are numerous, done by different people, and using different methods. I think my reading is correct, but in any event reducing my numbers by 50% would leave my argument intact.
4. This is mainly for ease of illustration. The Rand studies show that different types of cases have varing amounts of cost. One third is a conservative estimate.
5. "Most civil jury trials in Cook County produce small awards, often less than what it costs the taxpayers to put on the trial . . . the amount in dispute in most Cook County trials was almost certainly less than the combined cost to taxpayers and parties." *Comparative Justice*, Rand/R-3006-ICJ, Michael G. Shanley and Mark A. Peterson.

6. This is one part of the legal proceeding that is not very expensive.
7. This is not necessarily true, but there is no obvious reason that the lawyers' view of the matter would deviate from that of the party's in any consistent direction.
8. Using the referee's smaller estimates of cost, the bargaining range would be only $10,000, but the principal would be the same. (Tullock, 1980 and 1974)
9. It is not likely that we will make large errors in estimating our opponents legal expenses.
10. Possible but difficult in the United States.
11. In many cases, far more than this.
12. I myself have not actually testified in any recent hearing, but I have been hired as a professional witness and collected large fees for assisting in the preparation of cases which were then settled.
13. I am of course, aware of the fact that lawyers are engaged in many things other than trial.
14. See Wittman's, op. cit., for a claim that the data are not quite so evenly divided and then Priest for further examination of the empirical data arguing that they are about equal.
15. When I was in my very short period of legal practice, we sometimes offered to pay the filing fees of suits against our clients, a tiny amount.
16. Which of course, changes the likely outcome of the case.
17. American Insurance companies in making their decisions as to whether or not to settle cases, normally take into account both the skill and the disposition of the attorney with whom they have to deal.
18. I seem to be the only person so mystified.
19. As far as I know, this particular problem has not been addressed by the orthodoxy, but this surely is the explanation they would give if they did address it.
20. In some cases, the defendants are insurance companies who are not risk averse.

REFERENCES

Danzon, Patricia Munch, *The Disposition of Medical Malpractice Claims*, Rand Corporation: Santa Monica, CA, June 1980, p.v.

———, and Lillard, Lee A., *The Resolution of Medical Malpractice Claims*, The Institute for Civil Justice, Rand Corporation: Research Results and Policy Implications, Rand/R-2793-ICJ, pp. vii.

Kakalik, James S., Ebener, Patricia A., Felstiner, William L.F. and Shanley, Michael G., *Costs of Asbestos Litigation*, The Institute for Civil Justice, The Rand Corporation, Santa Monica, CA: 1983.

Priest, George L. "Reexamining the Selection Hypothesis: Learning from Wittman's Mistakes", *Journal of Legal Studies*, Vol XIV, (January 1985).

———, and Klein, Benjamin, "The Selection of Disputes for Litigation", 13, *Journal of Legal Studies*, 1 (1984).

Trubek, David M., Sarat, Austin, Felstiner, William L.F., Kritzer, Herbert M., and Grossman, Joel B., "The Costs of Ordinary Litigation", *UCLA Law Review*, Vol. 31, No. 1, Oct. 1983, pp 72–127.

Tullock, Gordon, *Trials on Trial*. The Columbia University Press, New York, NY: 1980.

———, *Trials on Trial*, Columbia Univesity Press, New York, 1980, pp. 52–64.

———, *The Social Dilemma*, Public Choice Monograph Series, George Mason University 1974, pp. 1–8.

Wittman, Donald, "Is the Selection of Cases for Trial Biased?", *Journal of Legal Studies*, Vol. XIV, (January 1985).

ECONOMIC EFFICIENCY AND THE COMMON LAW: A CRITICAL SURVEY*

Peter H. Aranson

1. THE COMMON LAW IN HISTORICAL PERSPECTIVE

Since the publication of Ronald H. Coase's "The Problem of Social Cost" (1960), law and economics scholars have paid increasing attention to the allocative consequences – efficiency – of the common law process in general, and to those of specific common law rules governing liability, in particular. This essay surveys those works that examine the general efficiency of the common law process,[1] and it considers various challenges to those works. First, though, we place the common law in historical perspective and consider alternative governmental approaches to its traditional subject matter.

1.1. Common law subject matter

As it developed after the Norman Conquest of England, the common law originally concerned nearly every area of law except foreign relations and the armed forces. The criminal law had common law origins, as did its various provisions guaranteeing the rights of the accused. Antitrust law, similarly, grew out of the common law. But today most writers regard as "traditional" the common law areas of property, contracts, and torts, and they ordinarily tack on to these categories the many concerns that arose in the parallel areas of equity law, such as divorce, wills and estates, and trusts. Indeed, Parliament merged the two bodies of common law and equity in the 1870s. Thus, in most common law countries, we now think of common law as governing people's day-to-day interactions in their capacities as private persons. Legislation explicitly and increasingly has preempted such former domains of common law as criminal law, antitrust, and broad areas of regulation.[2]

In common law nations, too, legislatures increasingly have adopted codifications of common law rules, mixed with rules whose origins are purely legislative. Most American states, for example, have adopted the Uniform Commerical Code as law. And most states also have enacted statutes concerning even specific non-criminal law subjects that formerly were nearly the exclusive domain of common law. Of course, some non-legislative "codification" had occurred earlier in the *Commentaries* of Blackstone, less systematically in the treatises of Bracton and Coke, and in specialized treatises in particular areas of the common law. But these enjoyed only such force of law as judges were willing to give them.

1.2. Common law process

Because of this infusion of non-legislative and legislative codifications into the traditional subject-matter domain of the common law, it may be misleading to refer today to a coherent and unalloyed body of rules governing the resolution of disputes arising from private interactions as *the* "common law." For example, a person who receives a worthless check in payment for services rendered may have a *private* right of action against its issuer under the common law of fraud or for a breach of contract or under the statute of frauds; the district attorney also may bring a criminal action against the issuer, pursuant to state legislation, for writing or passing a bad check.

What remains of the common law, therefore, is less a body of pure judge-made law and more a process that judges (and litigants) use to arrive at a decision in a dispute arising in traditional common law areas.[3] That process begins when a potential plaintiff to a possible lawsuit serves on a potential defendant a complaint alleging that the defendant has failed to perform a duty owed in general (under tort law) or in particular (under contract law), and as a consequence the plaintiff has suffered damages. The complaint also may set out the measure of damages and the relief demanded. Potential plaintiff and defendant then may try to negotiate a settlement out of court. Plaintiff's attorney also simulataneously might file a suit in an appropriate court, recapitulating the allegations in the complaint, citing the appropriate law, arguing that the plaintiff has standing to sue and has a justifiable cause of action, and informing the court why he believes that it is the proper forum for bringing this action. Settlement negotiations usually will proceed while these pretrial activities occur. Similiarly, defendant's attorney may then file an answer or a cross complaint with the court. Plaintiff's attorney may then file a reply to the cross complaint.

The court may hear and decide various pretrial motions (perhaps to dismiss part or all of the complaint or cross complaint, for an assortment of reasons, including the want of subject-matter jurisdiction, or lack of standing, or failure to state a proper cause of action). Pretrial discovery proceedings and conferences will occur. Eventually, if the litigants fail to settle out of court, and if the judge allows, then the trial occurs, the court reaches a judgment, and the losing party may decide to appeal the judgment to a higher (appellate) court.

The litigants' first important decision, to settle out of court or to continue with the trial through its completion, is one principal component in studies of common law efficiency. The judge's decision, to find for the plaintiff or the defendant, forms a part of the second principal component. Here, we come to the heart of the common law process. The judge at common law arrives at his decision by consulting the decisions of his and other courts in earlier cases with the same or similar fact patterns.[4] While there are variations in this process, nevertheless the judge's method of inquiry follows these lines. First, following a discovery of the facts, the judge must decide if (preempting) statute law governs his decision. If it does not, then he must find the most recent case eventually decided by the highest appellate court in his jurisdiction that most closely resembles the case at bar; ordinarily, he will apply the *precedent* set in that case to the instant dispute. If no such precedent is available, then the judge may look to the decisions of other courts or to legal writings, to find the law to apply to the facts. And if he discovers no such guidance in his inquiry, then he may recapitulate this entire process by searching for a close legal analogy in the case law. Failing to find such an analogy, the judge then may be free to decide matters for himself. That is, he will "make law."

Judges at common law can and do depart from precedent in deciding cases before them, but a stark rejection of precedent is uncommon. More often, a judge's refusal to follow precedent will incorporate an attempt, in some measure, to distinguish the fact pattern in the instant case from the fact pattern that prevailed in the case whose earlier decision set the precedent. Even then, the judge who wishes to depart from precedent will search for earlier cases, in which the "spirit" of the decision established the principle that he wishes to follow in the case before him. To do otherwise is to invite reversal by the appellate court.[5] Definitive decisions that establish or reverse precedents, in any case, ordinarily arise from the opinions of appelate courts.

1.3. Common law and civil law

Common Law, as applied in Anglo Saxon nations (except Scotland and Ireland) and in former British colonies (except Sri Lanka, South Africa, and Zimbabwe), and civil law, as applied in continental European nations and elsewhere, probably have similar historical roots in common law processes of judge-made law. The law merchant, other forms of customary law, and ecclesiastical law provided much of this base. Prerevolutionary northern France and the Hanseatic League had forms of common law. Southern France adopted many of the codifications of Roman law, which themselves were partly the product of earlier judges.

Today, though, common law and civil law differ in their most recent origins and in their respective processes. First, common law derives directly and consciously from the decisions of judges in earlier cases. To that extent, common law is a judge-made case law. But civil law derives directly from statutory codes, and thus it is the product of legislation. Of course, like common law, civil law is not a pure, unalloyed body of legislative codes. Civil law judges have shown an increasing reliance on precedents that they themselves have set. And the codes that the French National Assembly or the German Bundestag enacts represent the work of committees of judges.

Second, the difference in form between common law and civil law bespeaks a material degree of difference in substance. A judge at common law, following precedent, reasons from a specific rule in a prior case to the specific facts of the present case, and only then does he utter a generalization, but one whose application governs only the instant case case and (at the appellate level) ones very much like it. A judge in a civil law case first finds a general principle in a richly detailed and precise statute, which he applies to the case. In sum, in common law change is in the hands of the judges while in civil law it is in the hands of the legislature.

2. MODELS OF COMMON LAW EFFICIENCY

Because contemporary common law subject matter is an admixture of statutory and case law, it may seem surprising that modern scholars who study the efficiency characteristics of the common law process treat them as if they concerned pure case law alone. But the denatured state of common law subject matter poses no real problems for theoretical analysis. Indeed, if a legislature changes the law by invading common law territory, then models constructed in the same spirit as those that we review may indicate the allocative consequences of the resulting amalgam. Accordingly, we treat common law as if it derived from the same pure judge-made rules and processes that we have just described.

2.1. Rubin

We begin by considering Paul H. Rubin's (1977) models of the common law, because they stand first chronologically[6] and represent the point of departure for all other models. Our discussion of Rubin's models is more detailed than that of the other models, as his fully incorporate the nature of this body of work and explicitly identify the underlying assumptions, which the other models either accept or modify.

Rubin considers a simple tort case, in which A is the potential tortfeasor-defendant and B, the potential victim-plaintiff, for some kind of accident that imposes a cost of X each time that it occurs and injures B.[7] Now suppose that precedent in such cases would hold A liable, so that each time that the accident occurs he must pay X to B, either because of settlement negotiations or as the result of a judgment against him in a lawsuit. A then may adopt some accident-avoidance measures, which cost him S_A and lead to an expectation of $N_A = N_A(S_A)$ future accidents. T_A, A's total present value[8] of accident costs and prevention costs, then becomes

$$T_A = S_A + N_A X.$$

Presumably, A adjusts S_A to minimize T_A.[9] Alternatively, precedent in such cases may "hold B liable," meaning that B has no legal right to collect X from A if an accident occurs. B then might pay S_B to avoid such accidents, yielding him a total cost of

$$T_B = S_B + N_B X,$$

and B adjusts S_B to minimize T_B. Rubin assumes throughout that joint action to reduce N (or X) is impossible.

If T_A is less than T_B, then an efficient liability rule would favor B and place liability on the potential tortfeasor, A; if T_A is greater than T_B, then an efficient liability rule would favor A and place liability on the potential victim, B. Rubin also assumes that R, the probability that B will prevail at trial, is a function of precedent. Hence, if precedent favors B (A), then R exceeds (is less than) one-half. He similarly assumes that the parties know and agree on the value of R, and at this stage in the analysis, perhaps because transaction costs make it prohibitively expensive, one party may not contract away his rights under the rule to the other, even if the other party is the lower-cost accident avoider. We may thus interpret R as the probability that a judge, presented with the facts in the case, will follow precedent. R may equal one (zero) if precedent favors B (A). More often, R may not equal unity or zero, perhaps because precedent is unclear, because the facts do not fit precedent exactly, because the configuration of costs have changed materially since the precedent was first decided, or because judges occasionally may exhibit some tendency to ignore precedent.

At this point it is useful to summarize the assumptions that characterize Rubin's models:

A1. *Complete liability placement.* The common law rule places liability on either the plaintiff or the defendant, but not on both (for example, the courts will place either complete or no liability on a partially "responsible" plaintiff or defendant);

A2. *Exclusive avoidance.* Either one party or the other, but not both, will carry on accident (breach, or trespass)-avoidance activities;

B1. *Precedent and probability.* Until successfully challenged, *ceteris paribus*, precedent entirely determines the probability of future liability;

B2. *Probability and avoidance costs.* The probability of future liability, *ceteris paribus*, entirely determines future avoidance costs for one party or the other;

C1. *Probability and judgment.* Courts probabilistically follow precedent; R, the probability that plaintiff prevails, exceeds one-half if precedent favors plaintiff;

C2. *Agreement on R.* Both litigants know and agree on the value of R;

D1. *Change in precedent.* A single case that adopts a different rule than that found in precedent will change precedent entirely to that which the court enunciates in that case;

E1. *Equal court costs.* The parties face equal litigation costs;

F1. *Independent court costs.* Litigation costs are independent of the nature or stakes of the litigation;

G1. *Equal settlement costs.* The parties face equal settlement costs;

H1. *Independent settlement costs.* Settlement costs are independent of the nature or stakes of the dispute;

I1. *Liability contracting and high transaction costs.* Either because the legal rules governing the case do not allow it, or because transaction costs are high, litigants cannot contract away from the existing rule's assignment of liability;

J1. *Avoidance contracting and high transaction costs.* Either because the legal rules governing the case do not allow it, or because transaction costs are high, litigants cannot contract away from the existing rule's implications for the assignment of accident (breach or trespass)-avoidance activities.

Rubin's first model in this set, and the one on which most efficiency claims for the common law process rest, imposes two additional assumptions:

K1. *Future precedential interests.* Both parties have equal, nonzero interest in precedent;

L1. *Free-rider problems.* Neither party (with a nonzero interest in precedent) faces Pareto-relevant free-rider problems in assembling the resources to sustain litigation (up to the point of equal litigation costs (E1)).

These assumptions (A1–2, B1–2, C1–2, and D1–L1), taken together, describe a model of the common law process leading to the adoption of efficient rules (precedents). In particular, suppose that A has injured B, and that the present rule holds A, the tortfeasor, liable, but that the rule is inefficient, because T_A exceeds T_B. Let V_A and V_B, respectively, represent A and B's expected values if the case goes to trial. Then,

$$V_A = R(-X) + (1 - R)T_A - C, \tag{1}$$

$$V_B = R(X) + (1 - R)(-T_B) - C. \tag{2}$$

C in each instance is the (equal) court cost. As the result of a trial, A expects to pay B the amount X with probability R, but he also expects to be relieved of future avoidance and judgment costs, T_A, if the court reverses the precedent, which it will do with probability $1 - R$; and so for B.

If $-V_A$ exceeds V_B, then A and B will settle out of court, which implies that A will not challenge the precedent, and it will continue to stand. But if V_B exceeds $-V_A$, then A and B will go to trial and test the rule. This condition for trial implies that

$$(1 - R)(T_A - T_B) > 2C. \tag{3}$$

Notice that for any nonzero value of $1 - R$, the incentive to go to trial is an increasing function of $T_A - T_B$, the difference between the precedential value for plaintiff and defendant, and a decreasing function of litigation costs. If the rule is efficient in assigning liability to A, then $T_A - T_B$ is negative, the parties always will settle out of court, and the rule never will face a court challenge. But if $T_A - T_B$ is positive, measuring the level of the rule's inefficiency, then considering the value of R and litigation costs, some parties may go to trial, and eventually the rule will be changed to one favoring A, the efficient result. Future parties then will not find it rational to challenge the rule unless circumstances change to make the rule inefficient. This model thus predicts that precedent under a common law process will track efficient rules and create an efficient allocation of resources by placing liability on the party whose cost of bearing it is less.

This process is especially intriguing, because the model is essentially "judgeless." It is an "invisible hand" model, whose results depend entirely on the litigants' interests and incentives, to sue or to settle out of court. Judges even may decide cases randomly. But if parameters are otherwise stable, then disputants will only relitigate inefficient rules, which will represent an increasingly smaller proportion of the body of common law precedents.[10] Hence, the process need not depend on judges' "class interests" or concerns for efficiency.

A different model, and a different result, emerges if we modify either K1 or L1, or both, to reflect an asymmetry in future precedential interests or in present free-rider problems. In particular,

K2. *Asymmetric precedential interest.* One party has a nonzero interest in precedent while the other party has no interest in precedent;

L2. *Asymmetric free-rider problems.* One party faces no Pareto-relevant free-rider problems in assembling the resources to sustain litigation, but the other party faces such problems to the extent that he is entirely unable to represent any future interest in precedent.

If assumptions A1–2, B1–2, C1–2, and D1–J1 prevail, along with either assumption K2 or L2 (or both), then either equation (1) or (2) changes, as well as equation (3). Thus, suppose that A has no interest in precedent or cannot assemble sufficient resources to mount an adequate defense to the question of precedent. Equation (1) then becomes

$$V_A = R(-X) - C, \tag{4}$$

and equation (2) becomes

$$V_B = R(X) + R(T_B) - C. \tag{5}$$

A trial occurs if

$$R(T_B) > 2C. \tag{6}$$

Because equation (6) does not reflect A's interest in precendent, T_A, or because A has no such interest, a precedent in favor of A, when challenged at trial, eventually will be reversed in B's favor, provided that the values of R, T_B, and C so allow. If such challenges do occur, then precedent eventually will favor the party with the future interest in precedent, B in this example, if it does not already do so. Therefore, this model has no endogenous efficiency implications.

A third model assumes that neither party has a future interest in precedent, either because it is entirely absent or because of symmetric free-rider problems. In particular,

K3. *No precedential interests.* Neither party has a nonzero interest in precedent;

L3. *Symmetric free-rider problems.* Both parties face Pareto-relevant free-rider problems, making each entirely unable to assemble the resources to represent any future interest in precedent.

Again, if assumptions A1–2, B1–2, C1–2, and D1–J1 prevail, along with either assumption K3 or L3 (or both), a third model is described, in which V_A and V_B become respectively,

$$V_A = -RX - C, \tag{7}$$

$$V_B = RX - C. \tag{8}$$

A and B settle out of court if

$$RX + C > RX - C, \tag{9}$$

which is always satisfied, provided that C2, agreement on R, holds, which we assume to be true. Because neither A nor B will decide to challenge an existing precedent at trial, the precedent stands, and this model, like the previous one, has no endogenous efficiency implications.

Before we introduce the final model, it may be helpful to reflect on what we have learned. The essential differences among the three models concern the existence and location of a future interest in precedent or, what may be the same thing, each litigant's ability to represent that interest in the presence (or absence) of free-rider problems, because of which the present litigant cannot assemble others' future interests to attack or defend precedent. If both parties can and do express such an interest (K1 and L1), then the resulting rule eventually will be efficient if it is not so already. But if one or both parties remains unable or unwilling to do so, then the rule's efficiency or inefficiency is merely an historical accident.

To know the conditions leading to one distribution or another of interest in precedent or free-rider problems in a particular area of law requries some speculation. Rubin (1977) comments that we might find future interest on the part of "government agencies, labor unions, firms, and insurance companies (p. 53)," Hence, automobile tort law, for example, might be efficient, because insurance companies will represent both plaintiff (under a subrogation claim) and defendant. But product-liability law may reflect the interests of firms but not of consumers, short of class-action suits or appropriately designed legislative intervention (and assuming that market forces themselves do not already provide an appropriate set of incentives).

Whether the emergent precedents in any area of law are efficient, however, does not depend in Rubin's model on a full distribution of future interests or on the complete absence of free-rider problems. Instead, only an occasional set of litigants need have these characteristics for judicial activity to drive precedent toward efficiency. For example, if all suits have either two parties with future interests or two parties with no future interests in precedent, then precedent will converge to an efficient result, because of the actions of the interested pairs. Parties to similar disputes with asymmetric future interests, of course, may bias the results one way or the other. But the presence of litigants with symmetric future interests will tend to restore efficient rules.

Rubin's final model incorporates the possibility that one party may pay the other to adopt accident-avoidance activities, where the party paid is the less-costly accident avoider. In this model the basic assumptions, A1–2, B1–2, C1–2, and D1–I1 remain in effect. But we replace J1, "avoidance contracting and high transaction costs," with,

J2. *Avoidance contracting and low transaction costs.* Transaction costs are sufficiently low to allow future litigants to contract away from the existing rule's implications for the assignment of accident (breach, or trespass)-avoidance activities.

Rubin then assumes that K1 and L1 hold — both parties have equal, non-zero interest in precedent, and neither party faces Pareto-relevant free-rider problems. Further, let T_N be A's cost of paying B to engage in avoidance, given that T_A is greater than T_B. A pays B if T_N is less than $T_A - T_B$, provided that the rule (inefficiently) favors B. The two litigants' expected values of going to court if an accident *does* occur become,

$$V_A = R(-X) + (1 - R)(T_B + T_N) - C, \tag{10}$$

$$V_B = R(X) + (1 - R)(-T_B) - C. \tag{11}$$

So, A and B will go to trial if

$$(1 - R)T_N > 2C. \tag{12}$$

Here, A has reduced the cost of the inefficient rule, $T_A - T_B$, by paying B to accept avoidance costs. But A has not eliminated that cost entirely. T_N remains to be paid, and as T_N grows larger, perhaps as a function of increased transaction costs, the likelihood of a court challenge to the rule increases. For example, if the costs of A's transacting with relevant Bs increases, until $T_N = T_A - T_B$, then at that point A may sue or settle, rather than continue to pay B. The inefficient rule's deadweight loss continues under this arrangement, but the parties may arrive at a mutually preferred outcome by shifting avoidance activities to the superior (cheaper) risk-avoider. If an accident does occur under shifted avoidance, then the court would still apply liability to the inefficient avoider, the defendant, with probability R. If a court challenge shifts the rule to an efficient precedent, then all such avoidance-shifting arrangements will cease.

2.2. *Priest*

The second model, that of George L. Priest (1977), differs from Rubin's in several important respects. Priest implicitly adopts several of Rubin's basic assumptions, namely A1–2, B1–2, and C1–E1. But his model differs in these assumptions. First, the litigants need not agree on R. Indeed, Rubin (1977, pp. 62–63) sensibly claims that if Priest's litigants do agree on R, then no litigation would occur, and precedent would not change. Hence, Priest's model includes,

C3. *Disagreement on R.* Some parties disagree on the value of R.

Second, Priest claims that his model does not rely on the potential litigants' future interests in precedent, so precedent may tend toward efficiency under assumption K1 or K2 or K3. Priest's model also does not rely on the possibility or impossibility of payments to shift avoidance (I1 or I2), payments to shift liability (implicitly, J2), or the presence or absence of Pareto-relevant externalities (L1 or L2 or L3).

Instead, Priest's model relies on C3 and two additional assumptions. First,

J3. *Positive transaction costs.* Transaction costs are sufficiently great that the Coase theorem's implications (of contracting away liability) do not operate in some cases.

Second, reflecting Rubin's analysis, Priest assumes that,

M1. *Stakes increase with inefficiency of rule.* The stakes in cases in which precedent is inefficient exceed those in which it is efficient.

J3 prevents some parties from contracting before or after an accident, breach, or trespass, to shift liability or avoidance. The difference in stakes under efficient and inefficient rules, M1, then forms the prediction that potential plaintiffs and defendants will be more likely to litigate cases arising under inefficient than efficient rules. Disagreement on R, C3, then makes suit even more likely, as that disagreement expands the difference between V_A and V_B.

From this point on, Priest's analysis resembles Rubin's, except that the mix of efficient and inefficient rules is the outcome of a Markov process, in which the transition probabilities generate from the judge's bias toward efficiency. The speed of rule adjustment and the equilibrium steady-state mix of efficient and inefficient rules partly reflect the relitigation rate. For example, Table 1 reproduces Priest's calculations of the prevailing equilibrium proportions of efficient rules, assuming that potential litigants retest efficient rules in court at a rate of two percent. The interesting aspect of the table's entries is Priest's claim that relitigation rates may vary inversely with judges' biases *toward* efficiency. "The relitigation rate is an indirect measure of the extent of the inefficiency of individual rules. As rules become more inefficient and impose greater costs on the parties subject to them, the stakes of the disputes will increase and the litigation rate will rise (Priest, 1977, p. 71)." On this view, "[a]lthough it may initially seem paradoxical, as judges promulgate rules imposing greater inefficiencies on society, judicial influence on the proportion of efficient rules in force will decline because each of the rules individually will be less likely to avoid challenge (p. 71)." That is, as judicial bias toward efficiency declines, the relitigation rate of the increasing number of inefficient rules *perforce* increases.

2.3. Goodman

John C. Goodman's (1978) model rests on elements of Rubin's and Priest's works, but also on the theory of non-cooperative, continuous games. Goodman adopts assumptions A1 (complete liability placement), C1 (probability and judgement), and C2 (agreement on R), but he stands mute on A2 (exclusive avoidance), B1 (precedent and probability), and B2 (probability and avoidance costs). Court and settlement costs can vary in Goodman's model, which assumptions we denote:

E2. *Variable court costs.* The parties may vary their individual litigation costs;

G2. *Variable settlement costs.* The parties may face unequal and variable settlement costs.

Similarly, Goodman merely speculates about the relationship between private and social costs and benefits, so either L1 or L2 may operate.

Table 1. Equilibrium Proportion of Efficient Rules (%). Relitigation Rate of Efficient Rules Held Constant (2%).

		Relitigation Rate, Inefficient Rules			
		0.04	0.06	0.08	0.09
Judicial Bias	0.7	82.4%	87.5%	90.3%	91.3%
(% Efficient)	0.6	75.0	81.8	85.7	87.1
	0.5	66.7	75.0	80.0	81.8
	0.4	57.7	66.7	72.7	75.0
	0.3	46.2	56.3	63.2	65.9

Source: Priest, 1977, p. 71.

And future interests in precedent may affect neither, one, or both litigants, so K1 or K2 or K3 may prevail.

Goodman's model posits that a potential litigant's expected payoff from trial is a function of his and his adversary's investments in litigation and of any bias in the existing rule. In turn, willingness to pay for litigation is a function of its private benefits and the same bias. If no clear rule governs a particular fact pattern ($R = \frac{1}{2}$), then the party with the greater stakes will invest more in litigation and have a higher probability of winning in court. If this litigation sets a precedent, if the losing party (reflecting his lower stakes) is the lower-cost avoider, and if the ratio of the litigants' private benefits are roughly equivalent to the ratio of social benefits for similarly situated parties, then the rule will tend toward efficiency. Goodman also shows that differences in rates of return (capital-market treatment) or settlement-cost constraints as between the two litigants may remove any apparent connection between the ratio of private benefits and the resulting rule's efficiency.

2.4. Landes and Posner

Landes and Posner (1979) develop the most fully articulated model of the common law, in the same micro-analytic framework as Rubin and Goodman deploy. But the Landes and Posner model contains an explicit assumption about precedent formation that differs from D1, (complete) change of precedent, which Rubin, Priest, and Goodman use, namely:

D2. *Marginal chance in precedent.* A single judicial decision for (or against) an existing rule marginally and symmetrically increases (or diminishes) the probability that the rule will apply in all subsequent cases.

Similarly, Landes and Posner's model incorporates the possibility, unlike I1, contracting and high transaction costs, that in some cases the parties may be able to contract out of a liability rule's assignment:

I2. *Liability contracting and low transaction costs.* Because transaction costs are sufficiently low and/or rights are alienable, potential litigants may contract out of the liability rule.

The complete list of assumptions and their appropriate complements, which we have described to this point, allow Landes and Posner to generate sets of different predictions about litigation, with associated implications for efficiency. They begin with a model that imposes assumptions A1–2, B1–2, and C1–2, but D2 (marginal change in precedent) instead of D1, E2 (variable court costs), J1 (avoidance contracting and high transaction costs), G2 (variable settlement costs), and

I1 (liability contracting and high transaction costs). This last assumption, I1, or its variant, J3 (positive transaction costs), would seem to mark cases involving most tort law, more than property law, and even more than contract law. Indeed, Landes and Posner label their first model, imposing I1, as one in which there is "no contractural relationship between the parties (1979, p. 267)."

Under these conditions, if K3 (no precedential interests) or L3 (symmetric free-rider problems) prevails, then the parties will settle out of court, with no implications for efficiency. If K1 (future precedential interests) and L1 ((no) free-rider problems) hold, and if the parties' stakes overcome court costs and the like, then the disputants will sue rather than settle if the precedent is *efficient*, but they will settle if it is not. And if K2 (asymmetric precedential interests) or L2 (asymmetric free-rider problems) holds, then "the precedent will shift [marginally] in favor of or against efficient liability rules depending on [which party] has the greater stake (1979, p. 273)."[11]

Landes and Posner next consider a model in all respects like the previous one, except that I2 prevails instead of I1: the parties enjoy a contractural relationship that includes the possibility of bargaining away from the rule's current liability assignment. They arrive at four separate conclusions, as a function of changing parameters within their model.

First, from the structure of their model, they deduce that the possibility of contracting increases the likelihood of going to trial. Hence, if the existing rule is efficient (R exceeds $\frac{1}{2}$), then either "a more efficient rule will replace the market assignment of liability" (if the parties are in the neighborhood of a point in R in which they are nearly indifferent between contracting or suing), or "the existing rule will tend to become more efficient over time [if R is greater than the point of indifference between contracting and suing, so that the parties will sue] (1979, p. 276)." But if the existing rule is inefficient (R is less than $\frac{1}{2}$), then to the extent that the parties sue, they tend to reinforce the inefficient rule. The costs of inefficiency remain small in this instance, though, because the parties will tend to contract away from its liability assignment. Thus, what remains of the inefficiency is solely a transaction cost of contracting. While this process may have some unknown distributive consequences and rent-seeking costs, its allocative consequences merely reflect the transaction costs.

Second, Landes and Posner modify the preceding model, by substituting K2, asymmetric precedential interests, or L2, asymmetric free-rider problems, for K1, (symmetric) future precedential interests, or L1, (no) free-rider problems. Without contracting possibilities, the rule becomes more or less efficient as a reflection of which party, favored or unfavored, has the greater stakes. But with contracting, the interplay of stakes and probability in the face of an inefficient rule becomes irrelevant, because *ceteris paribus*, the parties will contract to assign liability in the direction of efficiency.

Third, if contracting and information costs decline (I2 prevails), then two results follow. (1) Suppose that R measures the probability that the rule assigns liability efficiently, and R_0 is the point above which the parties litigate and below which they contract to reassign liability. A reduction in contracting and information costs would raise R_0, and the range below R_0, in which the parties contract, would expand. (2) If R_0 exceeds one-half, which it is more likely to do under (1), the preceding set of conditions, and if transaction and information costs fall, then the remaining parties' decisions to litigate will increase the rule's efficiency, even though the number of such parties has declined. Thus, "there is a complimentarity between market and legal efficiency — the greater the efficiency of the market [because transaction and information costs decline] — the greater the tendency for a subset of legal rules to become more efficient (1979, p. 277)."

Finally, if R is significantly greater than R_0, then contracting away from the rule would become relatively more costly, and the findings of the analysis without contracting, those under I1, liability contracting and high transaction costs, would apply. But if R is significantly less than R_0, then the parties would always settle and possibly contract away from the rule's liability assignment, depending on the levels of transaction and information costs.

The authors next turn to the problem of making litigation expenditures endogenous to their model, by imposing E2, variable court costs. They conclude that if the stakes are symmetrical, then some litigants whom the rule inefficiently disfavors might litigate and spend enough to move the rule in the direction of efficiency. But if the stakes are asymmetrical, then inefficient rules will grow more inefficient (R will decline), but disputes occurring under efficient rules will be settled. These findings however, may vary with the values of the model's parameters.

2.5. Cooter and Kornhauser

The final two models that we consider here examine explicitly the evolutionary character of the common law. The first of these models, which Robert Cooter and Lewis Kornhauser (1980) develop, relies on three initial assumptions, some of which seem essentially definitional:

N1. *Finiteness and measurability.* The set of possible legal rules is finite, and a one-to-one and onto function maps the rules into an ordinal measure of "goodness" (for example, efficiency);

N2. *Measure and probability.* Let rule i + 1 be a "better" rule than rule i; the probability that a judge changes rule i to rule i + 1 and the probability that he changes rule i to rule i − 1 are positive;

D3. *Universal admissibility of change.* Every precedent has a nonzero probability of change.

Cooter and Kornhauser show that if these three assumptions hold, as well as Cl (probability and judgment) and Dl (complete change in precedent), then "the legal system tends toward a stable state in which each rule prevails a positive proportion of the time (1980, p. 144)." That is, these assumptions, as should be evident, are not sufficient to predict the adoption of preponderantly efficient rules. Stated differently, these assumptions describe a null model, in which neither judges nor litigants impose any interests or incentives on the common law process.

But if we modify D3 to,

D4. *Measure and restricted challenge.* Every rule but the "best" has a positive probability of challenge,

then the authors prove, in accordance with Rubin's and Priest's results, that "the legal system tends toward a stable state in which the best rule prevails 100 percent of the time (1980, p. 145)."

Two other optimistic results occur if we place some conditions on transition matrices, which express in their rows, for a given legal state, the probability that each rule will prevail. First, if C1, D1, N1–2, and D3 hold, and if

D5. *Measure and biased survival.* The "better the precedent the more likely that the legal rule will be good in the next period (1980, p. 147),"

then "[i]f a change occurs so that some legal rule is more likely to be replaced by a good rule than formerly, then the legal process tends towards a stable state which is better than the stable state of the original process (1980, p. 147)." Here, "better" means that more weight is placed, in terms of probability, on better rules than on worse rules.

Second, suppose that these assumptions hold:

D6. *Measure and biased change.*

(a) *Marginality restriction.* The probability that a judge adopts rule i + j, j greater than one, if rule i is the precedent equals zero;

(b) *Marginality symmetry.* The probability that the judge changes rule i to rule i + 1 equals the probability that he changes rule i to i − 1;[12]

(c) *Measure and biased probability.* The probability that the judge maintains rule j exceeds the probability that he maintains rule i if j exceeds (is better than) i;

D7. *Measure and biased challenge.* The probability that rule i is litigated exceeds the probability that rule j is litigated if j exceeds i.

If C1, D1, N1–2, D6, and D7 hold, then Cooter and Kornhauser prove that,

> The legal system has a stable state such that the proportion of time during which each rule prevails increases monotonically with the goodness of the rule. Furthermore, an increase in the probability of litigating any rule j, where j [is less than] n [the best rule], affects the stable state in such a way that (i) the proportion of time increases during which any rule prevails other than rule j, and (ii) the better the rule, the larger is the increase in the proportion of time it prevails (1980, p. 149).

The Cooter and Kornhauser theorems rely on an evolutionary model to search for the least restrictive, most general assumptions that can sustain a prediction of common law efficiency. Interpreted in this spirit, their findings seem pessimistic for common law efficiency, not because they never discover it, but because their assumptions clearly invoke some predictions about how potential litigants and judges will act. Their summary of these assumptions states the matter succinctly.

> Our theorems suggest that, if legal processes are simple, evolutionary forces can improve the law relative to what it would otherwise be. In particular, we have shown what consequences to expect *if* inefficient laws are litigated more frequently and *if* more is invested in overturning them than in defending them. However, we have offered no argument to prove that the frequency or intensity of litigation or investment in litigation varies systematically with the efficiency of the law. We have shown the consequences of evolutionary forces without demonstrating their presence in the law (1980, p. 150).

The relevant question then becomes whether models such as Rubin's and Goodman's have supplied the requisite "evolutionary forces," for the "consequences" to characterize the common law. It is evident that other models, such as those of Landes and Posner, might suggest otherwise.

2.6. Terrebonne

The final model that we review is R. Peter Terrebonne's (1981) attempt to meld an evolutionary game with potential litigants' decisions in common law processes. His first assumption merely states the availability of courts in which potential plaintiffs can press their claims. While all other models made such an assumption, Terrebonne's explicit identification of it may raise important questions. For example, are rules of standing themselves efficient or inefficient in any sense? Can one litigate the standing issue if preclusion is possible? Would the resulting (litigated) rules of standing be efficient or inefficient? And what would happen to the remaining body of common law precedents if legislatures began to restrict the courts' jurisdictions concerning particular kinds of disputes?

Terrebonne's analysis also assumes C2, that the parties know R uniquely and agree on its value. He also assumes what Rubin, Priest, and others have assumed implicitly to get to their conclusions, that,

O1. *Litigation and survival.* The probability that a rule survives varies inversely with the frequency with which it is litigated.

Similarly, Terrebonne assumes J3, the existence of positive transaction costs, to the extent that I1 and J1 hold: the parties cannot cooperate in any fashion to shift liability or avoidance activities.

Terrebonne's remaining assumptions are really definitions of (damage, avoidance, and litigation) costs and (litigation and avoidance) strategies, as well as descriptions of the game played between litigants randomly and exhaustively drawn in pairs from disjoint populations of "plaintiffs" and "defendants." Each time a pair is drawn, an accident (breach, or trespass) may or may not occur, as a function, for example, of avoidance costs.

Terrebonne then exhausts the potential orderings of costs and probabilities, to identify the possible combinations of "evolutionary stable strategies," those that realize a "higher average rate of return than any alternative strategy (1981, p. 401)." The results identify two cases in which the parties' joint strategy choices render an efficient resource allocation and a zero percent litigation rate, and two cases in which joint choices render an inefficient resource allocation and a 100 percent litigation rate, leading to a change of rule toward efficiency under O1. Terrebonne finds only a single case in which resource allocation is inefficient, but the litigation rate under it is zero percent. This result occurs if the avoidance cost is less than the cost of damages, if R is less than the ratio of litigation costs to damage costs for the plaintiff, and if R is less than the ratio of avoidance costs to damage costs, times the inverse of the proportion of plaintiffs that sue, for the defendant. But this result remains consistent with Landes and Posner's findings under similar conditions.

3. EXOGENOUS LIMITS ON COMMON LAW EFFICIENCY

Section 2 summarizes the state of our *general* theoretical knowledge about common law efficiency, inefficiency, or randomness with respect to tendencies toward efficiency. Here, we explore certain exogenous limits on common law efficiency, those which the models that we have examined do not incorporate, but which should be obvious to us from our survey, or which various authors have suggested independently. These include the variety of the models themselves, the problem of decentralized information and preference revelation, and the usefulness of the common law to make judgments about its own jurisdiction and that of the legislature.

3.1. Model variety

It should be apparent from our review of the six essays studied here, that we are beset with an embarrassment of richness and variety, and we have little guidance for selecting among the resulting menu of assumptions and the models that they might describe. Section 2 identifies eighteen assumptions or sets of assumptions, each with between one and nine imaginable (and sometimes opposite) variants. There are, all told, a resulting 5,971,968 possible systems of assumptions under which judicial activity with regard to a particular common law rule of liability might operate. These sets of assumptions do not include additional partitions, such as the presence or absence of appellate courts, or a characterization of the potential litigants' risk preferences (all of the models reviewed assume risk neutrality, but risk aversion might provide a useful substitute; it remains unclear, of course, whether the models' results might change under an assumption of risk aversion).

Occasionally we can state one or more of the assumptions or sets of assumptions listed in terms of another. For example, as we have already noted, high transaction costs (as, for instance, in tort law) may imply that I1 (liability contracting and high transaction costs), J1 (avoidance contracting and high transaction costs), and L3 (symmetric free-rider problems) operate. Certain of these assumptions also reflect an arbitrary polarization to achieve alternative binary conditions, even though there may remain an underlying continuous variable, such as the level of transaction costs or the range of disagreement on R. Finally, certain negatives of the principal assumptions might seldom apply.

Still, the number of possible systems of conditions seems unmanageably large for any *general* theory of the common law, and the research reviewed here considers only a very small sample of those systems, with substantial disagreement over which particular assumption seems more nearly appropriate. The potential for argument is potent, for example, in the conflict between Rubin's treatment of changes in R as a function of a single decision (D1, (complete) change in precedent), and that of

Landes and Posner (D2, marginal change in precedent). Surely, the results that emerge from the two essays are very different, precisely because this difference in assumption sometimes is driving those results to deductions that render entirely opposite conclusions.

We must stress that the problem of variety does not pose a challenge to the usefulness of the enterprise that this research undertakes, but only to the robustness of any conclusions drawn from it at this stage in its development. Indeed, the presence of such a variety of possibilities suggests just how quickly a profoundly extensive research agenda has developed. But its richness and variety also make it apparent that this body of research is in its formative years, and it awaits more general proofs of more general theorems, as well as far more empirical research linking assumptions to actual conditions and practices.

3.2. Decentralized information and preference revelation

A second challenge to claims for the possibility (or existence) of common law efficiency grows out of the Austrian contribution to the socialist calculation problem (Mises, 1981; Hayek, 1945). This literature observes that information about individual marginal valuations, expanded opportunity sets, and the like, is broadly and radically decentralized in the market, which makes economic calculation impossible for any central planning authority. But to the extent that common law courts, through whatever processes, would be conceptualized as mimicking putatively efficient market allocations through adjustments of precedent, to that extent these courts, at least implictly, would be about (if not explicitly in) the business of economic planning, with all of the attendent limitations – indeed, impossibilities – that the Austrian School has identified. Hence, the common law process would seem to be prevented from achieving efficient resource allocations.

In certain areas of common law, the courts have (increasingly less) recognized the information and preference-revelation problems in the rules that they apply. As Posner (1977) notes, "[t]he difficulties of legal determination of preferences or relative values may explain the tendency of common law courts to avoid major allocative judgments (p. 402)," and "it is desirable, so far as is consistent with achieving efficient use of resources, to minimize the necessity for broad cost-benefit analysis in legal decisions (p. 403)."

Mario Rizzo (1980a, 1980b), who has written extensively in this vein, suggests that information problems may go beyond questions of damage and cost of avoidance to the matter of relative negligence itself. Concerning his preference for strict liability in torts over a rule of negligence, Rizzo states the matter trenchantly:

> If . . . efficiency in the form of a judicial cost-benefit analysis represents an impossible *raison d'etre* for the law of torts, then it would seem that *even on economic grounds*, a system of strict liability is to be preferred to one of negligence. In a dynamic world in which the uncertainties of technological change, the ambiguities of forseeability, and the absence of a unique objective measurement of social cost all conspire to make the efficiency paradigm a delusion, the importance of certainty in the legal order is clear. Strict liability obviates or minimizes the need for courts to grapple, if only implicitly, with such impossibly elusive problems as forseeability, cheaper-cost avoider, social cost, and second best (1980a, p. 317).

Standing behind such claims is an implicit understanding that problems of information and preference revelation, first, do not affect the allocative efficiency of decentralized decision making in markets without Pareto-relevant external costs and benefits. Second, any legal attempt to resolve external-cost and benefit problems on a case-by-case basis through economic analysis (and possibly absent the possibility of alienating rights in liability or avoidance) remains fully subject to information and preference-revelation problems. Third, and accordingly, the preferred function of law is to declare a clear rule (in this frame of reference, a right), prudentially or otherwise, which sends decision making back into the market place, where the information for efficient action resides, dispersed and decentralized.

In short, the structure of the common law contains within it (and many of its rules give evidence of) an inherent economic rationale for the operation of *doctrine* instead of cost-benefit analysis. And the use of such doctrine as a substitute for efficiency-seeking rule adjustment, perhaps reflected in the permanence of some bodies of precedent, may appear to result in case-by-case inefficiencies writ small, when it is actually a reasonable response to the information-constrained abilities of courts to discern what efficient rules would require in each case. Devising doctrines that send decisions (for, example, how much to pay for accident avoidance) back to the market place, without further calculation, may thus promote efficiency writ large.

While it has much force, this criticism of common law efficiency enjoys no wider acceptance than does the Austrian School's critique of neoclassical microeconomics. The criticism itself is especially disturbing in the context of law. Suppose, for example that in an important question of liability, a judge had convinced himself beyond peradventure, that both parties adequately represented future interests, and that doctrine, as interpreted, placed liability on the higher-cost accident avoider. Should he follow doctrine, as subjectivists would prefer, and ignore his superior "knowledge of the particular circumstances of time and place," to invoke a familiar Austrian theme (Hayek, 1945)? Or, should he act on that knowledge and ignore doctrine?

Any answers to these questions must incorporate some measure of relative valuations of goals, which itself requires knowledge that neither side to this debate credibly might claim. Hence, we cannot answer them. But we can suggest that part of the difficulty in the Austrian criticism grows out of a simple confusion that besets both its advocates and detractors. That is a confusion between uncertainty as an explanatory variable and uncertainty as an *a priori* assumption. If one finds that judges, or even potential litigants themselves, are uncertain about costs and relative prices, then that condition might explain the common law's reliance on doctrine. This is an unobjectionable prediction, one subject to falsification, that grows out of the Austrian critique. One might even extend it into normative territory, to suggest that judges should uphold doctine if they are somewhat uncertain about a fact pattern to the contrary, or if the issue seems minor, merely to reduce the law's uncertainty. But to extend that line of reasoning to an *a priori* principle, upon which to base a constant body of doctrine, requires more knowlege than Austrian theory itself will admit.[13]

3.3. The boundaries of common law and legislation

The final set of criticisms involves the problem of defining – deciding upon – the common law's domain. As Section 1.1 points out, common law coexists with statute law, in a complex, poorly understood pattern of interaction. But both courts and legislatures face recurring decisions to allocate responsibility for certain areas and questions of law to one institution or the other. And sometimes courts (in American constitutional law cases) must declare whether the legislature itself has done something that is *ultra vires*, to borrow a phrase from corporation law, or whether the legislature legitimately has replaced a judge-made law with its own product, and if so, what it requires the courts to do. In either case the judiciary's demarcation of its own jurisdiction often will affect the precedents that it establishes, maintains, or changes. (Its decisions about jurisdictional matters themselves will form a body of precedent.) But we have no model of how common law courts decide such matters, so we cannot easily ascertain the efficiency properties of their own jurisdictional decisions that confine their choices (but see Landes and

Posner, 1975). Here, therefore, we shall rely on models that we have already reviewed, to speculate about jurisdictional and related adjustments, and to offer a critical interpretation, suggesting why those decisions themselves may be randomly (in)efficient. We separate our consideration into two parts. The first assumes that whatever division between courts and legislatures emerges grows out of public-interest considerations. The second assumes that the division grows out of political rent-seeking.

3.3a. Jurisdiction under a public-interest theory

The assumptions in all of the models reviewed concerning future interests in precedent, free-rider problems, transaction costs, and contracting out of avoidance or liability are intimately related, in that ordinarily they reflect large-number problems (Coase, 1960). These problems also form the intellectual justification for the existence of the state (Baumol, 1965; Buchanan, 1971): with large numbers of persons, free-rider or transaction-cost problems may make beneficial joint action too costly to undertake; people might then choose their own private consumption and production activities by adopting the level at which private marginal benefit equals private marginal cost; they do not perceive social costs and benefits, because it is too costly to negotiate among themselves, because they face free-rider problems in potential contracting and compliance, or because of any combination of these and related reasons. As a consequence, so the theory holds, Pareto-preferred allocations go unresolved, and the resulting allocation of resources remains inefficient. This general view of "market failure" is subject to severe criticism on its own terms (Aranson and Ordeshook, 1985, pp. 98–106). For example, many social-cost problems may have private solutions (Coase, 1974). Others may not present Pareto-relevant configurations of costs and benefits (West, 1967; 1976). This view nevertheless provides the *animus* for the "public-interest" theory of the state.

That theory, in its democratic version, holds that through the electoral registration of preferences, and the intermediation of legislative, executive, administrative, and judicial processes, citizens' preferences for the efficient production (suppression) of public goods (bads) find reflection in the public policies and body of legal precedents eventually adopted and enforced (Bowen, 1943). But this theory, too, is subject to severe criticism on its own terms (Aranson and Ordeshook, 1985, pp. 107–118; Aranson, forthcoming). First, citizens may underestimate the benefits (Downs, 1960) or the costs (Goetz, 1972; Van Wagstaff, 1965; Wagner,

1976) of public action, leading alternatively to the underproduction or overproduction of public goods and services. Second, neither the social-preference relation nor the social-choice function may identify an equilibrium set of public policies in either the electorate or the legislature (McKelvey, 1979; Riker, 1980), or even in the courts (Easterbrook, 1982). As a consequence of the resulting unpredictability, risk-averse voters may find their welfare diminished under the implied political lottery. Similarly, the notion of efficiency itself loses any meaning in such an environment.

In spite of these problems, we take the public-interest theory on its face and ask the next logical question, which both courts and legislatures must ask themselves as they face each new decision: what is the function of the common law within such an intellectual structure? Alternatively: given this intellectual structure, how do we divide the domain of social choice between common law and statute law?

An historical approach suggests how we might go about answering these questions within the structure of our models. Section 1 points out that many early societies had common law-like institutions (Landes and Posner, 1979; Posner, 1980). The law that evolved in these institutions at first largely concerned private disputes, such as those arising over private agreements, and then later expanded into cases of injury and crime. Indeed, until the middle of the nineteenth century, some common law courts in the American Midwest continued to decide on issues of public spending and construction of roads, canals, jails, courthouses, and schools (Brisbin, 1982). It is an artifact of this period that today the Massachusetts state legislature is known as the "General Court," that a committee of the British House of Lords exercises appellate review, and that in certain counties in the American South, grand juries choose the members of the county boards of education and advise local legislatures.

A "public-interest" theory of this historical pattern suggests that courts first were established to adjudicate private disputes. These nascent "political" institutions initially would rule on all disputes and on most other governmental matters, as there were no alternative forums. As these conflicts eventually came to involve larger numbers of people, the courts would continue to try to resolve them. In some jurisdictions, such as agricultural, sparsely populated areas (for example, the American Midwest), the courts eventually engaged in the full range of governmental activities. But in other jurisdictions, such as heavily industrialized or commercialized, densely populated areas (for example, the American Northeast or metropolitan London), it earlier might have become apparent that common law courts were not well suited for certain governmental tasks: those besides today's judicial functions that people would demand in more complex social and economic order. Hence, at some point specialized institutions, such as legislatures, executive branches, and bureaus and agencies, developed as people partitioned the set of governmental activities into judicial and nonjudicial categories.

This partition does not merely reflect problems of scale or specialization, *per se*, because if it did, then there would be a proliferation *and* persistence of courts in *all* areas of rule-creation and application, and little else.[14] Instead, under a public-interest theory, the partition might reflect a larger problem, that common law courts were relatively less-well suited than were these later-developed institutions, to resolve certain kinds of disputes, and more particularly, to perform certain governmental functions

The assumptions that Section 2 describes help us identify some necessary conditions about the areas of law that remained within the courts. Those areas would include disputes under which the assumptions leading to efficient resource allocations would be satisfied. The areas of law that "migrated" to other institutions would include those in which the conditions of common law processes could not imply that those assumptions prevailed. But as we shall find in considering rent-seeking explanations for jurisdictional change, these dividing conditions (assumptions) would be necessary but not sufficient for such a partition to occur. First, the political alternatives to common law processes might be equally inefficient. Second, both common law processes and their alternatives might yield equivalent resource allocations, but one system may be more costly to operate than the other.

In either case the models allow us to identify the assumptions under which the common law may depart from efficiency. But the problem remains that we have an embarrassing richness of models. For example, under Rubin's models, if K2 or K3 operate (asymmetric or no precedential interests), perhaps because of J3, high transaction costs, or L2 or L3, Pareto-relevant externalities (free-rider problems), then the common law may not achieve efficiency, and those subject areas affected may find removal to the political branches. Ordinary contract cases, involving no externalities in the parties' activities, then might remain under common law control (with occasional statutory codification). But "precedential decisions" governing property, tort, or contract law cases involving the potential for large external costs and benefits, such as zoning, accidents involving concentrated industries, or product liability "consumer contracts," respectively, might find removal to the legislature for the determination of general rules of application.

Our conjecture differs if we invoke Priest's model, however, for there J3, positive transaction costs, coupled with the notion of higher stakes in litigation brought under inefficient rules, would lead us to the opposite conclusion; namely, that precisely the law in those areas that Rubin's or Goodman's model implies would fall under the political branches, would remain under common law processes if Priest's model is the "correct" one.

Landes and Posner's model provides some additional guidance in three important respects. First, the central difference in their model is D2, marginal change in precedent, and therefore marginal change in R. Under this assumption efficient precedents are relitigated, and thereby grow more efficient, while no litigation occurs if the precedent is inefficient: the parties can only settle out of court, and the rule lies judicially dormant. This model contemplates, then, a greatly reduced social function for litigation, as compared with its function under the Rubin or Priest or Goodman model, which is to move the rule of liability toward efficiency. Accordingly, legislative processes might make relatively more public choices under the Landes and Posner model than under the others.

Second, Landes and Posner's model sometimes *explicitly* allows the parties to contract away from the prevailing rule's liability assignment. Including this strategy in the litigants' opportunity sets places a floor under common law efficiency, because in those areas of common law in which private liability reassignment is possible, *ceteris paribus*, at the margin the potential litigants may contract away from an inefficient rule's assignments. The other models do not include this explicit assumption (some of Priest's litigants might contract, while Rubin's can only contract away from the rule's avoidance implications). But allowing contracting would have the opposite effect on efficiency than the one that Rubin and Priest predict in its absence. If court costs net of expected stakes exceed contracting costs, then potential litigants might not go to trial, leaving the law inefficient, as compared with the possibility in the Landes and Posner model, that the parties might relitigate efficient rules and make them more efficient, and that at the margin, where R approximately equals one-half, further litigation may transform an inefficient or efficiency-neutral rule into an efficient one.

Third, common law rules that govern the possibility of contracting away from an inefficient rule may themselves help to demarcate the boundary between common law and statute law. Rules against such contracting ordinarily occur in circumstances in which the courts would hold them void as "contrary to public policy." The implication of such a rule is that there remain some external costs or benefits that did not enter the parties' calculations. That is, K2 or K3, or L2 or L3, along with J3, may operate. Notice that under these assumptions we do not expect common law rules to achieve efficiency. The process may be random. Yet it is in precisely those areas of law that the courts or legislatures might not allow the parties to contract away from the liability assignments of inefficient rules.

What, then, is the common law's domain under a public-interest theory? Plainly, all issues involving Pareto-relevant externalities (L2 or L3) or high transaction costs (J3 or its variants) would be subject to legislative, in addition to, or as a substitute for, common law governance. Similarly, if the parties have asymmetrical (K2) or no (K3) future interests in precedent, then the persistence of inefficient rules (by accident) may call for statutory resolution. Common law control would most likely prevail in those areas of contract law, and to a lesser degree in areas of property law, in which the parties ask the courts to perfect contracts. Tort law problems would tend increasingly to fall under statutory control, as would those areas of property law (zoning, for example) in which Pareto-relevant externalities may be present.

3.3b. Jurisdiction under a private-interest theory

The alternative theory of legislation grows out of the increasingly widespread understanding that the principal *animus* for members of the political branches is the public production of private, divisible benefits (Aranson and Ordeshook, 1985). The core of this theory holds that the same form of failure affects the political process as affects markets. That is, for a decision maker in a market relation, it may not be rational to incorporate in his decision calculus the social costs and benefits of his actions. Similarly, for a decision maker in a political relation, it may not be rational for him to incorporate in his decision calculus the social costs of (the fulfillment of) his political demands. It equally may not be rational for him to spend his own resources to promote efficient public policies that optimally produce (suppress) public goods (bads).

The legislation that results from this process follows one of two directions, depending on the configuration of preferences among the relevant actors. In the first configuration, a population of voters contains several interest groups. One group, say, engages public institutions to produce a good that for it is private and divisible, the cost to be spread over all members of the population. Under this concentrated benefits-dispersed costs configuration, relative to their added tax shares, members of the population face high transaction costs and free-rider problems, which effectively preclude opposition. Politicians cannot capture the benefits of providing public goods, because those benefits go to those who do not support the politicians with votes or money. But politicians can make a market in private goods, produced at collective cost. So they provide private benefits.[15] All interest groups are locked in this process, an n-person prisoners' dilemma, in which legislation begets increasing diminutions in welfare.

In the second configuration of preferences, there are two groups whose members demand partly to completely conflicting legislative decisions. Whichever group wins receives a concentrated benefit, while the other group pays a concentrated cost. The resulting public policy ordinarily imposes a dispersed cost on the population. The usual situation finds two firms or industries producing partially substitutible goods, or an industry or firm facing concentrated consumer groups (for example, those served by an airline route). Rather than rely on a market test, one firm asks, say, for policies that would impose differentially larger (regulatory) costs on the other. Because the legislature cannot create a policy that would satisfy both groups, it creates instead an uninstructed subordinate "legislature," a regulatory agency, and simultaneously offers the groups a regulatory (legislative) "lottery" over possible public policies (Fiorina, 1982; Aranson, Gellhorn, and Robinson, 1982). By comparison, under the first configuration of preferences, pork-barrel legislation or judicially enforced statutes seem more likely to emerge.

How might we interpret common law processes and their development under the interest-group theory of legislation? Here our speculations grow less certain. We must first decide on the extent to which the common law itself is or was in the past subject to the same kind of failure that appears to afflict both the market and the political branches. As Rubin (1982) points out, potential litigants under the common law may confront the same kinds of incentives that affect the decisions of interest groups in statutory development. His conjecture is that the common law first developed in small communities, in which there was little specialization. Hence, assumptions K1 and L1, J2 and I2 (full precedential interest, few free-rider problems, and nearly complete contacting) probably operated to provide conditions for efficient rules to develop in the common law *and* in the legislative process. Today, by contrast, and probably since the turn of the century, their opposites afflict both the judicial and political branches.

But a problem emerges with this explanation of judicial and statutory change. Suppose that Rubin's characterization of pre-twentieth century conditions is correct. If so, then we could not identify, in the theory's own terms, an explanation for the added shift from private to public law that occurred in *this* century. After all, under K2, for example, a potential litigant with a continuing interest in precedent would be in the same position as an interest group in the legislative process, in search of a concentrated benefit with dispersed costs. Before this century courts did some things, such as deciding who would be liable in an accident and what a contract meant, and legislatures did others, such as providing for the building of roads and a standing army. Today, though, while courts and legislatures may both find pleaders before them with asymmetrical interests, the ground of decision has shifted away from courts and into the political branches. Only later in this century did courts begin to "catch up" to the political branches in such areas, for example, as landlord-tenant law.[16]

We may offer three very general explanations for the observed pattern of change. First, legislators and others in the political branches, as owners of the firm that defines and reshapes private property rights, are residuals claimants for the policies that they generate. Judges are not, and indeed judicial canons of ethics prevent them from engaging in the overt and sometimes covert exchanges that occur in the legislative process. Hence, the efficient common law rules of the nineteenth century would find judicial protection into this century under the considerable inertia that may persist in a system of precedents. Legislative processes, by contrast, specialize in change.

Second, the rules of procedure that emerged in the common law also placed special-interest pleaders at a distinct disadvantage. Rules of standing, ripeness, and jurisdiction grew out of the same kinds of considerations that shaped liability rules themselves. For example, a rule of standing could open the court to a plaintiff damaged by an inherently dangerous activity.[17] But the *ex post* control implicit in such a rule could seldom find *judicial* transformation into *ex ante* regulation, where no actual injury had occurred. Nor is it apparent that *potential* victims of potential large-scale torts could resolve the substantial free-rider and transaction cost problems that might hinder *legislative* appeals. That result had to await the twentieth-century clash of firms and factor suppliers in search of anticompetitive advantage.

Third, the problem of jurisdiction itself, apart from the issue of standing, may become a crucial consideration in explaining the observed changes. In particular, as the jurisdiction or the electorate expands, the opportunities for both pork-barrel and regulatory policies grow apace, merely because free-rider and transaction cost problems for potential opponents of such policies at some point will gain relevance. Population growth itself, therefore, could partly explain a parameter shift, say, from K1 to K2 and from L1 to L2. But the matter does not end there, because jurisdiction size also may be an important strategic variable for any rent-seeking group to manipulate through its choice of a forum. For instance, such groups may shift their public-policy demands *out* of state and local courts and *into* Congress. (As we note in footnote 2, *supra*, an American federal court would be constrained by its own rules to apply state common law, as interpreted by state courts, and it could not embroider on that law unless federal law had pre-empted it.) Hence, the shift from the local judiciary to the federal legislature would represent an attractive stategy under a rent-seeking theory of legislation.

4. CONCLUSION

The general theoretical literature on the efficiency of the common law is extraordinary for its richness and for the future research opportunities, both general and specific, that it offers. In a way it seems peculiar that scholars have attacked the question of allocative efficiency first, before they have understood fully the demand and supply sides of the process, as they relate to specific areas of law, and then to the corpus of the law. It comes as no surprise that the attack did not result in clean, general theorems. Instead, it merely revealed the underlying contextual richness of an ongoing process.

This research strategy nevertheless has provided us with several benefits. First, it has restored to the common law the legitimacy that it has a social function, whether it performs that function better or worse than do other institutions in particular areas. Second, it has created, in an unusually short time, an incredibly diverse set of research agendas in particular areas of law, on the boundary between common law and legislation, in the courts' own rulings on procedure, and in the general area of overall efficiency problems. Finally, it has set out the importance of but limitations in empirical research, which ultimately must be responsible for testing the robustness of the emerging theories and models.

NOTES

* An earlier version of this essay, under the title "Doctrinal Judgments and Economic Judgments in Common Law and Constitutional Law," was prepared for delivery at a Joint Conference of the European Association of Law and Economics and the International Institute of Management; Berlin, Germany; June 24–26, 1985. The author thanks Goran Skogh, Cento Veljanovski, Jonathan Macey, and two anonymous referees for their comments and suggestions. He would like to hold them all responsible for any infelicitous aspects of this essay, and himself responsible for whatever virtue that the reader might find in it. But the customary law of his profession (probably efficiently) prevents such a transfer of responsibility, even if he and they otherwise might contract to a different allocation of liability.

1. See Rubin, 1977; Priest, 1977; Goodman, 1978; Landes and Posner, 1979; Cooter and Kornhauser, 1980; and Terrebonne, 1981.
2. Ineed, in the United States, a common law nation, federal courts have left the development of common law rules to state courts. Federal courts, as a rule, are not free to develop their own common law, but must apply the (common) law of the state in which a cause of action arises. See Erie R.R. Co. v. Tompkins, 304 U.S. 64 (1938). Federal courts may ignore the state court's rule only if federal legislation (or the Constitution itself) has pre-empted it. See, e.g., Middlesex County Sewerage Authority v. National Sea Clammers Ass'n, 101 S.Ct. 2615 (1981), and City of Milwaukee v. Illinois, 451 U.S. 304 (1981). But compare Silkwood v. Kerr-McGee Corp., 104 S.Ct. 615 (1984).
3. The following brief and greatly oversimplified description of common law processes will be familiar to scholars from common law nations. We include it here for continental scholars, who may not be quite so familiar with them.
4. The fact pattern in the instant case may be significant in two respects. First, the judge may have to decide on several procedural questions: does the plaintiff have standing? Is this the proper forum to bring this lawsuit? Has the plaintiff exhausted all avenues of relief and appeal (in a suit against the government). And, is this a justiciable issue? In doing so, the judge will consult a body of precedent in cases involving similar fact patterns. These are matters of jurisprudence, procedure, conflict of laws, and the like. But the judge will also consult precedent in similar cases in deciding what verdict to render in the instance case. Hence, precedent governs both the procedures the judge uses in the course of the trial and the actual decision itself.
5. This division of labor between trial courts and appellate courts leads to the generalization that the first decides questions of facts while the second decides questions of law (which the first then applies to the facts that it finds at trial). Like most other distinctions in this field, this one sometimes becomes blurred.
6. Richard A. Posner (1972, 1977) earlier had been struck by the apparent efficiency of common law rules of liabilty. He sought to explain this phenomenon as partly the product of judges' preferences for improving economic welfare. There at at least two theoretical problems with this explanation, although it may have some merit. First, it rests on a tautology: common law rules that judges adopt are efficient because judges wish to adopt efficient rules. Second, a problem of falsification emerges if, for example, (1) judges rely heavily on precedent, and (2) only efficient rules are (re)-litigated. The second condition may be likely to occur. See, e.g., Landes and Posner, 1979, p. 270, *passim.*, and the text at *infra*, Sections 2.4 and 3.3a.
7. This limitation to a tort context does not restrict the generality of the analysis, provided that in alternative contexts (e.g., contract and property law) the parties cannot contract away their rights under a particular rule of liability. See Posner, 1972, pp. 98–102.
8. We assume that these variables already incorporate whatever discounting may be required.
9. That is, A sets S_A so that $dT_A/dS_A = 1 + dN_A/dS_A = 0$. This formulation should satisfy the second-order conditions. For a more general discussion, see Brown, 1973.
10. In a later essay Rubin (1980) bolsters this argument by observing that if rules are efficient, then people should merely adjust their private activities to comport with something like a "reasonable man" standard. They will then find themselves litigating only inefficient precedents, which eventually will lead to an overturning of these inefficient rules.
11. As we note earlier, *supra* note 6, this combination of findings places extreme doubt

on evidence drawn from cases in support of the efficiency of the common law. If Landes and Posner's model is the "correct" one, especially insofar as D2 is concerned, then litigation would occur only in areas in which rules are already efficient, and the results of that litigation would go toward strengthening the areas' stocks of efficient precedents. Areas of law covered by inefficient precedents would tend to lie "dormant." Hence, evidence about efficiency gained from actual court decisions would merely reflect an artifact of potential litigants' decisions only to relitigate (increasingly) efficient precedents. Even scattered evidence of inefficient rules would become extremely damaging to the proposition that the common law adopts efficient rules.

12. Assumption D6(b) resembles assumption N2, but it is a stronger form of the assumption.
13. Rubin (1980) in a response to Rizzo's claim, places the argument in the context of "as if" assumptions in economics: judges need not have actual knowledge of costs, and so forth, as long as they act *as if* they do. At first glance, Rubin's response seems to be correct. But Rizzo's (and the Austrian School's) claim is deeper than Rubin supposes. For in the Austrian view, it is not even clear that an independent researcher could make such a judgment. Hence, any theory of efficiency seems unfalsifiable.
14. We do find in the United States today a Court of Claims, a Court of Customs and Patent Appeals, bankruptcy courts, and tax courts. But these courts seem more fully involved in rule application in specialized areas than in rule creation: they operate under federal statutes and regulations. Similarly, many federal regulatory agencies create rules and apply them in quasijudicial settings, with administrative law judges presiding. The European experience is not materially different. France, for example, long has had experience with special subject-matter courts. But under a public-interest theory, we may explain both developments as exploitations of specialization.
15. Constitutional provisions and some electoral control necessarily and partly constrain politicians to provide some public goods, such as national defense and public peace, as well as some quasi-public goods, such as schools, roads, public parks, and a patent system. But these programs are very much private in production, and especially in decisions concerning construction contracts and locations, and specific regulations of the private sector. The resulting resource allocation probably departs markedly in level, cost, and design from what an efficiency criterion would dictate.
16. See, e.g., Javins v. First National Realty Corporation, 428 F.2d 1071 (D.C. Cir.), *cert. denied*, 400 U.S. 925 (1970). For a discussion of this case and other similar changes in landlord-tenant law, see Rabin, 1984.
17. See, e.g., Fletcher v. Rylands, 3 H. & C. 774 (Ex. 1865).

REFERENCES

Aranson, Peter H., "The Democratic Order and Public Choice," in G. Brennan and L. Lomasky, eds., *Individual Liberty and the Democratic Order*, forthcoming publication.

———, Gellhorn, Ernest, and Robinson, Glen O., "A Theory of Legislative Delegation," *Cornell Law Review*, November 1983, **68**, 1–67.,

———, and Ordeshook, Peter C., "Public Interest, Private Interest, and the Democratic Polity," in R. Benjamin and S. Elkin, eds., *The Democratic State*, Lawrence: The University Press of Kansas, 1985, ch. 4.

Baumol, William J., *Welfare Economics and the Theory of the State*, 2nd ed. rev., Cambridge: Harvard University Press, 1965.

Bowen, Howard R., "The Interpretation of Voting in the Allocation of Economic Resources," *Quarterly Journal of Economics*, November 1943, **58**, 27–48.

Brisbin, Richard A., "The Delegation of Authority to State Bureaucracies during the Early Republic: Indiana, 1787–1850," Paper prepared for the American Political Science Association Annual Meeting, Denver Colorado, September 1982.

Brown, John Prather, "Toward an Economic Theory of Liability," *Journal of Legal Studies*, June 1973, **2**, 323–349.

Buchanan, James M., *The Bases of Collective Action*, New York: General Learning Press, 1971.

Coase, Roanld H., "The Lighthouse in Economics," *Journal of Law and Economics*, October 1974, **17**, 357–376.

———, "The Problem of Social Cost," *Journal of Law and Economics*, October 1960, **3**, 1–44.

Cooter, Robert, and Kornhauser, Lewis, "Can Litigation Improve the Law without the Help of Judges?" *Journal of Legal Studies*, January 1980, **9**, 139–163.

Downs, Anthony, "Why the Government Budget is Too Small in a Democracy," *World Politics*, July 1960, 541–563.

Easterbrook, Frank, "Ways of Criticizing the Court," *Harvard Law Review*, February 1982, **95**, 802–832.

Fiorina, Morris P., "Legislative Choice of Regulatory Forms: Legal Process or Administrative Process," *Public Choice*, 1982, **39**, 33–66.

Goetz, Charles J., "Fiscal Illusion in State-Local Finance," in T.E. Borcherding, ed., *Budgets and Bureaucrats*, Durham, N.C.: Duke University Press, 1977, ch. 10.

Goodman, John C., "An Economic Theory of the Evolution of the Common Law," *Journal of Legal Studies*, June 1978, **7**, 393–406.

Hayek, Friedrich A., "The Use of Knowledge in Society," *American Economic Review*, September 1945, **35**, 519–530.

Landes, William M., and Posner, Richard A., "Adjudication as a Private Good," *Journal of Legal Studies*, March 1979, **8**, 235–284.

———, "The Independent Judiciary from an Interest-group Perspective," *Journal of Law and Economics*, December 1975, **18**, 875–901.

McKelvey, Richard D., "General Conditions for Global Intransitivities in Formal Voting Models," *Econometrica*, September 1979, **47**, 1085–1111.

Mises, Ludwig von, *Socialism: An Economic and Sociological Analysis*, Indianapolis: Liberty Classics, 1981.

Posner, Richard A., "A Theory of Negligence," *Journal of Legal Studies*, January 1972, **1**, 29–96.

———, "A Theory of Primitive Society with Special Reference to Primitive Law," *Journal of Law and Economics*, April 1980, **23**, 1–53.

———, *Economic Analysis of Law*, 2d ed., Boston: Little Brown, 1977.

Priest, George L., "The Common Law Process and the Selection of Efficient Rules," *Journal of Legal Studies*, January 1977, **6**, 65–82.

Rabin, Edward H., "The Revolution in Residential Landlord-Tenant Law: Causes and Consequences," *Cornell Law Review*, March 1984, **69**, 517–584.

Riker, William H., "Implications from the Disequilibrium of Majority Rule for the Study of Institutions," *American Political Science Review*, June 1980, **74**, 349–366.

Rizzo, Mario J., "Law amid Flux: The Economics if Negligence and Strict Liability in Tort," *Journal of Legal Studies*, March 1980a, **9**, 291–318.

———, "The Mirage of Efficiency," *Hofstra Law Review*, Spring 1980b, **8**, 641–658.

Rubin, Paul H., "Common Law and Statute Law," *Journal of Legal Studies*, June 1982, **11**, 205–223.

———, "Predictability and the Economic Approach to Law: A Comment on Rizzo," *Journal of Legal Studies*, March 1980, **9**, 319–334.

———, "Why Is the Common Law Efficient?" *Journal of Legal Studies*, January 1977, **6**, 51–63.

Terrebonne, R. Peter, "A Strictly Evolutionary Model of Common Law," *Journal of Legal Studies*, June 1981, **10**, 397–407.

van Wagstaff, Joseph, "Income Tax Consciousness under Withholding," *Southern Economic Journal*, July 1965, **32**, 73–80.

Wagner, Richard E., "Revenue Structure, Fiscal Illusion, and Budgetary Choice," *Public Choice*, Spring 1976, **25**, 45–61.

West, Edwin G., "An Economic Analysis of the Law and Politics of Non-Public School 'Aid'," *Journal of Law and Economics*, April 1976, **19**, 79–101.

———, "The Political Economy of American Public School Legislation," *Journal of Law and Economics*, October 1967, **10**, 1010–128.

DEFAULT RISK AND THE OPTIMAL PRICING OF COURT ENFORCEMENT SERVICES

Hugh Gravelle

1. INTRODUCTION

All contracts in which the performance of the contracting parties is sequential embody default risk. There will be a stage at which one of the parties has performed his part of the contract and supplied something of value to the other but has not yet received contracted-for value in return. The first party will then face the risk that the second party will be unable, or unwilling, to carry out his obligations under the contract. The most obvious and most extensively analysed examples of this problem are credit contracts in which the borrower may fail to repay principal and interest to the creditor. However, sellers of *any* goods or services (including labour services) who provide them in advance or buyers who pay in advance, will be subject to the same type of risk.[1]

Most of the literature on *default risk* has examined its role in explaining credit rationing. Relatively little account has been taken of the fact that the party who has been defaulted against (henceforth the creditor) has remedies against the party who fails to honour his obligations (henceforth the debtor). These remedies may be privately provided, ranging from polite (or otherwise) requests for performance (henceforth payment) to physical assault, or they may be services supplied by the courts (ranging from judgement that a debt exists and must be paid to the provision of the services of court officials to enforce judgement and payment[2]). Remedies have two economically interesting characteristics: they may make the debtor worse off by an amount which exceeds the payment by the debtor and they impose costs on the creditor so that the net recovery is less than the payment by the debtor. Remedies are punishments as well as means of effecting costly transfers in the event of default.

The creditor's access to remedies will influence the debtor's behaviour in two ways. At the time when the debtor is due to repay or perform, the threat of the remedies will increase the likelihood that he will repay, since they increase the costs to him of defaulting. The availability of remedies will also affect decisions, made before the payment date, which alter the debtor's ability to pay. In earlier periods the debtor may work harder, exercise more care in supervising or choosing his investiments, or vary his consumption pattern, in order to increase the probability that he will have sufficient funds available to honour the contract. Remedies thus may reduce the moral hazard which arises when the creditor cannot monitor the debtor's decisions and the contract shifts some of the burden of poor outcomes from the debtor to the creditor.[3]

The use of remedies imposes costs on the creditor (phone calls, letters, time costs of visits, charges for court services . . .). This will limit the creditor's ability to make credible threats to the debtor about the consequences of default. If the creditor cannot commit himself in advance the debtor will realise that the creditor's decision on the remedies to pursue will be based on an assessment of their post-default costs and benefits. The creditor will be forced to ignore their effect on the default risk of this particular contract.

The inability to commit means that the feasible contracts between the two parties (which explicitly or implicitly specify the creditor's remedies) will be restricted to those in which the remedies are part of a consistent strategy[4]: they must be optimal given default. The greater the creditor's use of remedies expected by the debtor, the smaller will be the probability of default and, if contracts are competitive, the smaller will be the contractural repayment. Thus in states of the world in which the debtor does not default he is better off the greater the anticipated level of enforcement activity or remedies. But if he does default he is made worse off by a greater amount of enforcement. There will be a privately efficient amount of enforcement activity at which the debtor's expected utility is maximised, subject to some reservation level of the creditor's expected utility. It is not clear a priori whether this privately efficient enforcement activity is greater than, equal to or less than the consistent, *ex post* optimal, amount chosen by the creditor.

Public policy towards creditors' remedies can influence both the contracts concluded and the outcomes of the contract. The two obvious policy instruments are direct regulation of enforcement activities (whether debtors can be jailed for non-payment, how easily debtors can declare themselves bankrupt, the level and type of assets protected against seizure and so on) and the price which the courts charge for use of their enforcement services. By varying court charges or permitted remedies it may be possible to alleviate some of the private inefficiency which can result when creditors are unable to commit themselves to particular levels of enforcement in advance of default.

This paper models the behaviour of debtors and creditors when there is endogenous default risk and costly enforcement. It examines the consequences of different assumptions about the creditor's ability to monitor debtor behaviour and to commit his enforcement activities. The effects of variations in government policy instruments are analysed and welfare implications considered. Section 2 sets out the basic analytical framework, models the default decision and discusses the factors influencing the content of the contract. Section 3 considers the case of complete contracts when the creditor can observe debtor behaviour and commit his enforement level. Section 4 drops the assumption of observability and examines the implications of *moral hazard.* Section 5 deals with the case in which no creditor commitment is possible. In sections 2 to 5 there is only one type of enforcement activity (court services) and the government can commit itself, but can only control the price to be charged to the creditor for the use of its services. Section 6 extends the analysis by allowing for both private and *public enforcement* services, considers the choice between court prices and direct controls on remedies as policy instruments and examines the implications of lack of commitment by the government. The last section summarises the results and briefly discusses the justification for analysing court services as just another commodity like electricity or transport.

This introductory section concludes by briefly indicating the content of related work. One of the first papers to recognise that enforcement of contracts may be costly for both debtor and creditor is Leff (1970) in which attention is focussed on the post-default stage and the implications for contract price are not considered. A group of authors [Barro (1976), Benjamin (1978), Harris (1978)] examine the use of collateral in debt contracts and allow the value of the collateral to the debtor to exceed its value to creditor, but they assume that the transfer of collateral imposes no costs on the creditor. Thus the consistency problem does not arise. In Chiang and Finkelstein (1982) and Rea (1984) creditors can impose penalties on defaulting debtors but the penalties do not directly lead to any repayment by defaulters. The main interest in Rea (1984) is in the use of penalties to separate good and bad risks. The consistency problem is not considered in Chiang and Finkelstein (1982) even though punishment is costly for the creditor. Allen (1983) and Eaton and Gersovitz (1981) analyse the threat of future exclusion from the loan market as an incentive for repayment. The threat is assumed costless in Eaton and Gersovitz's model. In Allen (1983) the creditor is assumed to be able to commit himself and this credible threat and credit rationing of the debtor ensure that it is never optimal for the debtor to default. Stiglitz and Weiss (1983) show that intertemporal linkages in loan contracts whereby defaulters are refused future access to credit but those who repay are rewarded by future loans at lower rates, can be an effective and credible strategy for lenders seeking to limit moral hazard. Finally, Johnson (1978) contains a detailed discussion of alternative creditors remedies and proposals to restrict them but is not based on an explicit formal model and ignores the consistency problem.

2. FRAMEWORK OF THE MODEL

2.1. The default decision

Although the model is applicable to a wide variety of contracts, for definiteness it will be described in the context of the loan market. The debtor borrows a fixed sum in period 0, perhaps to finance the acquisition of consumer durables or other assets, and is contracted to repay R (representing principal and interest) in period 1. The debtor's period 0 income is certain and fixed but period 1 income y is random. Two alternative assumptions will be made about the distribution of period 1 income. It will usually be assumed that y is a continuous random variable with distribution function F(x, y) where x is care or effort by the debtor in period 0. Increasing x does not decrease period 1 income in any state of the world: $F_x(x, y) \leqslant 0$. The alternative assumption on period 1 income is that it can be either low (y^l) or high (y^h) with the probability of low income being F(x). Increases in effort reduce or do not increase the probability of low income ($F_x(x) \leqslant 0$)., One interpretation of this discrete case is that F(x) is the probability of *unemployment*, x a measure of *search intensity*, y^l unemployment benefit and y^h income if employed.

Since it is assumed that the debtor is always better off as a result of the loan contract and period 0 income is fixed, first period utility can be written simply as a strictly concave cardinal function of effort: $u^o = u^o(x)$, $u^o_x < 0$, $u^o_{xx} < 0$. In period 1 the debtor has a random income y and if he repays as contracted consumption is $y - R$. If he defaults his repayment to the creditor is g(a, y) where a is the level of court supplied remedies chosen by the creditor and $g_a \geqslant 0$, $g_y \geqslant 0$. The recovery function g(.) will vary with the legal rules which constrain the creditor's pursuit of the debtor. In most jurisdictions for example, the debtor has a level of protected assets below which he cannot be driven. Remedies impose an additional cost on the debtor, indicated by $\gamma(a)(\gamma' > 0)$. The costs can be pecuniary (time off work to attend court hearings, legal fees) or psychological (worry or guilt). When the model is extended to more than two periods γ could also include restricted future access to credit. The debtor's period 1 utility is $u(y - g(a), \gamma(a))$ if he defaults and $u(y - R, \gamma(0))$ if he repays. The period 1 cardinal utility function has $u_y > 0$, $u_\gamma \leqslant 0$, and is concave.

Default occurs if and only if

$$D = u(y - R, \gamma(0)) - u(y - g(a, y), \gamma(a)) = D(y, a, R) < 0 \tag{1}$$

It is assumed[5] that for all $a > 0$ and R there exists an income $\theta = \theta(a, R)$ such that $D = 0$ and that D is increasing in y at θ. Thus default occurs if and only if $y < \theta$ and the probability of default is

$$F = F(x, \theta(a, R)) \tag{2}$$

with default risk decreasing with creditor enforcement activity a ($F_y\theta_a < 0$) and increasing with contractural repayment ($F_yO_R > 0$).[6] In the discrete case it is assumed that $D(y^l, a, R) < 0 < D(y^h, a, R)$ for all a, R so that default risk depends only on effort.

Consider, for future reference, the debtor's marginal utility of period 1 income conditional on whether default occurs and define

$$u_y^l = (1/F) \int_{-\infty}^{\theta} u_y(y - g(a, y), \gamma(a))dF \tag{3}$$

$$u_y^h = (1/(a - F)) \int_{\theta}^{\infty} u_y(y - R, \gamma(0))dF \tag{4}$$

Since default occurs if and only if $y < \theta$ and u is concave it would seem plausible that $u_y^l > u_y^h$. Remember, however, that $u_\gamma < 0$ so that there will exist a range of y, when $a > 0$, such that the debtor repays R even though $y - R < y - g$. Then in some default states (values of y) u_y is smaller than in some non-default states and depending on the properties of the distribution function it is possible that $u_y^l < u_y^h$. This possibility is strengthened if $u_{y\gamma} < 0$ and weakened if $u_{y\gamma} > 0$ (as for example when γ is entirely pecuniary so that $u_{y\gamma} = - u_{yy} > 0$).

The debtor's expected utility, given the optimal period 1 default decision, is

$$V(x, a, R) = u^o(x) + \int_{-\infty}^{\theta(a, R)} u(y - g(a, y), \gamma(a))f(x, y)dy + \int_{\theta(a, R)}^{\infty} u(y - R, \gamma(0))f(x, y)dy \tag{5}$$

where f(x, y) is the density function corresponding to F(x, y) and $V_a < 0$, $V_R < 0$.

2.2. The creditor

The creditor is risk neutral and competition ensures that expected profit on the loan contract is zero. The *creditor* and the debtor both make the same correct assumption about the distribution of period 1 debtor income and the creditor knows $\theta(a, R)$ and thus the default probability $F(x, \theta(a, R))$ as a function of x. The creditor does not know the realised income y, only, by the default decision, whether $y < \theta$ or $y \geqq \theta$. When the debtor defaults the creditor can purchase remedies or enforcement services from the court at a price of p per unit. This payment is made by the creditor but it can be added to the debtor's required repayment. Gross recovery from the debtor with income y is $g(a, y)(g_a \geqq 0, g_y \geqq 0)$ so that net recovery after payment of court fees is $g(a, y) - pa$.

When a is chosen the creditor does not know y, only that $y < \theta$. Thus recovery is random since $g_y(a, y) \geqq 0$. Define expected recovery, given default, by

$$G = (1/F) \int_{-\infty}^{\theta(a,R)} g(a, y)f(x, y)dy = G(a, \theta, x) \tag{6}$$

where $G_a > 0$, $G_\theta > 0$, $G_\theta\theta_a < 0$, $G_\theta\theta_R > 0$. The direct *ex post* effect of a on recovery is positive as expected but a also has an indirect effect by influencing the critical minimum income θ at which the debtor repays. Since recovery increases with income, changes in θ will alter expected recovery given default. Thus $dG/da = G_a + G_\theta\theta_a$ is ambiguously signed. The effect of effort on recovery is also ambiguous without making stringent assumptions about F(x, y).

The contract will satisfy the expected profit constraint, expressed in terms of period 1 funds,

$$\pi = (1 - F)R + F(G - pa) - K = 0 \tag{7}$$

where K is the cost of the contract to the creditor and consists of administrative costs and the opportunity cost of funds lent to the debtor.

Substituting in (7) from (2) and (6) for F and G, contracts must satisfy

$$\pi = [1 - F(x, \theta(a, R))]R + F(x, \theta(a, R))[G(a, \theta(a, R), x) - pa] - K = \pi(x, a, R, p) = 0 \tag{8}$$

This must hold whatever the assumptions made about the parties' ability to specify x and a as terms of the contract. Note that since, *ceteris paribus*, an increase in default risk F would increase the breakeven R and an increase in R increases default risk, $\pi(x, a, R, p)$ will have to satisfy certain stability conditions if "plausible" comparative static responses are required. The precise stability requirements will however differ depending on whether a or x are controlled through the contract.

2.3. Credible threats

If the creditor can commit himself in period 0 to any level of enforcement activity in the event of default in period 1 the set of potential contracts is greater than if commitment is not possible. Without the ability to make credible threats or promises, which can alter *debtor* behaviour and the terms of the contract, the creditor will choose a so as to maximise net recovery $G - pa$ in the event of default. Let a^o denote this consistent but myopic level of enforcement. If a could be varied as part of the contract then the privately efficient contracted-for enforcement a^c may be greater or less than a^o (see sections 4 and 5).

Consider a possible debtor-creditor contract in which $a^c > a^o$. Such a contract is not consistent and will not be made, since both parties will realise that a will not equal a^c, (but a^o) if default occurs, despite the contractual obligation on the creditor to choose a^c. When default has occurred a can no longer affect contractural repayments R or debtor effort x. The debtor's utility given default is clearly decreasing in a so he will not wish to press the creditor to honour the contract concerning a^c. The creditor's post default optimal choice of a is just a^o so he will not wish to honour his promise of a^c. Thus neither party will wish to ensure that $a = a^c$ rather than $a = a^o$.

If $a^c < a^o$ the debtor will wish to see the promise a^c fulfilled. If the creditor reneges and chooses a^o the debtor can ask the court to enforce this term of the contract. But to succeed the debtor must be able to produce evidence which will satisfy the court that $a > a^c$. When the court is the only supplier of remedies to the creditor (sections 2 to 5) this presents no problem but when remedies are also privately supplied (section 6) it may be more difficult to prove that the creditor is violating the promise regarding a^c. The debtor may also incur non-recoverable costs in suing and may choose not to enforce a^c.

If the debtor and creditor cannot bind the creditor to an $a \neq a^o$ it may be possible for the creditor to commit himself by entering into an additional contract with a third party. In this contract the creditor promises to choose a^c if default occurs. If he reneges and chooses $a \neq a^c$ then he has to pay the third party a large sum (sufficient to ensure that

a^c is preferable to a^o). In effect the creditor commits himself by posting a bond redeemable only if he carries out his promise to choose a^c.[7] In order for this bonding contract to ensure a^c it is necessary for the third party to be able, at low enough cost, to observe default and the level of a and to produce evidence on these to the court. If $a^c > a^o$ both creditor and debtor have an incentive to conceal from the third party the fact that a^c has not been chosen. If $a^c < a^o$ the debtor at least has an incentive to inform the third party if a^o is chosen but difficulties of proof may remain, especially when a is a vector of public and private enforcement activities.

Commitment may or may not be possible depending on the costs of monitoring a, although contracts with $a^c < a^o$ appear more likely to be credible. In what follows a variety of cases are therefore considered, corresponding to different extreme assumptions about monitoring costs.

2.4. Time horizon

The assumption that there are only two periods can be relaxed without affecting the qualitative nature of the results in the paper. With more than two periods both debtor and creditor will take account of the fact that their actions under one contract may affect their payoffs under future contracts. The debtor who defaults may find that he is denied access to credit in the future or has to pay higher interest rates [Allen (1983), Stiglitz and Weiss (1983), Eaton and Gersovitch (1983)].

The future repercussions of default on the debtor would be reflected in the model in this paper in a larger $\gamma(a)$: a greater cost of default without a corresponding increase in recovery for the creditor. Default risk would be reduced but the inefficiencies associated with moral hazard and lack of commitment would remain.

For the creditor an extension of the time horizon has more important consequences because it creates an additional means whereby the creditor can commit himself. The effects of current behaviour on reputation for honouring contracts [Kreps and Wilson (1982)] and on the willingness of debtors to repeat their contracts [Telser (1981)] increases the range of credible promises or threats. If these effects are large enough to make any promise or threat credible then the analysis of sections 3 and 4 will apply. Where they are insufficient the results in section 5 on the no-commitment case will be relevant.

3. COMPLETE CONTRACTS

3.1. Single contracts

In this section it is assumed that the creditor can observe the debtor's care or effort x and that commitment is possible. The debtor will thus be able to choose a contract, specifying R, a and x, to maximise his expected utility V(x, a, R) subject to the creditor's breakeven constraint (8). The Lagrangean for the debtor's problem is

$$£ = V(x, a, R) + \lambda\pi(x, a, R, p) \tag{9}$$

Assuming a non-corner solution, the necessary conditions are

$$V_x(x, a, R) + \lambda\pi_x = 0 \tag{10a}$$

$$V_x(x, a, R) + \lambda\pi_a = 0 \tag{10b}$$

$$V_R(x, a, R) + \lambda\pi_R = 0 \tag{10c}$$

plus the constraint. The creditor's and debtor's marginal rates of substitution between each pair of contract terms will be equated.

Since the debtor and creditor can make privately efficient contracts about all the variables under their control (x, a, R) affecting their utility or profit it might appear that there is no reason why the price of court services p should not be equal to marginal cost: the usual welfare conclusion for public firms where there are no second best or distributional problems should hold. The court's profit on the sale of its enforcement services is pa – C(a) (where C is cost). This profit is earned, with probability F, if the debtor defaults. Let σ be the marginal social value of expected profit on the sale of court enforcement services. The social welfare maximand is

$$V(x, a, R) + \sigma F[pa - C(a)] \tag{11}$$

It is assumed in sections 2 to 5 that private contracts cannot be directly altered by public policy. Hence there is no direct control of x, a or R by policy makers. The policy instrument available is the price of enforcement services, p, and (11) is maximised subject to the privately efficient debtor-creditor contract defined by (10) and (8). It is assumed that the policy maker can commit himself in period 0 to the price to be charged in period 1 if default occurs. (See section 6 for the implications of the policy maker's inability to commit.)

The socially optimal price will satisfy[8]

$$\lambda Fa + \sigma\left[F\left(a + (p - C')\frac{da}{dp}\right) + (pa - C)\frac{dF}{dp}\right] = 0 \tag{12}$$

where use has been made of the envelope property in the debtor-creditor privately optimal contract problem ($dv/dp = \lambda\pi_p$) and $\pi_p = -Fa$. Define $\eta = d\log(Fa)/d\log p$ as the price elasticity of expected demand-for enforcement services[9], $\alpha = d\log(C/a)/d\log a$ as the elasticity of the average cost of enforcement services and $\eta_F = d\log F/d\log p$ as the elasticity of default risk with respect to price. Then rearrangement of (12) yields[10] the optimal percentage deviation of price from marginal cost

$$\frac{p - C'}{p} = \frac{-1}{\eta}\left[\frac{\sigma - \lambda}{\sigma} + \alpha\frac{C}{pa}\eta_F\right] \tag{13}$$

This resembles the usual pricing rule [see, for example, Rees (1984)] in that the price-marginal cost margin is inversely related to the price elasticity of expected demand but has two distinctive features. In the usual public firm case λ is the marginal utility of income to the consumer of the public firm's products. In the case of enforcement services λ is the marginal value to the debtor (consumer) of additional creditor income, i.e. of a relaxation in the creditor's profit constraint. It is *not* the expected marginal utility of period 1 debtor income (Eu_y).

The other unusual feature of (13) is that the elasticity of average cost affects the optimal price. The intuition behind this is that when the privately optimal debtor-creditor contract is made both parties ignore the indirect effects via F of their contract on the expected public sector surplus $F(pa - C)$. To see this most clearly consider the case in which income is discretely distributed and default risk $F = F(x)$ does not depend on a or R. If the social welfare maximiser could directly control x (and thus F), as well as p, the first order conditions on the social welfare function would be

$$V_x + \lambda\pi_x + \sigma F_x(pa - C) = 0 \tag{14a}$$

$$\lambda\pi_p + \sigma F\left[a + (p - C')\frac{da}{dp}\right] = 0 \tag{14b}$$

(Recall that the contract on a, R would be chosen to maximise V s.t. $\pi = 0$ for given x, so that the envelope property ensures that the indirect effects of x and p on V, via a and R, can be ignored.) With direct planner control of x and thus default risk F, the optimal price satisfies exactly the usual inverse elasticity formula and if $\lambda = \sigma$, then $p = C'$. When x is not directly controllable by the planner, the price must be chosen allowing for its additional indirect effects on expected public sector surplus via x and thus F. If $p = C'$ and average cost is decreasing then $F_x(pa - C) > 0$ (since $F_x < 0$). The privately optimal choice of x, which ensures that $V_x + \lambda\pi_x = 0$, means that x is too small because losses are made and increases in x reduce their probability. Thus, if privately optimal x declines with p, a price below marginal cost is indicated. Conversely if average cost increases with a ($\alpha > 0$) p should exceed marginal cost to reduce a and thus x in order to increase default risk and the chance of earning the surplus pa $-$ C > 0. The importance of the cost structure in determining p depends both on the magnitude of α and on how large profits are relative to total revenue (reflected in the C/pa term).

3.2. Mutliple contracts

If there are n *ex ante* identical pairs of contracting debtors and creditors the social welfare function will be $nV + \sigma[pnFa - EC(\sum_i a)]$. This differs essentially from the single contract case only in the term $EC(\sum_i a)$ which is the expected cost to the public sector of supplying enforcement services. Unless C is linear ($\alpha = 0$) $EC(\sum_i a) \neq nFC(a)$ and hence optimal price will depend on the number of contracts. In general, even if debtor default risks are independent, the optimal price formula will be quite complex since it will involve the derivative with respect to p of

$$EC\left(\sum_i a\right) = \sum_{k=0}^{n} \binom{n}{k} F^k(1 - F)^{n-k}C(ka) \tag{15}$$

where both F and a are functions of p. The optimal price will depend on marginal cost at every possible output level. If each debtor and creditor generate a demand for enforcement that is 'small' in relation to total demand then the difference between expected marginal cost and marginal cost at expected output will be 'small'. To capture the idea that each pair of contractors is small suppose that each demands $a(p, n) = a^c(p)/n$ if default occurs. Then because the $a(p, n)$ are identically and independently distributed we can use the law of large numbers to show that plim $C(\Sigma a) = C(E\Sigma a) = C(Fa^c)$. Then expected budget surplus can be written as $Fap - C(Fa)$ for large n and so the marginal social value of p is

$$n\lambda\pi_p + \sigma\left[Fa^c + (p - C'(Fa^c))\frac{d(a^cF)}{dp}\right] \tag{12'}$$

and since $\pi_p = -Fa(p, n) = Fa^c(p)/n$ we get the optimal pricing rule

$$\frac{p - C'}{p} = -\frac{1}{\eta}\frac{\sigma - \lambda}{\sigma} \tag{13'}$$

No account is taken of the elasticity of average cost because actual total demand is almost surely equal to expected total demand.

The remaining sections of the paper will consider the case of a single debtor-creditor pair. If $\alpha = 0$ then the results apply to any economy in which the debtor-creditor pair is replicated n-fold since the social welfare function is not essentially altered. If individual demands for enforcement are small relative to total expected demand then the single pair results also apply irrespective of the cost structure provided that we set $\alpha = 0$ in the optimal pricing formulae.

4. MORAL HAZARD

It is now assumed that x is not observable by the creditor so that it is not controllable by the contract between debtor and creditor. Commitment by the creditor is still possible. The debtor will choose his first period care taking the (a, R) terms of the contract as fixed and ignoring the effect of x on the creditor's profit. The choice of x will maximise V(x, a, R) for parametric a and R. Denote this level of care as

$$x = x^{o}(a, R) \tag{16}$$

The choice of contract terms (a, R) will thus maximise $V(x^{o}(a, R), a, R)$ subject to $\pi(x^{o}(a, R), a, R, p) = 0$ and will satisfy

$$v_a + \lambda(\pi_a + \pi_x x_a^{o}) = 0 \tag{17}$$

$$v_R + \lambda(\pi_R + \pi_x x_R^{o}) = 0 \tag{18}$$

plus the constraint.[11] The debtor and creditor cannot control care by a contract but they take account of the effect of (a, R) on x in their privately efficient contract.

Using the envelope property of the privately optimal contract, the marginal value to the debtor of an increase in enforcement price is $\lambda\pi_p = -\lambda Fa$. This is identical in form to the case in which there is no moral hazard and x is a term in the contract. Since the marginal expected public sector surplus $d[F(pa - C)]/dp$ is also identical in form, *the optimal price must satisfy the same conditions irrespective of whether there is moral hazard.* The particular optimal level will of course differ because x^{o} and the contract termns (a, R) will differ and so will their responses to changes in p. However exactly the same formula ((13) or (13′)) must hold in both cases. In particular if $\sigma = \lambda$ and $\alpha = 0$ p should equal $C'(a)$ even if there is moral hazard.

The rationale for this result is that enforcement price p has no direct effect on the level of care. Care depends on p only through the influence of p on the privately optimal (a, R). These terms are fixed by the contract after taking into account their effect on x^{o} (a, R). Moral hazard is privately optimally mitigated, though not eliminated, by the parties through their contact and variations in p do not constitute an additional direct means of affecting care. Enforcement price is not an effective instrument for improving the choice of care. The parties are made worse off by the creditor's inability to monitor x but this moral hazard will not influence the socially optimal price of enforcement.

5. CONTRACTS WITHOUT COMMITMENT

5.1. The default game

When commitment is not possible the creditor's credible choice of enforcement a takes account only of its effect on his recovery given that default has occurred. He will ignore the effect of a on default risk because, without commitment, a is chosen *ex post* i.e. after the debtor has defaulted. Thus when default occurs the creditor will choose a to maximise recovery (defined by (6)), less enforcement costs: $G(a, \theta, x) - pa$, where the effects of a on θ and x are ignored. Let this consistent choice of a be denoted a^o. Then

$$a = a^o(x, \theta, p) \qquad (19)$$

since in maximising $G - pa$ the creditor takes θ and x as unalterable by the choice of a made after default i.e. without commitment.[12]

If x is not controlled by the contract because it cannot be observed by the creditor then x and a are determined in a non-cooperative game. In this game the creditor must adopt the role of Stackelberg follower because he moves last (choosing a) and cannot commit himself. He cannot observe x when he moves (otherwise x would be a term of the contract) but he has full information about the debtor's preferences and probability beliefs. Hence he can predict what x would be rational for the debtor at the first stage of the game. The debtor is also fully informed about the creditor's preferences and probability beliefs and is aware that the creditor has the same information about the debtor and that the creditor believes the debtor will act rationally. The debtor will therefore choose x to maximise $V(x, a, R)$ subject to the creditor's consistent choice of a i.e. subject to (19). Thus the debtor adopts the role of Stackelberg leader and takes the effect of x on a into account in determining his optimal first period move:

$$x = x^*(R, p) \qquad (20)$$

The debtor-creditor contract is made in the light of both parties knowledge of its effect on the outcome of the subsequent non-cooperative game. The contract maximises V subject to the profit constraint, (19) and (20). With three choice variables (x, a, R) and three constraints the optimisation problem is trivial and one could solve the constraints for (x, a, R) as functions of p, substitute into V and obtain dV/dp directly. It is more instructive to impose the constraints explicitly and to consider the Lagrangean

$$L = V(x, a, R) + \lambda\pi(x, a, R, p) + \mu[a^{\circ}(x, \theta, p) - a] + \varrho[x^{*}(R, p) - x] \tag{21}$$

Using envelope properties of the optimised value of L gives

$$\frac{dV}{dp} = \lambda\pi_{p} + \mu a^{\circ}_{p} + \varrho x^{*}_{p} \tag{22}$$

which differs in two respects from the analogous expressions in sections 3 and 4, where commitment was possible. Lack of commitment means that variations in a have direct impact on V which have not been accounted for, via the contract, in the repayment term R. Since the no-commitment constraint is an equality μ may be positive or negative. If $\mu > 0$ the debtor would be willing to accept a larger level of enforcement because he places a high value on the resulting reduction in R. (See below for a diagrammatic illustration of this point).

The other distinguishing feature of (22) is that, despite the fact that the debtor controls x, its marginal value to him is not zero. x affects V directly but also influences π and a° and the debtor cannot trade off x against R. If x was observable by the creditor *or* if commitment was possible its marginal value would be zero. Only when there is no commitment will moral hazard have any impact on dV/dp and thus on the optimal price. Section 4 showed that if commitment is possible a and R are chosen by the debtor taking into account their effects on x (via (16)) and so the indirect influence of p on x (via a and R) does not create any additional benefit for the debtor. If x *is* observable and hence can be controlled by contract the constraint (20) does not arise and $\varrho \equiv 0$.

There are two other circumstances in which the effect of p on x can be ignored. Suppose that the recovery function g(a, y) does not depend on y: $g = g(a)$. Then inspection of (6) shows that $G(x, \theta, a) = g(a)$ and so the consistent choice of a, now maximisng $g - pa$, depends only on p: $a = a^{\circ}(p)$. The debtor's choice of x in the non-cooperative game now maximises V with a unaffected by x and so x satisfies (16): $x = x^{\circ}(a, R)$ and does not depend directly on p. Thus the Lagrangean is $V + \lambda\pi + \mu[a^{\circ}(p) - a] + \varrho[x^{\circ}(a, R) - x]$ and $dL/dp = dV/dp = \lambda\pi_{p} + \mu a^{\circ}_{p}$.

Second, suppose that we endow the debtor with rather less rationality and assume he ignores the effect of x on a. Then (16) again describes his

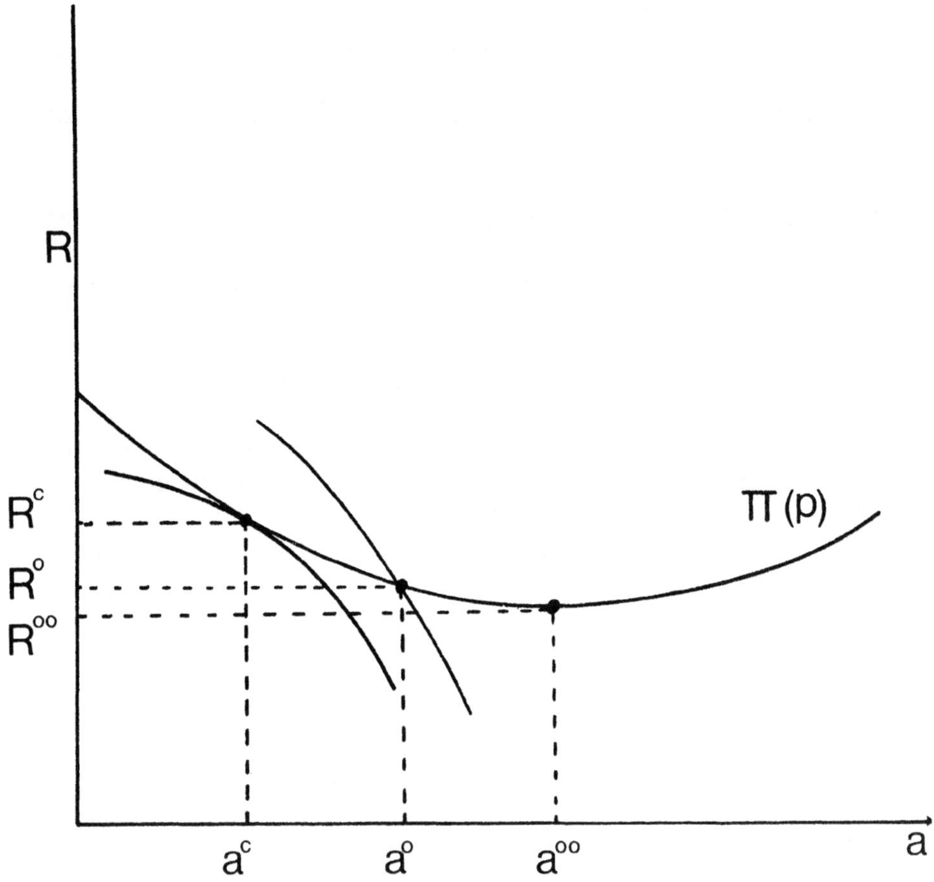

Figure 1.

reaction function and (a, x) is determined as the Nash equilibrium[13] of the non-cooperative game. If (16) holds to constrain x then p has no direct influence on x and dV/dp again reduces to $\lambda\pi_p + \mu a_p^o$.

Figure 1 illustrates the commitment and no commitment contracts in a simple case in which x has no effect on default risk and is hence fixed at zero. The line $\pi(p)$ is the locus of (a, R) satisfying the profit constraint $\pi(0, a, R, p) = 0$. If y does not affect recovery $G = g(a)$ and the consistent choice of a satisfies

$$g'(a) - p = 0 \tag{23}$$

This is a^o in the figure and the resulting breakeven R is R^o and at (a^o, R^o) the debtor's indifference curve v^o cuts $\pi(p)$ from above.[14] If commitment was possible all points along $\pi(p)$ would be feasible and the debtor would choose (a^c, R^c) where V^c is tangent to $\pi(p)$. In this case shown $a^c < a^o$ and the debtor would prefer a lower level of enforcement than the no-commitment level a^o. The first order conditions from the choice of contract when $a = a^o(p)$ and x^* is fixed imply

$$\mu = V_a + \lambda\pi_a = V_a + V_R \frac{\partial R}{\partial a} \tag{24}$$

where $\partial R/\partial a = -\pi_a/\pi_R$ is the slope of $\pi(p)$. In figure 1 since V^o cuts $\pi(p)$ from above $-V_a/V_R < \partial R/\partial a$ and so $\mu < 0$. The debtor would prefer an a^c less than a^o if commitment was possible.

It is clear from the figure that with different preferences or profit constraint a^c could exceed a^o: the debtor would prefer a larger a because he places a high value on the consequent reduction in R. Only if default risk does not depend on a will a^o exceed a^c irrespective of preferences. If a^o lies on a negatively sloped portion of $\pi(p)$ then it is possible for $a^c > a^o$. Since $V_R < 0$, π_R must be positive at a^o.[15] Then the sign of the slope of $\pi(p)$ is determined by

$$\pi_a = F_\theta\theta_a[g - pa - R] + F(g' - p) \tag{25}$$

The consistent choice of a, satisfying (23), gives $\pi_a = F_\theta\theta_a(g - pa - R)$. If additional a reduces default risk then $\pi_a > 0$ at a^o (since $g - pa - R < 0$) and $\pi(p)$ is negatively sloped. If F is unaffected by enforcement (the discrete case) then $\pi_a = 0$ at a^o and the consistent choice of a is at a^{oo} in figure 1. It then must be the case that $a^c > a^o$ and $\mu < 0$.

Note that, although $\lambda\pi_p = -\lambda Fa < 0$, $\mu a_p^o + \varrho x_p^*$ may be positive if $\mu < 0$. Thus, unlike the case when commitment is possible and unlike the usual public enterprise case, the "consumer" of the public sector services (the debtor) may actually prefer a higher price rather than a lower one. Although an increase in p will make him worse off by raising R it will also reduce enforcement given default and the net effect may be to raise his expected utility. If the standard public firm model an increase in price merely makes consumers worse off.

5.2. Optimal pricing without commitment

Turning to the socially optimal price (i.e. taking also into account the public sector surplus $F(pa - c)$) assume that there exists a finite p_{max} such that the demand for enforcement services a^o is zero if and only if $p \geqslant p_{max}$. Consider first a positive socially optimal price less than p_{max}.

The marginal social value of p is

$$\lambda \pi_p + \mu a_p^o + \varrho x_p^* + \sigma\left[F\left(a^o + (p - C')\frac{da^o}{dp}\right) + (pa^o - C)\frac{dF}{dp}\right] \quad (26)$$

and setting this to zero and rearranging yields

$$\frac{p - C'}{p} = -\frac{1}{\eta}\left[\frac{\sigma - \lambda}{\sigma} + \frac{\alpha C}{pa}\eta_F + \frac{(\mu/\sigma)}{pF}\eta_o + \frac{(\varrho/\sigma)x^*}{Fap}\eta_x\right] \quad (27)$$

where $\eta_o = \partial \log a^o/\partial \log p$, $\eta_x = \partial \log x^*/\partial \log p$.[16] This differs from (13) or (13′) in containing terms reflecting the influence of p on enforcement and effort. η/σ and ϱ/σ have the dimensions of prices of enforcement and effort and can be interpreted as shadow prices. Thus the optimal price-marginal cost deviaton will depend on how responsive a^o and x^* are to the price of enforcement (reflected in the elasticity terms η_o, η_x) and on how important their shadow values ($\mu a/\sigma$) and $\varrho x/\sigma$) are relative to total expenditure on enforcement (pa). Optimal price thus depends on how inefficient the contract is compared to the case in which commitment is possible and how responsive the contract is to the price of enforcement.

Figure 2 illustrates one type of solution in the simple case in which x is fixed at zero. Increases in p shift $\pi(p)$ upwards and $a^o(p)$ to the left tracing out the policy relevant locus AA which shows the set of (a, R) achievable by variation of p. In the example shown the debtor's indifference curves cut the $\pi(p)$ loci from above (so $a^c < a^o$ at all p) and as p is increased along AA the debtors utility increases because the effect of p in reducing a outweighs the consequent increases in R. Since $dV/dp > 0$ the optimal price p* will be greater than the price which maximises expected public sector surplus.

Consider an example in which the optimal price is p_{max} i.e. price is set so high that the creditor prefers not to use any remedies at all: $a^o = 0$.[17] Assume x does not affect F, income is either y^l or y^h (so that default risk does not vary with x, a or R), $\alpha = 0$ and $\sigma = \lambda$. Then (26) reduces to

$$\mu a_p^o + \sigma(p - C')Fa_p^o \quad (28)$$

and $\sigma = \lambda = u_y^h$, $\mu = V_a = F(u_y^l\gamma' - u_y^l g')$ (where superscripts indicate $y = y^h$ or y^l).[18] Substituting in (28) gives (since $g' = p$)

$$[(u_y^h - u_y^l)p + u_y^l\gamma' - u_y^h C']a_p^o F \quad (29)$$

as the marginal social value of p. Now it is plausible though (as the discussion of (3), (4) in section 2.1 indicated) not certain, that $u_y^h \leqslant u_y^l$. Then, (29) is positive for all $p < p_{max}$ (since $a_p^o < 0$ for $p < p_{max}$), and so the optimal price is p_{max} (or any $p > p_{max}$).

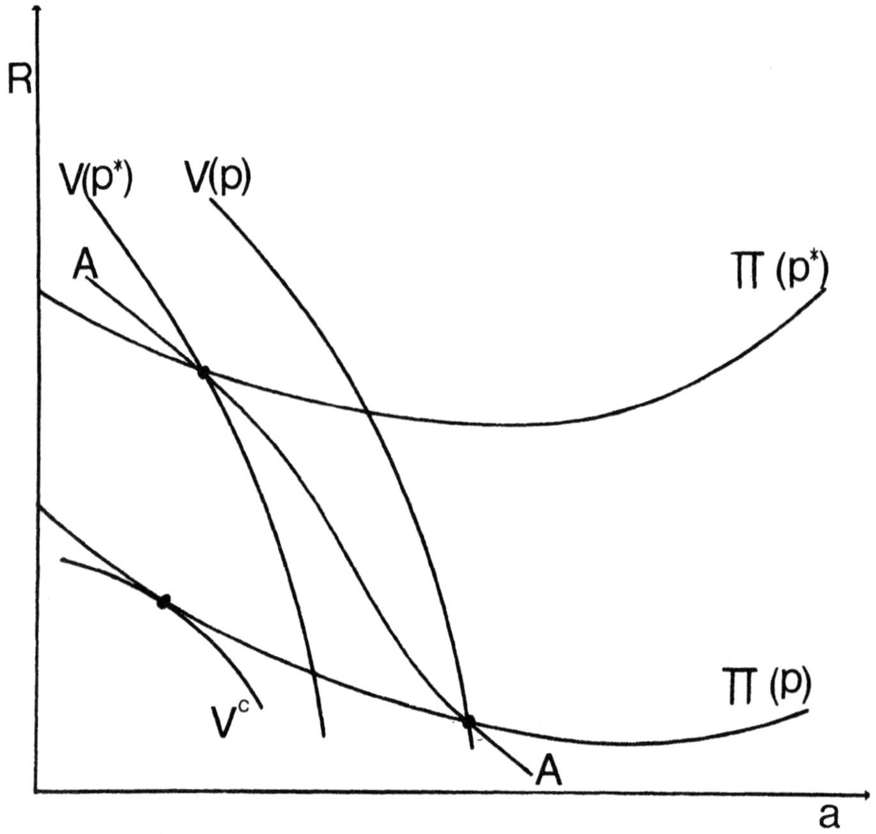

Figure 2.

One of the crucial assumptions in this example is that default risk is exogenous and unaffected by the price of enforcement services. The cost to the debtor of increases in p is the resulting increase in R. When F is fixed this cost is reduced because the reduction in a^o does not raise F and so reinforce the direct effect of p on R.

6. SOME EXTENSIONS

6.1. Private and public enforcement

As suggested in the introduction, creditors may use public or private enforcement procedures to recover in the event of default. To examine the implications of the existance of private remedies let $a = (a_1, a_2)$ now denote the vector of public (a_1) and private (a_2) enforcement services used by the creditor and $p = (p_1, p_2)$ be their prices. The cost function for a_i is $C_i(a_i)$. Recovery now depends on income and both public and private enforcement activities: $g(a_1, a_2, y)$. Expected recovery given default is

$$G(a_1, a_2, \theta, x) = (1/F) \int_{-\infty}^{\theta} g(a_1, a_2, y)f(x, y)dy \tag{30}$$

The no-commitment enforcement vector maximises (30) less $\Sigma p_i a_i$ so that $a_i = a_i^0(x, \theta, p_1, p_2)$. Without commitment and observation of effort the Lagrangean for the contract problem is now

$$\begin{aligned} L = {} & V(x, a_1, a_2, R) + \lambda\pi(x, a_1, a_2, R, p_1, p_2) \\ & + \sum_i \mu_i[a_i^o(x, \theta, p) - a_i] + \varrho[x^*(R, p) - x] \end{aligned} \tag{31}$$

and the effect of marginal increases in the price of public enforcement services is

$$\frac{dV}{dp_1} = \lambda\pi_1 + \mu_1 a_{11}^o + \mu_2 a_{21}^o + \varrho x_1^* \tag{32}$$

where the subscript 1 on π, a_i^o and x^* denotes the partial derivative with respect to p_1. Letting σ_i be the marginal social value of expected profit on the sale of the i th enforcement service the social welfare function becomes $V + \Sigma\sigma_i F[p_i a_i^0 - C_i(a_i)]$. Then, assuming an interior solution, optimal p_1 satisfies

$$\begin{aligned} & \lambda\pi_1 + \sum_i \mu_i a_{i1}^o + \varrho x_1^* + \sigma_1 F a_1^o \\ & \quad + \sum_i \sigma_i \left[(p_i - C_i') \frac{d(a_i^o F)}{dp_i} + \alpha_i C_i \frac{dF}{dp_1} \right] = 0 \end{aligned} \tag{33}$$

where α_i is the elasticity of C_i/a_i.

The deviation of price from marginal cost of public enforcement services will now also depend on the effects of p_1 on no-commitment demand for private enforcement services and on supply conditions in the private sector. If $dF/dp_1 > 0$, public and private enforcement are substitutes ($d(a_2^o F)dp_1 > 0$), $\alpha_2 > 0$ (diseconomics of scale in private enforcement, and a_2 is produced by a monopoly supplier, ($p_2 > C_2'$), then this will tend to raise p_1. Increasing p_1 increases $F(p_2 a_2 - C_2)$ for given (p_2, a_2) by raising F and it increases the output of a_2 thus reducing the welfare losses from monopolisation of private enforcement. This upward influence on p_1 will also be increased if $\mu_2 > 0$ and $\partial a_2^0/\partial p_1 > 0$.

If private enforcement is supplied competitively then $p_2 = C'_2$ and rents are encorporated in firms costs, so that $C'_2 = C_2/a_2$. The effect of p_1 on the private enforcement sector can then be neglected and the only difference between (33) and (26) will be the presence of the term involving μ_2. If μ_1 and μ_2 are of the same sign (for example $a^c < a^o$ so that $(\mu_1, \mu_2) < (0, 0)$) and $a^o_{21} > 0$ the choice of p_1 will have to balance two effects. Increasing p_1 will reduce a^o_1, which is desirable since $\mu_1 < 0$ but will increase a^o_2, which is undesirable since $\mu_2 < 0$.

Publicly supplied enforcement activities may be more easily monitored and it may be possible for there to be commitment on a_1 but not a_2. Then $\mu_1 = 0$ so that, if $\sigma_1 = \lambda$, $\alpha_1 = 0$ and $a^o_{21} > 0$ p_1 should be set below marginal cost if $a^o_2 > a^c_2$ in order to discourage the use of private enforcement services.

6.2. Price versus quantity control

The analysis so far has considered the choice of p subject to the constraint that the level of a is determined by the optimisation of the creditor (if there is no commitment) or by creditor and debtor (if commitment is feasible). Thus a could only be indirectly influenced by variation in the price charged by the court. Let us consider first whether the ability also to impose direct controls on enforcement activities increases the optimised value of the social welfare function. It is obvious that abolition of the constraint on a cannot decrease the optimised value of the social welfare function but the issue is not trivial because in the standard public sector pricing problem the ability to control quantities as well as prices does not increase the optimised value of the social welfare function. The ability to fix prices and quantities, rather than just prices, merely creates the possibility of lump sum transfers. Since in deriving efficient pricing rules it is assumed either that lump sum taxes are feasible or that distribution is irrelevant, relaxation of the constraint that quantities are determined solely by consumers' private optimisations is of no value.

With the supply of public enforcement services there will in general be a gain in being able to control both p and a. The optimal price p* when a is not directly controlled maximises $V + \sigma F(pa - C) \equiv W(a(p), p)$ and so satisfies $W_a(da/dp) + W_p = 0$. The price and enforcement activity when p *and* a are policy instruments are p**, a** satisfying $W_a = 0$, $W_p = 0$. Then $W(a(p^*), p^*) < W(A^{**}, p^{**})$ unless $W_a(a(p^*), p^*) = 0$. But[19]

$$W_a = \mu + \sigma\left[F(p - C') + (pa - C)\frac{dF}{da}\right] \tag{34}$$

and there is no reason in general why this should equal zero at p* satisfying (27) or (13). Even if $\sigma = \lambda$ (the equivalent of the standard assumption in the efficient pricing literature) (27) implies $W_a = 0$ only if $\mu = 0$ and $\alpha = 0$ or if the discrepancy between a^c and a^o generates a μ which just offsets the effect of p on expected public surplus. If commitment is not possible there are in general benefits from having an additional policy instrument (control of enforcement activity). Even if a and p are separately controllable it will not necessarily be the case that (a**, p**) ensure that $\mu = 0$ (i.e. that $a^{**} = a^c$). Setting

$$W_p = \lambda\pi_p + \sigma\left(Fa + (pa - C)\frac{dF}{dp}\right) = 0 = W_a \tag{35}$$

does not imply $\mu = 0$ unless $\lambda = \sigma$ and $\alpha = 0$ so that $p^{**} = C'$.

It is possible that direct control of a alone, with p fixed (at p^o say), will yield a larger W than with p controllable but a not. With sufficient continuity $W(a^*, p^o) > W(a(p^*), p^*)$ must hold for some $p^o \equiv p^{**}$, where a* maximises $W(a, p^o)$. For example, assume F is unaffected by x, $\mu < 0$, $\alpha = 0$, $u_y^l > \sigma > u_y^h = \lambda$, and that $p^* = p_{max}$, so that the solution in figure 3 obtains. Since $\sigma > \lambda$, $p^{**} < (C/a) = C'$.[20] In the figure $\mu < 0$ at a**, R** but this is inessential. Now fix $p^o = C/a$ and consider the choice of a along $\pi(p^o)$. Since $C' = C/a$, if a* is positive it must be such that $\mu = 0$ i.e. $a^* = a^c$. It is clear from the diagram that the debtor must be better off at (a*, R*) than when $p^* = p_{max}$. Since $a^o(p_{max}) = 0$ public sector surplus is zero at p_{max} and at $p^o = C/a$. Thus $W = V + \sigma F(pa - C)$ is greater at (a^*, p^o) than at (a^o) than at $(a^o(p_{max}), p_{max}) = (a(p^*), p^*)$. In this case direct regulation of enforcement is preferable to indirect control via the court's charge for its enforcement services.

6.3. No commitment by the policy maker

It has been assumed so far, that the debtor and creditor both believe that the policy maker can commit his choice of policy instruments. Since the optimal policy is time inconsistent the assumption is crucial and we therefore briefly examine the implications of dropping it. The policy maker's objective function at time 0 is

$$W = V + \phi\pi + \sigma F(pa - C) \tag{36}$$

where ϕ is the marginal social value of creditor profit. Now when commitment is possible for the policy maker p is chosen (committed) at time 0 to maximise W and the optimal rules of earlier sections follow.21 If policy commitment is not feasible then p will in fact be chosen in

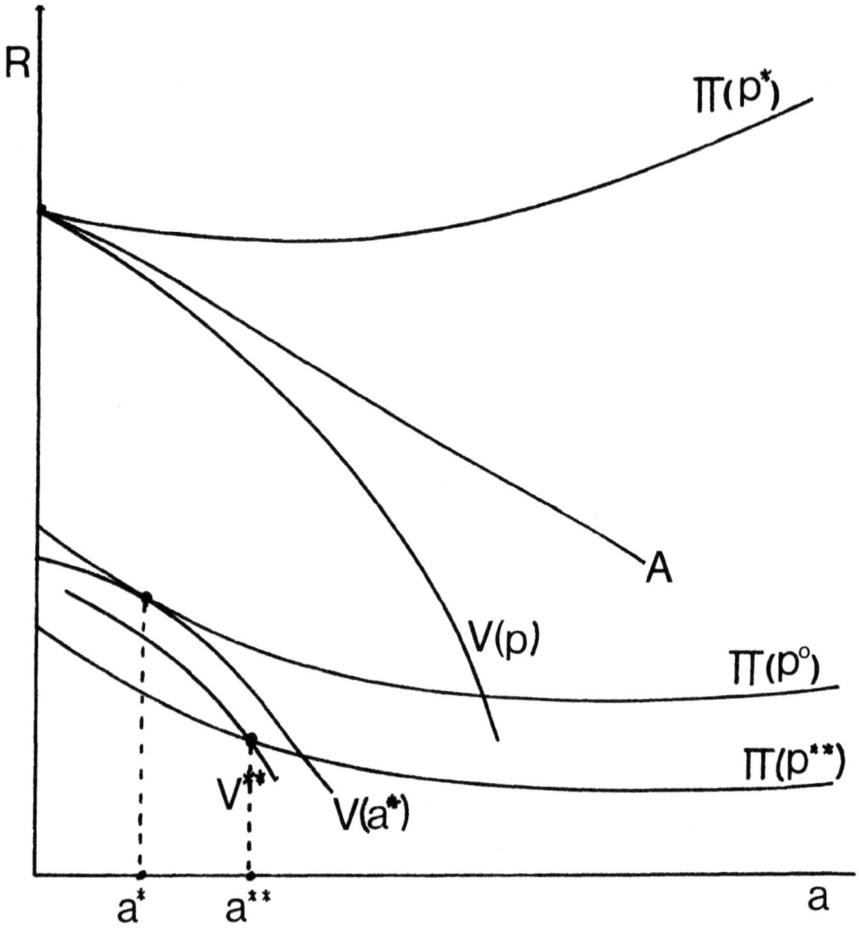

Figure 3.

period 1 if the debtor defaults. But then the *ex post* objective function is

$$(1/F) \int_{-\infty}^{\theta} u(y - g(a, y), \gamma(a))f(x, y)dy + \phi G - \sigma C + (\sigma - \phi)pa \tag{37}$$

For simplicity it is assumed that debtor and creditor treat p as a (correctly anticipated) parameter and so do not attempt to exploit the policy maker's inability to commit p. If the creditor is also unable to commit then $a = a^o(x, \theta, p)$ and this dependence of a^o on p is taken account of by the policy maker. The optimal consistent p is defined by

$$(1/F)V_a a_p^o + (\sigma - \phi)a^o + \sigma(p - C')a_p^o = 0 \tag{38}$$

and so

$$\frac{p - C'}{p} = -\frac{1}{\eta_o}\frac{\sigma - \phi}{\sigma} - \frac{V_a}{\sigma pF} \tag{39}$$

where $\eta_o = \partial \log a^o/\partial \log p$.

Several features of (39) should be noted. First, the consistent price-marginal cost deviation is not affected by the elasticity of average cost or the elasticity of default risk with respect to p. Since p cannot be committed it can have no influence on default risk F and so can influence expected surplus F(pa − C) only by its direct affect on a. Second, the consistent price is not influenced by whether x is controlled by the debtor contract (i.e. by the presence of moral hazard). Since x is determined in period 0 and p in period 1 p cannot, without policy maker commitment, affect x. Third, if we assume distributional neutrality in the sense that $\sigma = \phi$, then the consistent price must exceed marginal cost. The consistent price is chosen *ex post*, when only its effect on utility given default is relevant and larger a reduces post-default utility. Hence, with $a_p^o < 0$, p should exceed marginal cost. If an additional £1 is more highly valued in the hands of the public sector than the creditor ($\sigma > \phi$) this will further raise p and, if ϕ is small relative to σ, price could be above the level necessary to maximise *ex post* public sector surplus. Fourth, the optimal price with policy maker commitment (even assuming $\sigma = \phi$) may be larger or smaller than the consistent price. If, for example, $\mu > 0$, $\eta_x > 0$ and $\alpha \to 0$ then the optimal commited price defined by (27) will also exceed marginal cost and could exceed the consistent price.

7. CONCLUSIONS

7.1. Summary of results

The civil courts sell many of their services and it is illuminating to analyse their pricing rules using the standard normative approach usually applied to more conventional public firms. This paper has concentrated exclusively on the courts' provision of enforcement services i.e. remedies to creditors who are faced with a defaulting debtor. Although the contracting parties were conveniently labelled debtor and creditor the analysis applies unchanged to *any* contract in which there is default risk. The normative approach was deliberately simplified to make the results more easily comparable with the standard public enterprise results and to emphasise the peculiar positive features of enforcement services which distinguish them from other publicly supplied commodities.

The efficient (i.e. ignoring distribution) pricing rules derived differ from the standard policy prescriptions in a variety of ways:

(i) since the price of enforcement affects default risk and thus the profit of the court on the sale of enforcement services, price can diverge from marginal cost even if the debtor-creditor contract is complete and efficient. The divergence depends on whether marginal cost exceeds or is less than average cost but will tend to zero as the number of contracts becomes large;

(ii) if the creditor cannot commit himself and thus is restricted to credible threats regarding enforcement, the credible enforcement level may be too large or too small. Thus price will be partially determined by its effect on consistent enforcement and may be raised above or set below marginal cost depending on whether consistent enforcement is greater or less than the amount the parties would have contracted for if commitment was possible;

(iii) if the creditor is unable to observe debtor activities which influence the probability of default and if commitment is not possible then the price of enforcement services should also be influenced by its effect on such debtor behaviour via the consistent level of enforcement;

(iv) the price of public enforcement will be affected by the presence of private enforcement services, even if such services are supplied competitively, if commitment is not possible;

(v) if the debtor-creditor contract is privately inefficient, compared with the contract when commitment is possible, then the policy maker's ability to control enforcement activity directly in addition to price will raise social welfare. (By contrast in the standard public firm case there is no advantage in being able to control price and quantity because consumers choose quantity efficiently given the price);

(vi) when the policy maker cannot commit himself to p in advance of default the credible price will exceed marginal cost.

7.2. Should public enforcement services be priced?

This paper has assumed that the contract enforcement services of public courts can usefully be subjected to the kind of normative policy analysis often applied to more conventional commodities. We conclude with a brief justification of this approach. A common initial reaction to the suggestion that the services of courts ought to be priced is that this amounts to restricting access to "justice" and that this is *ipso facto* bad. This objection is however based on a semantic confusion. It is important to distinguish between two interpretations of "justice". First, justice is often used as a handy portmanteau term for the services of courts and, in this sense, carries no normative overtones. Second, justice is a criterion for evaluating social institutions. Clearly anything which reduces the amount of justice in the second sense is, by definition, to be deplored. However before one can conclude that a particular method of allocating justice in the first sense (i.e. of court services) is worse than another it is necessary to assess the effects of the different allocation methods on the supply of court services and to evaluate those effects.

Civil courts provide three types of services: (a) specification of legal rules or property rights, (b) arbitration of disputes over facts, so that the appropriate legal rules may be applied and (c) the enforcement of legal rules or rights. The services are supplied (i) to parties whose dispute has arisen from their contractual relationship and (ii) where there is no contract between the parties. Since court services are costly some allocation mechanism is required. The standard objections to use of prices as rationing devices for government services are that individuals are incompetent, that it has deleterious effects on income distribution, that there are significant beneficial externalities associated with the consumption of the services or that the services are public goods (e.g. defence).

Some of these objections are relevant for some court services but they do not appear to be particularly compelling for the type (c) (ii) services (enforcement of contract terms) considered in this paper. It is not obvious why the incompetence argument should be stronger for individuals' decisions on enforcement of contracts than for their other choices. The distributional consequences of a positive price for court enforcement services are unlikely to be very great and not clearly regressive or progressive. Tax payers who would otherwise finance the services are better off. The positive enforcement price will increase the contract price required by firms. Individuals with low default risks will lose relative to those with high default risks.

Enforcement services are not public goods: an increase in consumption by one individual will reduce the amount available for consumption by others. There are some potential externalities associated with court enforcement services in that many people might feel that they are a substitute for a much less desirable activity: private enforcement. This would imply, *ceteris paribus*, that court enforcement services should have a lower price than otherwise but whether it should be zero or not would depend on the cross-price demand elasticities and the magnitude of the externality.

The enforcement services of public courts are indeed an unusual type of commodity, for the reasons discussed in the earlier sections, but this does not imply that their price cannot be evaluated using a standard normative framework. The objections to this approach can be more validly addressed to the framework itself than to its application to court enforcement services.

NOTES

* I am grateful to Bruce Ackerman for helpful comments and suggestions on an earlier draft.

1. A number of authors have considered a rather different type of contract risk in which nothing of value has been transferred at the time when one party unilaterally breaches the contract (for example a seller finds he can get a better price elsewhere). The issue here is what type of legal remedy should be granted to the offended party: specific performance (make the other party carry out the original contract), reliance damages (equal to any costs incurred by plaintiff as a result of relying on the contract) or expectations damages (equal to the plaintiff's profit if the contract is performed). [See Rogerson (1984), Shavell (1984)]. The question of enforcement does not arise in these papers. It is assumed that both parties are aware of the legal situation and if a breach occurs (when specific performance is not the rule) the defaulter will pay the appropriate damages without there being any recourse to the courts to enforce the remedy laid down by the law.
2. In England and Wales in 1982, 1,804,000 summonses for debt were issued in the County Courts and there were 1,263,000 applications by creditors for the main types of enforcement against debtors (warrants of execution, of delivery, of possession, attachment of earnings and oral examinations). Creditors pay fees for these services. In a sample of cases from one County Court total court costs were nearly 40% of the amount recovered [Cotterell et al., (1986)].
3. See Stiglitz and Weiss (1981) for an analysis of asymmetrical information as an explanation for credit rationing.
4. Kydland and Prescott (1977) examine the implications of lack of commitment for policy choices.
5. If $g(a, y)$ is continuous and non decreasing in y and attains a maximum of $R + pa$ (i.e. contractual repayment plus enforcement costs) for some y such that $F(x, y) < 1$ then $D(y, a, R) > 0$ for some y. There will also be some low y such that $g(a, y) = 0$ (because the court fixes a protected level of assets on income for the debtor). If $\gamma(a)$ has a sufficiently low upper bound then there will be some low y for which $D(y, a, R) < 0$. Provided u, γ and g are continuous there must exist a $y = \theta$ satisfying $D(\theta, a, R) = 0$ for all $a > 0$ and finite R. Assuming that u, g, γ (like all other functions in this paper) are differentiable up to any required order and, as elsewhere in the paper, letting subscripts denote partial derivatives

   $$D_y(\theta, a, R) = u_y(\theta - R, \gamma(0)) - u_y(\theta - g, \gamma(a))(1 - g_y)$$

   Now $R > g$ at θ because of the other costs of enforcement γ. Hence $u_{yy} \leqq 0$ and either (i) $u_{yy} < 0$ and $g_y(a, \theta) \geqq 0$, or (ii) $u_{yy} = 0$ and $g_y(a, \theta) > 0$ are sufficient for

   $$D_y(\theta, a, R) > 0.$$

6. Use of the implicit function rule on $D(\theta, a, R) = 0$ gives $\theta_a < 0$ and $\theta_R > 0$ since $D_y(\theta, a, R) > 0$, $D_a = u_y(y - g, \gamma)g_a - u_g\gamma' > 0$ and $D_R = -u_y(\theta - R, \gamma(0)) < 0$.

7. Allen (1983) assumes that the creditor can commit himself in this way but does not discuss the monitoring problem. Williamson (1983) examines the use of hostages (bonds) in some detail. The monitoring problem does not arise in his model because the hostages (sunk costs) are automatically forfeit if default occurs. Bruce Ackerman suggested in his comments on the first draft of this paper that the payment of "retainers" to the law firms by creditors is a form of commitment *ex ante*. If default occurs the additional cost of enforcement *ex post* is much reduced and so threats made *ex ante* are more credible.
8. It is assumed in this section that the optimal price is such that a is positive. An optimal solution could have $p < 0$ (i.e. the creditor is paid to enforce) if the weight attached to public sector losses is small and the debtor values reductions in R relatively highly compared with increases in a.
9. As in the standard public enterprise model it is assumed that an increase in price reduces (expected) demand aF. Since p affects a, x and R this imposes restrictions on da/dp and dF/dp. It is plausible that $da/dp < 0$ and that $dF/dp = F_x(dx/dp) + F_\theta(\theta_a(da/dp) + \theta_R dR/dp) > 0$.
10. Rewrite the last term in the square brackets as

$$(p - C')a\,(dF/dp) + (C'a - C)dF/dp = (p - C')a\,(dF/dp) + \alpha C(dF/dp)$$

and use $d(aF)/dp = a(dF/dp) + F(da/dp)$ to collect $(p - C')$ terms.
11. Plausibly $x_a^o > 0$ and $x_R^o < 0$ but restrictions on F(x, y) are necessary to ensure this. In the discrete case where $y = y^l$ or y^h inspection of V_{xa}, V_{xR} shows that those properties do hold.
12. a^o satisfies $G_a = p$ and from (6) it is clear that $a_\theta^o > 0$, $a_p^o < 0$ but that a_x^o can be positive or negative.
13. The Nash equilibrium is stable if $1 - a_\theta^o\theta_a - a_x^o x_a^o > 0$.
14. V_a, V_R are both negative but the quasi-concavity of V in a and R shown in figure 2 requires restrictions on $\gamma(a)$ and g(.) as well as the concavity of u in y and γ.
15. An optimal contract cannot have $\pi_R < 0$ because then both parties prefer a smaller R.
16. Note that these are 'partial' elasticities in that in θ, x are held constant in evaluating $\partial x^*/\partial p$. By contrast in evaluating da^o/dp in η, θ and x are allowed to vary with p.
17. When $a = 0$ it is necessary to assume that the utility function is directly dependent on whether default occurs, i.e. that there is some loss of utility attached to default even if the creditor does not utilise any of his remedies. If not default occurs whatever the income level.
18. The first order conditions in the contract problem include $V_R + \lambda\pi_R = 0$, $V_a + \lambda\pi_a - \mu = 0$ and with F fixed $\pi_R = (1 - F)$, $\pi_a = F(g' - p) = 0$ (since $a = a^o(p)$).
Since $V = u^o(0) + Fu(y^l - g(a), \gamma(a)) + (1 - F)u(y^h - R, \gamma(0))$, $V_R = -(1 - F)u_y^h$,

$$V_a = F(u_\gamma^l\gamma' - u_y^l g').$$

19. If a is directly controlled and the policy maker can commit himself x is determined by $V_x = 0$ if x is not observable. Hence the absence of any term in (34) reflecting the influence of a on x^o.
20. Since $\sigma > \lambda$ and $dF/dp > 0$, (54) is zero only if $pa < C$.
21. Remember that *ex ante* π is constrained to be zero and so did not need to appear explicitly in the social welfare function used in previous sections.

REFERENCES

Allen, Franklin, "Credit rationing and payment incentives", *Review of Economic Studies*, 1983, **50**, 639–646.

Barro, Robert J., "The loan market, collateral, and rates of interest", *Journal of Money, Credit and Banking*, 1976, **8**, 439–456.

Benjamin, Daniel K., "The use of collateral to enforce debt contracts", *Economic Inquiry*, 1978, **16**, 333–359.

Chiang, Raymond and John M. Finkelstein, "An incentive framework for evaluating the impact of loan provisions on default risk", *Southern Economic Journal*, 1982, **49**, 962–969.

Eaton, Jonathan and Mark Gersovitz, "Debt with potential repudiation: theoretical and empirical analysis", *Review of Economic Studies*, 1981, **48**, 289–309.

Cotterell, Roger, et al., "The recovery of judgement debts in the county court: some preliminary results", to appear in I. Ramsey, ed., *Debtors and Creditors*, Abingdon: Professional Books, 1986.

Harris, Richard, "The consequences of costly default", *Economic Inquiry*, 1978, **16**, 477–496.

Johnson, Robert W., "Cost/benefit analysis of creditors' remedies", *Credit Research Center Monograph No. 12*, 1978, Purdue University.

Kreps, David M. and Robert B. Wilson, "Reputation and imperfect information", *Journal of Economic Theory*, 1982, **27**, 253–279.

Kydland, Finn E. and Edward C. Prescott, "Rules rather than discretion: the inconsistency of optimal plans", *Journal of Political Economy*, 1977, **85**, 473–492.

Leff, Arther Allen, "Inquiry, ignorance and spite: the dynamics of coercive collection", *Yale Law Journal*, 1970, **80**, 1–70.

Rea, Samuel A., "Arm-breaking, consumer credit and personal bankruptcy", *Economic Inquiry*, 1984, **22**, 188–208.

Rees, Ray, *Public Enterprise Economics*, Weidenfeld and Nicolson, London, 1984.

Rogerson, William P., "Efficient reliance and damage measures for breach of contract", *Rand Journal of Economics*, 1984, **15**, 39–53.

Shavell, Steven, "The design of contracts and remedies for breach", *Quarterly Journal of Economics*, 1984, **1**, 121–148.

Stiglitz, Joseph E. and Andrew Weiss, "Credit rationing in markets with imperfect information", *American Economic Review*, 1981, **71**, 393–411.

———, "Incentive effects of terminations: applications to the credit and labor markets", *American Economic Review*, 1983, **73**, 912–927.

Telser, L.G., "A theory of self-enforcing agreements", *Journal of Business*, 1980, **53**, 27–44.

Williamson, Oliver E., "Credible commitments: using hostages to support exchange", *American Economic Review*, 1983, **83**, 514–540.

TRANSACTION COST AND COMMUNICATION: A THEORY OF INSTITUTIONAL CHANGE, APPLIED TO THE CASE OF PATENT LAW

Michael Hutter

1. INTRODUCTION

In part 2, I will sketch a theory which is capable of handling the methodological problems one encounters in explaining the production of institutions. Two basic propositions are developed. In part 3, I will apply the theory to explain changes in the patent law, using one specific case study and the outlines of a few other cases to demonstrate the validity of the propositions. Part IV offers a few inferences that may be drawn from the exercise.

2. THEORY

2.1. Communication, persons and conversations

25 years ago, Ronald Coase (1960) began his extension of the traditional framework of microeconomic theory by discussing the stylized case of a conflict between a farmer whose fields had been damaged by the cows of a rancher. The social problem of finding a solution to this conflict is, as Coase stressed, a reciprocal one: both parties have to find and accept a common constraint. The constraint will help to save the costs of future conflicts – but finding the constraint is a costly process. In consequence, one can hypothesize that the shape of institutions observed depends on the transaction costs which these institutions save, and on the transaction costs which are expended to bring the institutions into being and to maintain them. In a post-Coasean world, the entire institutional environment of a transaction – like the resolution of the conflict between the farmer and the rancher – is the result of former transactions involving the processing of information. And that is where the difficulties begin.

A theory which explains institutional change in an evolving, uncertain world depends crucially on the emergence of new information. The process in which new information emerges is called communication. The process of communication consists of (1) sending of suggested message by Alter – (2) information registration by Ego – (3) inference of understanding of Ego by Alter. (See, for an authoritative exposition of this topic, Luhmann, 1984).

In this view, information is one phase of a communication process which has to be produced in its entirety. Only within this envelope of mutual understanding can an economy function in a world of basic uncertainty. Neo-classical models take this understanding as given. The more general theory, instead, includes the process of inventing information.

An application of this theory of communication to the farmer-rancher case leads to the following sequence of argument: When the farmer talks to the rancher, he might begin by making a remark that refers to the damaged crops. The farmer then waits for the rancher's reaction. From this reaction, for instance, a remark that indicates defensiveness, guilt, surprise, etc., the farmer will infer the rancher's understanding of his initial message. Seen from the rancher's perspective, the farmer's message was noted as something that made a difference to the rancher, i.e.,something he did not "overhear". It informed him about the extent of the damage, about the farmer's opinion on it, about the farmer's strategy for dealing with it, and a number of other issues. In turn, the rancher's reaction informs the farmer about a number of points which allow him to better predict the future development of the transaction. It follows that design of message and inference of understanding are activities which are indispensable for the registration of information.

There are many communication processes that may safely be thought of as a transfer of information. Both the message forms used and the expectations of understanding have been so standardized that they demand litle effort and attention, However, our concern is with *new* information. How does it happen that, during a negotiation, something is said that never was said before and something is understood that never was understood before? This temporal aspect of information invention demands attention to the steps of that basic process.

Extending the economic theory of information to an economic theory of communication introduces, in consequence, an obstinate epistemological problem: If new information can be generated, then not only the institutions, but also the language in which these institutions are communicated appear to be subject to an economic actor's cost decisions.[1] Unlike the objects of the physical world, language can not be assumed to exist in the environment of an individual actor. At least two actors have to suppose each other's autonomous unity in order to initiate a process in which new information is generated. Every actor has to work on being recognized, on "having a voice", and every social actor has to work on being able to recognize new partners of communication, and on engaging them in conversation.

These seem to be trivial activities. But the appearance is deceptive, based as it is on a long tradition of careful neglect. Especially in research-intensive industries, participation in various strands of communication has become more important to the survival of companies than the techniques of manipulating and distributing material products. When communication instead of production shapes the output – as it is the case in industries "manufacturing" computer programs, circuits or pharmaceuticals – the total costs of production consist primarily of transaction costs.

To take these basic considerations into account, I will now develop a few definitions. An actor is called "autonomous" if its messages appear to be determined by an internal source rather than being a reaction to a source outside. A company, for instance, is able to interact with other economic actors through innumerable conversations, exchanges of letters, telexes, etc., all carried out through different individuals, and yet it is able to retain its identity as an autonomous actor. Even a system as large and seemingly amorphous as the legal system is able to interact with economic, political, scientific and other types of systems through various types of legal persons, and yet retain the independence of its logic, the strict self-determination of its language.

I will call these autonomous actors "persons" in order to distinguish them from the anthropomorphic "individuals". Basically, persons are suppositions of their conversation partners. It is the observing system which uses the mode of identification to attribute autonomy to a cluster of events.[2]

From the perspective of communication theory, every person consists of nothing but messages. Seen from the inside of a person – within a company, a court of Law, a university, etc. – these messages gain meaning through the context to which these messages refer. Such a context of communication will be called a "conversation".

The recognition of conversations gives us the opportunity to observe the change of an institution, like the Law, from two complementary positions: Taking the outside position, a person can see the Law's change through the evolution of other persons: courts, companies, pressure groups, schools of doctrine, etc. Taking the inside position, the Law's change is perceived through the evolution of language: changes and additions in legal codes, changes in the dominant interpretation of these codes, etc.

2.2. Two propositions

Proposition 1 (Outside observation): If the communication between persons increases in value, new persons will emerge. Persons which interact primarily with social systems (as opposed to biological or psychic systems) will be called "conversation circles." Out of the many variations of conversation circles appearing, some are selected for the internal communication of the observed system. Over the course of decades, new conversation circles establish themselves as participants in the economic as well as in the legal conversation, while others lose that ability and fade away.[3]

Proposition 2 (Inside Observation): A conversation is a set of all messages referring in some way to transactions. It will find new messages which carry meaning in conversations of its environment in order to increase the probability of realizing its own internal value.

The processing of new information in a conversation involves three steps:

1. A *case* serves as a vehicle of communication. All the messages that constitute a certain sequence are seen in the context of a basic interaction, a conflict, an exchange, etc.
2. A *code* is used to translate the case into a form that is understandable to other autonomous systems. Usually, a mixture of jargons and dialects is available for this task. *Media* are used to transport the message to the other system – through the air, through newspapers, through legal briefs.[4]
3. Only the response of the other system shows whether change has been induced. One can illustrate that process by comparing it with a therapy in which the therapist induces change in the patient: the task of the therapist consists in involving the patient in a conversation in the course of which the patient begins to re-interpret his or her own context, and thus begins to see future events "in a new light". Bateson (1954) has shown that play is a major form of such context creation in all societies. Therapeutic interaction is such a play-like, continuous activity. There must be a flow of variation of cases entering the internal conversation. Some of these cases are selected to go through internal translation and transmission. In turn, a few of the selected cases become elements of the

"doctrine". They are retained as vehicles to reproduce the mapping of new horizons into the self-interpretation of the autonomous systems involved in the conversation.

The response of the other system (in our case: the Law) has to be retranslated and transmitted, in turn, through codes and media. Then it will be available as part of the context, as a "matter of course" to new cases created.[5]

3. TESTING

3.1. Choosing a study case

My investigation was limited to the history of pharmaceutical patent law after 1945. Although the scope of the study was international, most of the material was compiled in three countries which allowed a comparison of widely diverging Economic, Legal and Political circumstances: the Federal Republic of Germany, the United States of America and the Republic of Italy.

The following sources were used for data collection:

a. Personal interviews with several dozen participants in each of the three countries: Heads of pharmaceutical company patent departments, patent agents and lawyers, association staff, judges, patent office representatives, etc.

b. Internal communication documentation of all participants. Although most of this material is not accessible or confidential, diverging standards of confidentiality have helped to obtain some letters, memos and protocols of meetings.

c. Publications by conversation participants.
This category includes annual reports of patent offices, associations and companies, as well as the vast literature in professional journals. These contributions are predominantly authored by patent lawyers and agents. They serve, beyond the topic of an article, to advertise the skills of the author.

For the purposes of this paper I will limit the exposition to a single case. Three other cases will then be sketched out briefly in order to compensate for some of the shortcomings of this particular case as an expository device.

The case involved a conflict between the General Electric Company (GE) and the US Patent and Trademark Office (PTO) in which GE claimed that it was denied lawful property rights by the PTO.

3.2. The story

During the 1960s, the previously assumed distinction between the categories of natural and man-made substances began to dissolve due to new knowledge of genetic structures and the ability to manipulate the reproduction of organisms. In the USA, the issue came up in connection with the Plant Variety Protection Act of 1970, which specifically did not extend patent protection to artificial cultivation of plants. This, however, left open the protection of man-made organisms when direct changes of genetic material take place. In consequence, there remained uncertainty as to patent protection for such products.

In 1972, GE filed under the name of its employee A. Chakrabarty a patent application which included a number of claims to a product, man-made organisms, i.e. bacteria capable of breaking down oil spills, and procedures for its use. The examiner and the Board of Appeals of the PTO rejected these claims.

It took six years to have the conflict between GE's and the PTO's interpretation of the law decided by the first appropriate court, the Court of Customs and Patent Appeals (CCPA). The CCPA was a court that specialized in conflicts between the government and private parties. The formulation of the case thus was eased by the fact that patent cases and their specific problems are well known to the court. With less experience in this conversation, however, is the Supreme Court. When a case similar to Chakrabarty reached the Supreme Court in 1979 (In re Bergy) the Supreme Court, not surprisingly. saw an analogy to a recent case in which it had rejected a patent claim for a computerized method used in alarm devices (*In re Flook*). Having been asked to reconsider, CCPA in a second opinion, pin-pointed the issue even further, using both *Chakrabarty* and *Bergy* (see U.S. CCPA (1979)). Before the Supreme Court heard the case again, *Bergy* was dropped in order to focus the issue even further. Now, in 1980, the Supreme Court affirmed the CCPA decision (see U.S. Supreme Court, 1980). In 1981, the PTO issued the patent to GE and began to examine the backlog of over a hundred similar applications. Subsequent decisions, however, are still restrictive. There is, for instance, a lack of clarification with respect to the deposition provisions for live organisms.

The costs of the entire case are not known. One may estimate from similar cases, however, that GE paid no less than two million dollars in the process. The costs to everyone involved, including the court system, may be of the same magnitude. The value of the actual patent to GE was relatively small. A product invented nine years earlier was obsolete by the time the patent was granted; Chakrabarty's procedure of dealing with plasmids, however, is still in use.

This short account of the struggle that led to a new form of transaction involving products of great importance for some sectors of the chemical industry shows the vast difference in detail between Coase's rancher and farmer and Real Life's GE and PTO. Real Life's detail is so finely tuned, that descriptive language can hardly do without the terminology developed in the legal discourse. In Coase's case, this detail is seemingly avoided by using a bucolic case, presumbaly "known" to everyone. But the fault is of the same order as in the case of the Robinson Crusoe paradigm: *The characters are stripped of their social environment. Thus, their names have no more meaning, they can not evolve any further.* Simplicity is bought at the price of choosing an extreme stationary case which, as an explanatory tool, distorts the issue beyond recognition.

Following the argument in part 2, I will now interpret *Diamond vs. Chakrabarty* – this whole story spanning nine years – as one instance, one glimpse of the "conversation net" in performance. I will show how patent property circles retold the story so that the transaction form for microorganisms has since been changed in the US and, as a consequence, in other nations.

The task at hand consists in (1) identifying the major participants in the conversation according to Proposition 1 and 2 reconstructing the course of the argument from PTO's original rejection to PTO's final acceptance of the contested claims according to Proposition 2.

3.3. Identifying conversation circles

In this section, conversation circles will be simply identified. Their emergence and reproduction will not be discussed in detail.

The list of participants starts with two courts. Both consist of a fixed, uneven number of members who decide by simple majority. Every court has its internal conversation. In *Chakrabarty*, the diverging positions are revealed on the Supreme Court through the texts of Chief Justice Burger's majority opinion and Justice Brennan's dissenting opinion. On the CCPA, they are revealed through the text of Judge Rich's majority opinion.[6]

Within the PTO – itself an agency of the Dept. of Commerce – we find three participating sections: One is the *office of the examiner*. In a standard application case the entire conversation would be limited to the examiner and the patent agent of the applicant, who would then arrive at final "claim language". This process would entail transaction costs in the minimal sense of using existing forms. Here, however, we deal with the invention of new transaction forms. Therefore, we find a second participant, the *Board of Appeals*, whose members are not disclosed in the case. A third one is the *Legal Office of the PTO* which speaks for the agency before the CCPA. Before the Supreme Court, the Legal Office is aided by the office of the *Solicitor General.* In all the proceedings, the PTO is addressed as representing "The Government". Even this brief analysis shows the variety of persons involved in speaking with the voice of the legal fiction "Government".

The respondent, GE, is represented by two sections: its *legal department*, counselled by a number of *specialist law firms*, and its *patent department*. To leave it at that, however, would be too narrow a view. There is reason to believe that GE kept discussing the case and its strategy within various conversation circles. One indication available are some statements made at a panel discussion (see Banbury Report (1982)).

Beyond these immediate participants, a number of actors can be identified through their use of the *amicus curiae* procedure which allows interested parties to make their position officially known to the court by filing briefs. This, of course, leaves out all unofficial and oral arguments brought forward. One can speculate, however, that those parties filing *amicus curiae* briefs were in turn selected through discussion in various conversation circles.

For the second CCPA decision, briefs were filed by the *University of California*, the *American Patent Law Association* (APLA), *Genentech Inc.* and the *Village of Belle Terre, L.I., N.Y.* The Genentech brief also called to attention three resolutions of the *American Bar Association* (ABA), Section of Patent, Trade-mark and Copyright Law.

For the Supreme Court decision, additional briefs were filed by the *People's Business Commission* (PBC, a consumer advocacy group), the *New York Patent Law Association* (NYPLA), the *Pharmaceutical Manufacturers' Association* (PMA), a *Group of Research Oriented Associations*, the *American Society for Microbiology* and an individual molecular *biologist*. (See Bureau of National Affairs, 1980).

Only one of the briefs, that of the PBC, spoke against affirming the CCPA decision. All the others supported it. It is easy to show that either GE or other research-oriented chemical firms were well represented within these organizations which "spoke up". Representation, however, does not make those organizations decoys for GE. The point of the argument is that GE is encouraged to bring forward its claim in all these circles. It may convince other participants in order to be able to speak with the voice of these circles, which are recognized by the Law's sensors, the courts. In many instances, *the professional clubs are already waiting for a case which can serve as a vehicle for existing problems*, since it is only through the appearance of appropriate topics they can reproduce themselves.

In conclusion, we find that a case superficially involving two parties was taken up by "social persons" of various organizational forms. *They created the necessary outside identity for economic actors to enter a conversation which, as its result, changed their own constraints.*[7]

3.4. Reconstructing legal change

I will now turn to Proposition 2. A sequence from original *case* to a change of *context* back to *cases* under new constraints is expected.

The question whether forms of life are statutory subject matter[8] remained moot as long as there did not exist an actual claim for such an invention. Once basic research – i.e., research on the level of (nonpatentable) "ideas" – had progressed enough, a number of patent claims were made that touched on the issue. As is to be expected, the applicant interpreted the statute positively to include his claim. The examiner interpreted it negatively, excluding claims to product and processes involving microorganisms. There were three cases contending for use as the basis for legal conversation: *Flook*, *Bergy* and *Chakrabarty*. *Flook* proved inacceptable because it involved a computerised method, i.e., an "idea"; *Bergy* was withdrawn before its Supreme Court hearing in order to concentrate the decision on Chakrabarty's claims; thus, *Chakrabarty* emerged as the paradigmatic case.

It took nine years to translate the *economic* question of property rights on certain research results into a language that allowed to answer a question that was internal to the *legal* system: are life forms patentable subject matter? The "coding process" went through the following stages:

June 72	Application for claims (GE)
?	Reasons for rejection (PTO)
?	Reasons for appeal of rejection (GE)
May 76	Reasons for rejection of appeal (PTO/Board of Appeals)
?	Reasons for court appeal of PTO rejection (GE)
March 78	Reasons for reversal of rejection (CCPA 1)
April 78	Appeal of reversal via certiorari (Government)
June 78	Vacation of judgment and reconsideration in light of *Flook* (Supreme Court 1)
November 78	Reaffirmation of reversal (CCPA 2)
June 80	Affirmation of reversal of rejection of claims (Supreme Court 2)

In 81	Grant of claims (PTO 2)
In 81	Issue of other claims upheld until *Chakrabarty* decision (PTO 3).

In order to perform this exceedingly complex task, a highly sophisticated "due process" and a highly sophisticated body of patent law literature had been developed. Were it not so, any attempt to change the PTO's attitude on any issue would be doomed to failure; the PTO's interpretation would be truly an "external constraint" to GE and any other research-oriented firm.

Translating the claim into legal code, however, is not sufficient to induce a change internal to the legal system. Such a change requires a change of the context in which the legal system – represented by the group called "Supreme Court" – *understands* the question of patentability.

In *Chakrabarty*, we can identify the phase of the conversation during which this shift in context occurred: It is marked by the dialogue *CCPA 1 – Supreme Court 1 – CCPA 2 – Supreme Court 2.* The question was first formulated by the *CCPA.* The Supreme Court responded that the answer to the question had been enunciated in *Flook.* The CCPA replied that it had been misunderstood and rephrased the question. Now the Supreme Court understood why the CCPA had held that "living things" are patentable. The Court reiterated the CCPA's opinion in the following words:

> "Congress thus recognized that the relevant distinction was not between living and inanimate things, but between products of nature, whether living or not, and human-made inventions. Here, respondent's microorganism is the result of human ingenuity and research." (U.S. Supreme Court, 1980)

Note that the courts had followed the classic procedure of "retelling the story with new emphasis".[9] This emphasis was now on "unanticipated inventions" rather than on "exclusion from subject matter". Both interpretations are possible, and the choice depends clearly on the court's perception of the present sitaution. We find that the conversation partners were able to invent legal analogies to inventive activities that had taken place first in the scientific and secondly in the economic system. The result was an adjustment of the legal language to that invention, mapping, as it were, uncertainties into the Law which correspond to the horizon of new possibilities opened by the invention.

The *Chakrabarty* case offers the opportunity to pursue the process of understanding, of "changing one's mind", even one step beyond the Supreme Court's decision as a whole. Just as a good therapist would try to pinpoint his messages to certain "triggers" within the patient, one would want to pinpoint such triggers or points of leverage within the Club called Supreme Court. In other words, one doesn't need to change the mind of everyone in the club to get a new answer. It is sufficient if the internal conversation can be steered in a different direction.

The mechanics of this shift are quite simple in *Chakrabarty*: The court had voted 3 : 6 in *Flook*; if the CCPA's decision in *Chakrabarty* was to be affirmed, a 5 : 4 majority was necessary. Therefore, two judges had to change their minds. To speak of a "judge" as an individual, however, is but a remnant of an old terminology. What is meant, given the context of a social system, is the conversation on *Chakrabarty* that took place in a specific judge's office, to which the individual judge and one or more law clerks contribute.

Now, we have reduced the "inventive step" of initiating this particular change within the legal system to its bare essentials. Judge Rich put it into a nutshell a few years after the Supreme Court's decision:

> "The basic purpose of the *Chakrabarty* opinion . . . was to hook at least a couple more law clerks . . . all I wanted was two more dissenters, which would make a majority, and that is what we got." (Banbury report (1982), p. 267)

Retranslating the legal change into the code of the economic system began as soon as the Supreme Court's opinion on the question was out. The economic value of patent applications held up by the PTO in attendance of a final decision on *Chakrabarty* increased and this increase was even reflected in the stockmarkets. The PTO has since adjusted to the new language by issuing patents on life forms, but it has taken a restrictive attitude in interpreting the court's decision with respect to higher life forms (see Adler (1985), esp. FN 63).

The PTO's behavior is hardly surprising. Although the legal question was one of patentability of living things, the factual basis was provided by microorganisms. It would be naive to assume that an issue as sweeping as this one would be settled on such a narrow base. We can rest assured, however, that the continuing flow of inventions in the field of biotechnological research will provide enough material to maintain an ongoing conversation around this issue, with new legal solutions, followed by technical inventions, followed again by new legal solutions.

3.5. Sketches of other cases

I will now extend the empirical base of observation through references to a few other case studies.

One might question how good an example *Chakrabarty* is, given the wide variety of transactions in which communication between economic and legal persons takes place. Most of the significant changes in the law occur through transactions that also include the political system in the conversation. *Chakrabarty* is unusual in its avoidance of political discourse, even though we find clear references to the Law-making powers of the parliamentary process, and to the distinctions between judicial and political tasks.

Furthermore, significant changes in the Law involve more varied participants in the conversation than *Chakrabarty* suggests. In political cases individuals tend to disappear more completely in a conversation between the circles which have evolved to produce specific issues.

I will refer to three cases that have also had a significant effect on the Law's response to the Economy's actions in their respective societies. They might be helpful in giving a somewhat broader view of the immense variety of actions constantly going on in order to produce and reproduce an institutional environment. All cases, however, are chosen from the field of pharmaceutical patent law. This allows us to register connections between these cases, rather than to study them in isolation.[10]

The Patent Term Restoration Act (PTRA)

In September 1984, Congress passed a law (P.L. 98–417) providing that a patent may be extended for a period of up to five years if the patented drug (or other item subject to regulatory review by the Food and Drug Administration) has undergone regulatory review. Increasing delays for Food and Drug Administration drug review had led to a number of remedies being discussed in and around the research-oriented drug industry. One of the proposed strategies was the extension of the patent term in proportion to regulatory delays. A first attempt, narrowly focused at convincing the chairman of the decisive House Subcommittee, failed in 1982 because a coalition of clubs, led by the association of generic drug companies, was formed and able to introduce distributional issues into the legislative procedure. A second attempt, adding legislative changes beneficial to the generic drug industry, was initiated in 1983 and signed into law in 1984. The first decisions of the PTO relating to the "Drug Price Competition and Patent Term Restoration Act" indicate that the agency intends to interpret the law in a rather restrictive manner. The costs of the "PTRA project" are distributed over a wide range of participants: Pharmaceutical manufacturers, patent departments, trade associations, bar associations, citizen groups, various Committees of Congress, newspaper houses, etc. The PTRA story demonstrates the breath of conversation and the cost of working in the political system, especially when distributional issues are tied to the proposed rules and, thus, to the expected changes of rights. Expenditures for the entire project will by far exceed the costs mentioned because all these expenses are still *preliminary* to the actual process of communicating with the Law. After the instrument for such a discourse has been forged in the political discussion, the phase of internal legal conversation is now just beginning: Cases have to turn up which allow a testing of diverging interpretations of the Law. In the coming years, we will be able to witness this process of developing the argument for a broad interpretation of patent term extensions in order to convince the appropriate courts.

The "Vorabgesetz"

In 1967, the German Bundestag passed a law that provided for a number of measures aimed at lessening the work load of the German Patent Office. Among these measures was the elimination of §1 sec. 2 n. 2 of the Patent Law which prohibited product patent claims for chemically manufactures substances (see, for a concise history, Bruchhausen (1977)).

In this case, the proponents of chemical product patent claims were successful in "implanting" the rule change into a "carrier project" which immensely reduced their own cost contribution. The suggestion, first introduced by one of the members of the Bundestag's Judicial Committee (Rechtsausschuß) in October 1966, became law less than a year later. The "Vorabgesetz" also demonstrates the effort necessary to turn a change in the political system into a change in the legal system: it took another four years to obtain a final response on the extent of product claims from the (specialized) chamber of the high court (Bundesgerichtshof) of the Federal Republic (BGHZ 58, 280, 287ff. – Imidazoline).

The innovative impact of these two cases on their respective legal systems diverges widely. The "Vorabgesetz" remedied a given exception within the Patent Law (which, by the way, the chemical industry had managed to introduce eighty years earlier). The PTRA, however, opened a new horizon of possibilities connected with flexible patent terms.

Sentenza No. 20

In 1978, the Italian Corte Costituzionale ruled that Art. 14 of the Italian Patent Law, prohibiting the patentability of drugs, was unconstitutional. (See Floridia (1983) for a comprehensive history and a clear analysis of contemporary problems).

As in *Chakrabarty*, the story of the case involves a lower court, the Commisione dei Ricorsi, capable of reframing the context of the drug patent prohibition and finding new language which convinced the higher court to reinterpret the constitution. Unlike the Vorabgesetz, the change was accomplished in the center of the legal system, eliminating the need for a lengthy process of legal interpretation. However, one had to expect grave disruptions of the market through conflicts in interpreting forfeited and violated patent claims. Unlike its US equivalent in the case of the PTRA, the Italian economy was unable to rely on the country's political system to solve these problems. As a consequence, we are able to witness in Italy the process of an industry inventing its own rules of conduct, without the aid of the political system, in a broad discussion involving all kinds of companies, associations, coalitions and commissions. The self-imposed constraints, approved by a number of representative bodies of associations in 1984, imitated the political process: it was agreed to act as if the norms suggested to parliament (the "Pittella bill") were actually in force. The costs of this process of self-regulation were high in terms of involvement of industry representative, media use, etc. A smoothly operating political system, however, was not among the alternative technologies available to the proponents of rules for the transitory period.[11]

Today, one finds that the Italian courts have begun to tackle a number of issues which are also part of the contemporary discussion in other legal systems, relating to the state of technical art in the pharmaceutical field. The slow process of adapting the rules to a change in context has begun.

4. A FEW INFERENCES

The presentation of the cases so briefly discussed above was intended to widen the perception of the reader to other situations in which transaction costs of considerable magnitude are expended in order to achieve new forms of transaction in the future. It was also intended to demonstrate the fluidity of the process and the speed of development in just one small subsection of an economy's institutional environment. Rather than drawing conclusions, I would like to indicate a few inferences which can be drawn.

1. The theory widens the field of economic investigation to a vast range of institutions. Empirical investigation, due to the complexity of the production process and our minute knowledge of it, focuses on qualitative comparative studies of carefully selected cases instead of the traditional quantitative method. Most visible and common are expenses made for changes of separable *rights*, for instance, industrial property rights. Closer scrutiny of concrete examples reveals, secondly, continuous variations and tests of *rules*, and, thirdly, frequent

attempts to talk the legal system into new *interpretations of itself*. The proportion of cost expended for each of these three types of transaction form changes is unknown.

2. The process of communication between Economy and Law is not a mere translation of economic issues into legal language, the Law is not just a tool to solve economic conflicts. Such a view overlooks the "Unity of the Law": Every autonomous system reproduces itself only through its own elements. Once a case has led to a new interpretation of what is "just" – for instance, the justice of not denying patents to inventions involving life forms – the legal system will behave according to that new interpretation irrespective of the action's economic value.

From the perspective of the Law, therefore, one might say that the Law feeds on cases like the ones originating in and formulated by the Economy. Whether the Law prospers is quite dependent on the quality of cases brought forward. If most cases involving new issues are settled out of court, for instance, the Law will lose its ability to provide guidelines for new actions in non-legal systems. Thus, the economic system becomes quite literally one of the "sources of justice". Since it is only one of the institutions in the environment of the Law, it reaches only certain sections of it, whereas other sections will change in the course of conversation with the State, other nations, the church, etc. It is part of the internal performance of the Law to reconstruct these varying contributions, using the basic distinction of "just" and "unjust". From the perspective of the Economy, Law is one of the sources of value in an Economy. Interpretations found within the Law, once they have been translated into expectations of future rights, open new possibilities for creating economic value.

NOTES

* Financial support for this project by the Deutsche Forschungsgemeinschaft is gratefully acknowledged.

1. There has been some recognition that "institutions" seem to change appearance, depending on whether they are interpreted from without – as organizations – or from within – as a code of behavior. See, recently, Vanberg, 1983, and, a while ago, Commons, 1923, on this topic.
2. Note that the legal system already a century ago developed the notion of fictitious actors called "legal persons".
3. We will see that the economic conversation circles communicate mainly with corres-

ponding sensors in the legal system: Specialized courts, bar associations, etc. They also communicate with firms whose employees contribute the majority of the conversation circles' internal communication. Those governing the firms know that they finance the existence of organizations with independent behavior. But exactly this independence allows effective communication between the systems: Any message by the economic sensor can be read by the legal sensor as the result of a generalization of various producers' perspectives, which helps to clarify whether it is actually the case that something "new" has happened in the environment of the legal system that requires a corresponding new way to acknowledge understanding.

4. The "price system" is, of course, the prime example of a code developed within economic systems. One might use the theory of communication to explore the production and the maintenance of that code. The focus of this paper, however, lies on the less formalized, more ordinary-language-oriented codes used in communicating with non-economic actors.
5. See Hutter, 1987, for a more detailed development of these propositions.
6. It should be noted that Rich was one of the leaders in the statutory revision of US patent law, and that he has been a dominating voice in the patent conversation ever since.
7. It is noteworthy that the strategy claims chosen for extending patent claims to microorganisms was to induce institutional change through the legal system. One could have dealt directly with the political system by introducing an amendment to the patent statute into the parliamentary process. In the early years of the patenting of life forms discussion, both conversations were pursued. But when it became clear that there was a good chance of a Supreme Court decision, resources were shifted to the legal strategy, which is decidedly cheaper and quicker than the political process, but which has much narrower effects in changing the *valid* language of institutional constraints.
8. Section 101 of the US Patent Statute (35 USC) reads:

   > "Whoever invents or discovers any new and useful process, machine, manufacture, or composition of matter, or any new and useful improvement thereof, may obtain a patent therefore, subject to the conditions and requirements of this title."

9. For this procedure only arguments are acceptable that relate to some fictitious "original intention" of a fictitious person called "Congress", construed as an eternal body that originated with the Founding Fathers. Apparently, this archaic, ritualistic procedure is necessary to prevent social destabilization: If interpretations were not tied to "original intention", any spurious situation could lead to an elimination of laws.
10. For a broader treatment of these cases see Hutter, 1987.
11. The amazing ability of the Italian pharmaceutical industry to assume political functions may be explained by two conditions, one historical, the other geographical. Firstly, Italian society has been accustomed to political instability and weakness. Secondly, Italy is a "small pond", compared to the number of participants in the German and US drug law discussion. This has led to clear hierarchies and structure, and it allows close contact between all participants of the process.

REFERENCES

Adler, R.: "Technology Transfer, National Innovative Capacity and Germplasm Conservation: Recommendations for an Integrated Biotechnology Policy". *Rutgers Computer and Technology Law Journal*, Sept, 1985.

Banbury Report 10: *Patenting of Life Forms*. Cold Spring Harbor, 1982.

Bateson, G.: "A Theory of Play and Fantasy". In: Steps to an Ecology of Mind. New York: Ballantine, 1972.

Bruchhausen, K.: "Der lange Weg zum modernen Patentrecht für chemische Erfindungen". *Gewerblicher Rechtsschutz und Urheberrecht*, 1977, 297–304.

Bureau of National Affairs: "Briefs filed in Chakrabarty Case", *Patent Trademark and Copyright Journal*, No. 465, 2.7.1980.

Coase, R.: "The Problem of Social Cost", *Journal of Law and Economics*, Vol. 2, 1960, 1–40.

Commons, J.R.: *Legal Foundations of Capitalism*. Madison: Univ. of Wisconsin Press, 1924.

Floridia, G.: "Il Brevetto di Farmaco in Italia: Analisi e Prospettive". *Studi in onore di Remo Franceschelli*, Milano: Giuffré, 1983, 751–820.

Hutter, M.: *Die Produktion von Recht*. Forthcoming.

Luhmann, N.: *Soziale Systeme*. Frankfurt: Suhrkamp, 1984.

U.S. CCPA: *In re Bergy, Coats and Malik*. 201 USPQ 355 (1979).

U.S. Supreme Court: *Diamond v. Chakrabarty*. 206 USPQ 193 (1980).

Vanberg, V.: "Der individualistische Ansatz zu einer Theorie der Entstehung und Entwicklung von Institutionen", *Jahrbuch für Neue Politische Okonomie*, Bd. 2, Tübingen: Mohr, 1983, 50–69.

PART THREE

ECONOMICS OF LEGAL REGULATION

REGULATORY MEASURES TO ENFORCE QUALITY PRODUCTION OF SELF-EMPLOYED PROFESSIONALS – A THEORETICAL STUDY OF A DYNAMIC MARKET PROCESS

J.- Matthias Graf v.d. Schulenburg*

The market for services of self-employed professionals is characterized by a high degree of consumer uncertainty as to the service quality. This is attributable to the experience-good character of services provided by doctors, dentists, lawyers and other self-employed professions. Therefore, measures are imposed to ensure high service quality on these markets, i.e. governmental agencies and professional associations supervice the quality of services provided by the self-employed professions. This article analyses mechanisms for enforcing quality production in a dynamic market process. The analysis leads to a criticism of existing regulatory measures and proposes a policy of market-oriented quality enforcement also for services which the consumer has difficulty to evaluate in advance.

1. INTRODUCTION

It is a rather common phenomenon that consumers have only little information about the available quality of certain goods. In many cases, the consumer can only judge about the quality after consumption. This is certainly true for meals served in restaurants, physician's and dentist's services. This quality uncertainty has significant consequences for the market structure and the market process. Consumers spend time and money to obtain information about the suppliers in the market. They share their experiences about physicians, lawyers, dentists and hosptials, and they consult agents and consumer journals to obtain more informa-

* I would like to thank Manfred Holler, Kornelius Kraft, Harris Schlesinger, Göran Skogh, Thomas von Ungern-Sternberg and Peter Zweifel for valuable comments on earlier versions of this paper.

tion about certain markets. However, some suppliers try to benefit from the consumer's lack of full information by selling low quality products.

This is why consumers build up long-term relations with high quality suppliers or pay attention to brand names. In addition, governmental agencies and professional organizations take regulatory measures to impede low quality producers[1]. They may initiate quality control procedures[2], quality standards and barriers to entry. An alternative is to regulate the professional education as well as to protect legally professional titles. For example, the titles of medical doctor, dentist, or lawyer can only be legally borne by a person who underwent professional training at an approved university. In addition professional associations create protected titles and appoint qualified professionals to use that title.

Many of the above regulatory measures represent strong limitations to competition which may be desirable from the viewpoint of the specific profession or sector, but which – from a general economic viewpoint – lead to misallocation. This raises the question of whether the above regulatory measures are efficient in guaranteeing high quality services of self-employed professions, or whether market-price mechanisms would do the better job.

This paper addresses this question, using a simple model of a market process. The discussion is centered on those professional services whose quality can typically be judged only after purchase. Special attention is paid to the role of administrated prices in quality enforcement. Preceeding the model analysis, and for the purpose of better classification and motivation of the chosen approach, existing results concerning the functioning of markets in the presence of quality uncertainty are briefly presented. In the last section implications are drawn regarding quality-enforcing policies for the self-employed professions.

2. QUALITY UNCERTAINTY AND INFORMATION STRUCTURE

First let us explain the quality concept employed in economic theory. We define a high-quality product as one that is preferred by all consumers over a similar product with low quality, and if production cost for high quality lies above that for low quality. This is not a trivial definition, though it may appear so at first sight. In his 'New Approach to Consumer Theory', Lancaster (1966) pointed out that consumers buy products for their features and that products usually have more than one. A dress for instance may have a stylish cut, be particularly warm and difficult to clean. In this case a price system can still be inferred, as

Rosen (1974) showed with his concept of hedonic prices, but the product quality can no longer be clearly determined since consumers will weigh the various product features differently according to the preferences. In addition, there are product features which are differently valued by consumers but do not entail different production costs. Some people prefer red, some prefer blue cars although both colours have the same production cost. It is assumed, therefore, that the products offered on the considered market can be clearly categorized according to quality whenever all information on the product features are available.

The full-information condition, however, is not exactly fulfilled when quality uncertainty exists. Assume that only the seller knows the quality of his products and the buyer is uncertain about the product quality. In this case, which seems to be typical for most markets, we have an asymmetrical information structure. Different types of goods may be distinguished: The quality of some commodities can be inspected prior to purchase. These so-called "search goods" confront the consumer with the task of minimizing the cost of searching for a high-quality seller by employing adequate search strategies. Chan/Leland (1982), Wiggins/Lane (1983) and Vany/Savings (1983) have studied the conditions of a market equilibrium for search goods. An interesting question discussed in that literature is whether the consumer can lower the search cost by using the producer's advertising efforts as an indicator of quality.

The latter point is also of relevance for goods and services whose qualities can be judged only after purchase.[3] Using a classification by Nelson (1970), these goods may be called "experience goods". Most services and in particular services of self-employed professionals are "experienced goods". In his classic paper, 'The Market for Lemons', Akerlof (1970) has argued that the market mechanism will only provide an incentive to sell high-quality goods if a long term relationship between the seller and the buyer has been established; i.e. if, in case of repurchase, the buyer remembers the seller and chooses the one whose product he found satisfactory. Taking this assumption Klein/Leffler (1981) and Ungern-Sternberg/Weizsäcker (1981) have analysed two market mechanisms which ensure high-quality production. First, producers invest in goodwill, so their name or brand will be associated with high quality. Second, the above-described mechanism of repeated purchase enables sellers of high-quality products to build up a circle of steady customers, whereas low-quality sellers will have mainly chance customers. If the product price is high enough, high-quality sellers obtain a rent (price-premium mechanism).

In addition to search and experience goods, there are further cases in which the consumer has difficulty in evaluating the quality even after purchase, such as for "faith goods" and "confidence goods", terms introduced by Darby/Karni (1973)[4] and Blankart/Pommerehne (1985), respectively. The quality evaluation of "faith goods" depends on the consumption of other goods as well. For example, some medication will only be effective if the patient keeps to bedrest. Other medication loses effectiveness if the patient consumes alcohol. The quality of "confidence goods" can often not be evaluated even after purchase, i.e. the buyer must be able to rely on their high quality, since quality deficiency may have fatal consequences. Let us give the examples of a parachute, a life-vest, an airplane or watch service. In the case of these goods it is advisable that the consumers not only buy the goods but in addition control the production process.

The following analysis concentrates on markets for services of self-employed professionals which are typical "experience goods". These are the markets for services of office-based physicians, dentists, lawyers, physiotherapists, tax accountants, and other self-employed professionals. Klein/Leffler (1981) and other authors have shown that a supplier has an economic incentive to offer high-quality services if the expected discounted profits are hgiher than in the case of low-quality production. However, the existing models are based on assumptions, which make it difficult to draw conclusions concerning the dynamics of markets for services of self-employed professional.

First, an unlimited time horizon is assumed to exist for the producer[5], although practice time for self-employed professionals is limited. Second, Klein/Leffler (1981) presuppose that consumers are well informed about the production conditions, the producer's objectives, his time preference and his degree of risk aversion[6], but that they are uncertain about the quality of the services offered. Given such knowledge and a specific price, the consumer can anticipate whether the supplier has decided to produce high or low-quality services. This assumption is unsatisfactory insofar as a consumer will hardly have all the above information except for that on the product quality chosen by the supplier. Third, a similar behaviour of all suppliers is assumed[7], although observation shows that in many markets suppliers of both high and low-quality goods are simultaneously active. Apart from different personal characteristics (time preference, objective function, etc.) of the suppliers this may also be attributable to their time of entry into the market since markets are dynamic. Fourth, either a given number of suppliers is assumed[8] or totally free market entry[9]. Both prohibitively high entry cost and free market entry are extreme cases. Furthermore, in practice the entry of new suppliers takes place successively because it takes time to acquire the necessary technical, organisational and sector-specific know-how (university education, in-practice training). This aspect as well requires a dynamic market analysis. Fifth, in general the use of a static equilibrium model is inadequate to analyse the features of dynamic markets.[10]

In the following section, a model is presented which takes into account some of the aspects mentioned above. A supplier will be considered who has just entered a certain market. He finds already a specific market configuration and makes his production decisions accordingly. These in turn are facts for those suppliers who enter the market later. Market structures neither appear from nowhere nor are arranged by an invisible hand for all time to come, but are formed in the historical course of time.

3. THE MODEL

Let us suppose a product can be offered in two different qualities, $\bar{q}$ and q, where $\bar{q}$ stands for high, and q for low quality. The price p is exogenously determined. The cost function is:

$$C(q, x) \tag{1}$$

where x denotes the quantity of the product. The cost function has the following characteristics:

$$C_x(q, x) = c(q), \text{ and}$$

$$c(\bar{q}) > c(q),$$

i.e. the marginal costs are constant, but high-quality production causes higher cost than low-quality production. This results in a smaller profit margin for high-quality production if the price is given. The supplier in question who is entering the market, finds N producers of whom (for whatever reason) $\bar{N}$ producers have decided for high quality, and N producers for low quality, where:

$$N = \bar{N} + N. \tag{2}$$

To simplify, let us assume that the decision for a specific quality is irreversible, i.e. a producer will stick to the quality chosen until he leaves the market. The high costs of switching to a different product quality may serve as an explanation.

There are D consumers in the market. Each consumer remains T periods in the market. After T periods he or she leaves the market because of death, moving, or a change in preferences. During each period he buys one product unit from the supplier. If he is satisfied with the quality, i.e. if the quality is $\bar{q}$, he will repurchase from the same supplier during the periods to come. If he is dissatisfied, he will switch to another supplier during the next period, i.e. buy from one of the N – N* remaining suppliers. N* stands for the number of suppliers from whom the consumer already bought and whose product quality he found to be q^{11}. For simplicity it is assumed that there is no information flow among consumers and suppliers are not allowed to advertise. If the population is stable, each period D/T consumers leave the market and D/T new consumers enter it. The latter will choose randomly one from the number of existing suppliers so that each supplier can expect to have D/(T N) new customers per period. Each supplier is assumed to have a planning horizon of W periods. Given this market structure, in each period there are three groups of consumers.

(a) New consumers (NC) who enter the market and buy for the first time. Given a stable population we receive NC = D/T.
(b) The old consumers, i.e. repeat buyers (RB) who have been dissatisfied and continue to search for a high-quality producer. The following equation holds for repeat buyers.

$$\mathrm{RB} = \mathrm{f}(N/\mathrm{N}, \mathrm{T}, \mathrm{D})$$

$$\text{with } \partial \mathrm{f}/\partial(N/\mathrm{N}) > 0$$

$$\partial \mathrm{f}/\partial \mathrm{T} \begin{cases} > 0, \text{ if T} < N \\ < 0, \text{ if T} > N \end{cases}$$

$$\partial \mathrm{f}/\partial \mathrm{D} \geqslant 0$$

$$\mathrm{RB} = 0 \text{ for T} = 1 \text{ or } N = 0.$$

The number of dissatisfied consumers rises if the relative number of low-quality suppliers increases. In this case the average search process of consumers lasts longer. If T < N, the probability is positive that consumers leave the market without having found a high-quality supplier, i.e. who only have received low-quality products.

(c) The third group consists of satisfied repeat buyers (SB) who have found a high-quality supplier

$$\mathrm{SB} = \mathrm{g}(N/\mathrm{N}, \mathrm{T}, \mathrm{D})$$

$$\text{with } \partial \mathrm{g}/\partial(N/\mathrm{N}) < 0$$

$$\partial \mathrm{g}/\partial \mathrm{T} > 0$$

$$\partial \mathrm{g}/\partial \mathrm{D} > 0$$

In other words, the higher the share of low-quality suppliers, the smaller the number of repeat buyers because there are more dissatisfied consumers in the market still searching for high-quality. The total demand on the market is then given by

$$D = NC + RB + SB \tag{3}$$

The question is, under which conditions will a new supplier entering the market decide for high-quality production given a specific market constellation? Obviously, his decision will depend on his expectations for future sales quantities as well as on the future market configuration. Let us assume that the quantity sold is $\bar{x}$ if high-quality production is chosen, and x if low-quality production is chosen. The new supplier entering the market at time t will then decide for high quality if

$$\int_t^{t+W} e^{-r\tau}\, \bar{x}(\tau)\,(p - c(\bar{q}))\, d\tau > \int_t^{t+W} e^{-r}\ \ x(\tau)\,(p - c(q))\, d\tau \tag{4}$$

holds, where r denotes the discount rate[12], and the duration of professional activity. Since both NC and RB consumers choose their suppliers randomly, low-quality suppliers as well as high quality suppliers can expect the same number of NC and RB consumers. Therefore, $\bar{x}(\tau)$ and $x(\tau)$ will differ only in the number of satisfied repeat buyers $SB_i(\tau)$[13]. This allows us to reformulate (4) as

$$\int_t^{t+W} e^{-r\tau}\, SB_i(\tau)\, d\tau > \frac{p - c(q)}{p - c(\bar{q})} > 1. \tag{5}$$

Inequality (5) leads directly to the following conclusion already derived by Klein/Leffler (1981): The lower the discount rate r, the higher the probability that a supplier decides to produce high-quality goods. Hence differences in individual time preference may be seen as one reason for the simultaneous existence of high- and low-quality suppliers in an experience-goods market[14].

Inequality (5) shows, in addition if r is not too high, and $T > 1$, there is always a price level where it is worthwhile for the supplier to decide for high-quality production. During the first period of his professional activity, the new supplier can expect to find $(NC + RB)/(N + 1)$ customers. If he produces high quality, these customers will repurchase from him in the following periods, so that SB_i will increase with τ for a quality supplier. Otherwise SB_i is zero. Since

$$\lim_{p \to \infty} \frac{p - c(q)}{p - c(\bar{q})} \to 1 \tag{6}$$

and $SB_i(\tau) > 1$ for $T > 1$ and $D > N$, there will exist a price for which (5) is fulfilled. In this case the price will produce a quality-enforcing premium. In experience-good markets, therefore, profits may help to solve the moral hazard problem caused by an asymmetrical information structure, and provide an incentive for high-quality production.

If the supplier decides for high quality, $SB_i(\tau)$ is positive and obviously depends also on the relative number $\mathcal{N}/N$ of suppliers who produce low quality, on the total demand D, as well as on the number of purchases consumers make during their lifetime. This is captured in equation (7).

$$SB_i = h(\mathcal{N}/N, T, D, \tau.) \tag{7}$$

$$\text{with } \partial h/\partial \mathcal{N}/N < 0$$
$$\partial h/\partial T > 0$$
$$\partial h/\partial D > 0$$

If the market structure remains constant over time, SB_i rises during the first T periods after entering the market and levels off at a specific value afterwards (see Figure 1a).

$$\partial SB_i/\partial \tau \begin{array}{l} > 0 \text{ for } \tau < T \\ = 0 \text{ for } \tau > T \end{array}, \; t < \tau < t + W$$

Once a circle of steady customers has established, in the periods $\tau > T$ the same number of new consumers join as old ones leave. Figure 1a shows how the number of consumers varies over the supplier's professional life-cycle. At point t, the time when the supplier enters the market, his sales will be the same whether he decided for low or for high-quality production. In the subsequent periods, $\bar{x}$ will always be higher than x due to the number of SB_i-consumers. Taking the given price-level and the cost function we can calculate the profit-path over time. Figure 1b illustrates this point and shows that the discounted value of the profit differences is equal to the rent a supplier receives if he decides for high quality production. Therefore the greater the relative number of low-quality suppliers, the higher the probability of new suppliers to decide for low quality as well. Hence, from the viewpoint of market dynamics there is a self-enforcing tendency towards low quality if the number of high-quality suppliers falls below a critical level. A relatively high price level may counteract this tendency. This result may be surprising since, in a market with a relatively large number of low-quality suppliers, a high-quality supplier should have good sales chances. But it is also easier for a low-quality supplier to survive because, in such a market, x will be relatively high compared to $\bar{x}$. This is why in a market

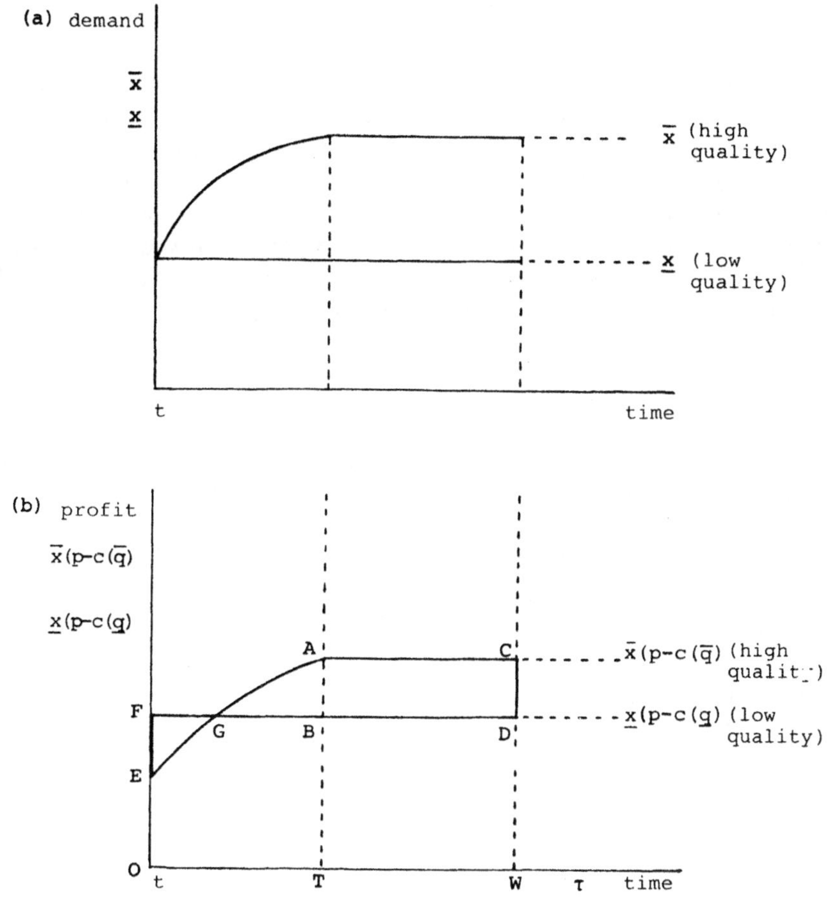

GBDCA-EGF = quality rent (if discount rate r=O)
OT = stage of expansion
TW = steady-state stage

Fig. 1a and 1b. Quality Incentives Through Market Forces.

with many low-quality suppliers there are so many dissatisfied buyers that a new supplier can always count on a sufficient number of chance customers. This reduces the incentive to produce high quality. Low quality supersedes high quality, if the number of low-quality suppliers exeeds a certain number.

From equation (7) also follows that the higher the number of repurchases per consumer T, the population number D, and the time horizon of the supplier W, the higher will be the probability that a supplier entering the market decides for high-quality production.

4. POLICY IMPLICATIONS FOR A DYNAMIC MARKET PROCESS

The above model of the decision problem of a supplier entering an experience-goods market allows us to infer the conditions for a quality-enforcing price policy in a dynamic market process. Two assumptions will be made: First, the government is in a position to control prices.[15] Second, during each period a specific number of new suppliers enter the market while a specific number of old suppliers leave. How does the price policy have to be designed in order to provide incentives for continued quality improvement rather than deterioration?

(5) to (7) can be simplified by writing,

$$g(\mathcal{N}/N, T, D) > f(p) \text{ with } \partial f/\partial p < 0. \tag{5'}$$

Obviously prices must be fixed in such a way as to ensure that (5′) is always fulfilled for those suppliers who enter the market. However, the governmental price agency will be interested in maintaining supplier profits at a level no higher than necessary for quality enforcement.[16] If the quality-ensuring price policy starts at the point of time 0, the features of optimal price-setting can be formulated as a problem of control:

$$\min \int_0^\infty |g(\mathcal{N}(t)/N(t), T, D(t)) - f(p(t))|dt. \tag{8}$$

subject to

$$g(\mathcal{N}(t)/N(t), T, D(t)) - f(p(t)) > 0 \text{ for all t} \tag{9}$$

where $\mathcal{N}(0) = \mathcal{N}_o$, $N(0) = N_o$
$D(0) = D_o$

$\mathcal{N}_o$, N_o and D_o describe the given market-structure at the time when the quality-ensuring price policy starts. (8) and (9) are fulfilled if the control variable p(t) is chosen so that

$$g(\mathcal{N}(t)/N(t), T, D(t)) - f(p(t)) = a > 0 \tag{10}$$

where a denotes a small positive unit which lies just above the perceptivity threshold of the supplier. By differentiating (10) with respect to t we obtain[17]

$$\dot{p} = \frac{-\dfrac{\partial g}{\partial(\mathcal{N}/N)}\dfrac{\dot{\mathcal{N}}}{N^2}N + \dfrac{\partial g}{\partial D}\dot{D}}{\dfrac{\partial f}{\partial p}}. \tag{11}$$

p denotes the optimal change in price p just sufficient to control product quality where the price at time t can be determined by equation (10).

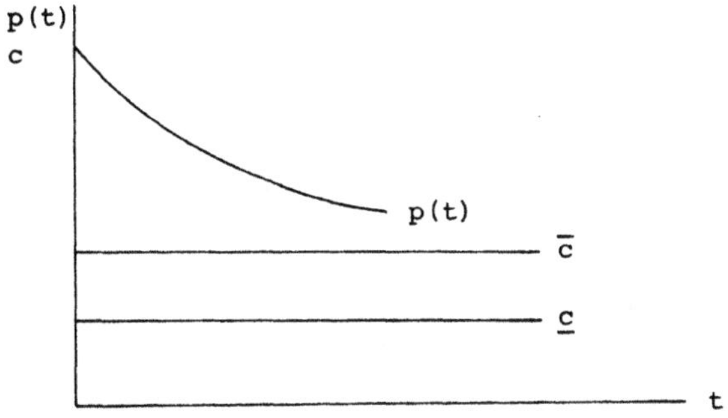

Fig. 2. Quality-enforcing Price Policy over Time.

Obviously $\dot{p}$ is negative if $\dot{N}$ and/or $\dot{D}$ are positive, i.e. the number of suppliers and/or the population increase. If this is the case, the price can be reduced continuously and the critical quality-ensuring price-level converges to the marginal cost $\bar{c}$ (see Figure 2). The higher $\dot{N}$, the quicker this process can develop. Contrary to the widespread opinion that market entry barriers help to ensure high-quality production, it is precisely the facilitation of market entry that raises the chances of successful quality-enforcing price policy[18].

In other words, in growing markets, the critical price-level decreases just sufficiently to motivate for high-quality production. Entry barriers increase the cost of quality-enforcing price policy.

5. ADMINISTRATED VERSUS MARKET PRICES

So far we have postulated an administrated price, i.e. a given price. The question arises whether in the case of experience goods, the market dynamics alone would create a price level that motivates high-quality production. Existing studies on experience-goods markets contribute little to answer this question because they postulate either a completely nonelastic demand, or a given total demand. These assumptions facilitate the analysis as they do not require an exact discussion of the demand curve and its relation to different qualities.[19] However, it remains unclear whether a price level will come about which is high enough to motivate high-quality production.

To solve this problem additional assumptions are necessary. Klein and Leffler (1981) postulate that the consumer is informed about the production cost if the quality is high or low. In this case it is easy for consumers to anticipate that suppliers will offer low quality if their price is not significantly higher than $\bar{c}$ (or, in the case of a U-Shaped cost function, lies above the marginal cost minimum for high quality). Therefore, the consumers will not be prepared to pay more than c (or the marginal cost minimum for low quality).

A different market process seems to be more realistic. Let us assume for a moment that there is only very little flow of information among consumers about the qualities offered on the market. Each consumer must then gain his own experience and is running the risk of buying low quality until he finds a high-quality supplier. If, however, perfect information flow would exist, low-quality suppliers would be pushed out of the market immediately. The assumption of limited information flow or positive information cost can be viewed as analogous to that of lacking possibilities to arbitrage or to positive transaction cost. Whoever is informed about high-quality suppliers is not able to pass information on easily. In such markets suppliers may differentiate prices according to different consumer groups.[20] In our model we have distinguished between three groups of consumers. Those who did not yet find a high-quality supplier (first-time buyers and dissatisfied repeat buyers) are presumably only prepared to buy at a 'trial' price p which lies below $\bar{c}$ since they cannot know whether they will receive high or low quality. In case they are satisfied, the next time they will be prepared to pay a higher price which includes a quality premium. Since suppliers anticipate such behaviour on part of the consumers, the expected higher price paid by satisfied steady customers motivates them to offer high quality.

6. IMPLICATIONS FOR QUALITY ENFORCEMENT FOR SERVICES OF SELF-EMPLOYED PROFESSIONALS

Services of self-employed professionals – such as physicians, dentists, lawyers, etc. – are frequently named as an example of experience goods.[21] Interestingly, these are precisely the markets for which quality-enforcement regulations have been demanded and forced through by the professional associations.

We have been able to show, however, that administrative prices are a sufficient tool to ensure high quality. Since prices for services of self-employed professionals are frequently administered, i.e. determined by governmental authorities or by means of negotiations[22], a price level could be fixed on these markets to provide an incentive for high-quality production. We have shown that market-entry barriers both hinder and increase the costs of a quality-enforcing price policy.

However, if suppliers are free to change their decision regarding the quality level, the incentive to offer high quality diminishes as time advances because the remaining time of his professional activity decreases. Therefore, routine checks of professional qualification could be necessary to ensure high quality over time, as is the rule with pilots.

One limitation, of the above model framework should be mentioned. The assumption of a constant marginal cost may not hold for self-employed professionals. Their costs consist of two components, money and personal work input. The evaluation of the work time depends on the relative value of leisure and is, therefore, not independent of the market price p. As a result, the costs of self-employed professionals are also a function of the market price, so that, in an extreme case, (6) need not necessarily converge to one. The result could be that there is no quality-enforcing price.

7. SUMMARY AND OUTLOOK

In this paper an attempt has been made to study the mechanisms which could lead to quality enforcement for services of self-employed professionals. This permits us to evaluate existing regulatory measures imposed for the purpose of quality enforcement. Markets for services of self-employed professionals are frequently characterized by administrated prices, entry barriers, training and practice regulations as well as by quality standards and controls. In this paper we have shown that, in a dynamic market process, the price mechanism itself is sufficient to motivate new suppliers to produce high quality. Contrary to the common opinion that entry barriers contribute towards quality enforcement, it is precisely the facilitation of market entry which raises the possibility of a successful quality-enforcing price policy. Regular quality control is justified as an additional measure since the economic incentive derived from the repeat purchase mechanism will diminish as the time horizon of the supplier decreases.

NOTES

1. Such measures are known to have been taken since antiquity. For example under Louis XIV carpet weavers were not allowed to work after 5 p.m. because the risk of low quality was higher when working with candle light.
2. For example in the U.S. Professional Standard Review Organizations were founded in 1972 to control the quality-cost relation of physician services.
3. Cf. Ungern-Sternberg/Weizsäcker (1981) and Conrad (1982).
4. Cf. also Hauser (1979).
5. We can work with the usual assumption of an infinite time horizon only if it is possible for a physician or a lawyer to sell his office and his goodwill. However, there

is only limited possibility for self-employed professionals to sell their goodwill since their name functions like a brandname.

6. For all models risk-neutral behaviour on part of the producers is assumed, i.e. maximization of expected profit instead of expected utility.
7. Holler (1984) sets aside this assumption by working with varying time preferences.
8. See e.g. Ungern-Sternberg/Weizsäcker (1981).
9. See e.g. Klein/Leffler (1981).
10. Recently the necessity of a dynamic analysis has been recognized (cf. e.g. Shapiro (1983): "Product quality choices by sellers are fundamentally dynamic" (21)). Nevertheless, there is not usually much attention paid to the dynamics of markets with quality uncertainty (see e.g. Wigging/Lane (1983): ". . . dynamic effects are beyond the scope of our one-period model" (882)).
11. It is implicitly assumed that the consumer is informed about the two different qualities available on the market. It is always worthwhile for him to keep searching until finding a high-quality producer. However, if there are several levels of quality, the expectations concerning the quality distribution are of importance to decide whether continued search is advisable. See Shapiro (1982) who analyses the case of incorrect quality expectations.
12. We implicitly assume risk-neutral behaviour (see above).
13. SB denotes the total number of satisfied repeat buyers, whereas SB_i denotes that number which falls to the supplier i ($i = 1, \ldots, N$), so that $\sum SB_i = SB$.
14. Cf. Holler (1984), 479.
15. This assumption applies for many trades and self-employed professionals in several countries where fees and prices are fixed by governmental or quasi-governmental agencies.
16. By means of sunk cost the expected profits could be skimmed off (for instance by means of a licence). Ungern-Sternberg/Weizsäcker (1981) and Klein/Leffler (1981) pointed this out.
17. A dot denotes a partial derivative with respect to time, e.g. $\dot{N} = \partial N/\partial \tau$.
18. For example, it has always been claimed by professional associations that an 'oversupply' of physicians would decrease the quality of physicians services.
19. Cf. e.g. Leffler (1982).
20. For a detailed discussion of the conditions for price differentiating behaviour see Schuelnburg (1984), especially the annex.
21. Cf. e.g. Leffler (1982): "physicians' services bought by the visit, and tennis lessons by the hour" (956); Shapiro (1982): "medical and legal services" (20); Chan/Leland (1982): "market for professional services – doctors, lawyers, contractors, etc." (499); Wieland (1984) explicitly refers his analysis to the market for physicians' services.
22. E.g. the fee schedule for physicians, dentists, physical therapists, and lawyers.

REFERENCES

Akerlof, G.A. (1970), The Market for Lemons: Quality Uncertainty and the Market Mechanism, *Quarterly Journal of Economics*, **84**, 488–500.

Blankart, C.B. and Pommerehne, W.W. (1985), Zwei Wege zur Privatisierung öffentlicher Dienstleistungen: Wettbewerb in einem Markt und Wettbewerb um einen Markt – eine kritische Beurteilung, in: Monissen, H.G., Milde, H. (Hrsg), *Theo-*

retische Grundlagen einer rationalen Wirtschaftspolitik (Festschrift für G. Gäfgen), Stuttgart: Kohlhammer.

Chan, Y.-S. and Leland, H. (1982), Prices and Qualities in Markets with Costly Information, *Review of Economic Studies*, **49**, 499–516.

Conrad, K. (1982), Advertising Quality and Informationally Consistent Prices, *Zeitschrift für die gesamte Staatswissenschaft*, **138**, 680–694.

Darby, R.R. and Karni, E. (1973), Free Competition and the Optimal Amount of Fraud, Journal of Law and Economics, 16, 67–88.

Hauser, H. (1979), Qualitätsinformationen und Marktstrukturen, Kyklos, **32**, 739–763.

Hey, J.D. and McKenna, C.J. (1981), Consumer Search with Uncertain Product Quality, *Journal of Political Economy*, **89**, 54–66.

Holler, M.J. (1984), Markets as Self-Policing Quality Enforcement Systems, Trappl, R. (Ed.), *Cybernetics and System Research* 2, Amsterdam: North-Holland, 477–481.

Klein, B. and Leffler, K.B. (1981), The Role of Market Forces in Assuring Contractual Performance, *Journal of Political Economy*, **89**, 615–641.

Lancaster, K. (1966), A New Approach to Consumer Theory, *Journal of Political Economy*, **74**, 132–157.

Leffler, K.B. (1982), Ambiguous Changes in Product Quality, *American Economic Review*, **72**, 956–967.

Rosen, S. (1974), Hedonic Prices and Implicit Markets: Product Differentiation in Pure Competition, *Journal of Political Economy*, **82**, 34–55.

Shapiro, C. (1982), Consumer Information, Product Quality, and Seller Reputation, *Bell Journal of Economics*, **13**, 20–35.

Shapiro, C. (1983), Optimal Pricing of Experience Goods, *Bell Journal of Economics*, 14, 497–507.

Ungern-Sternberg, T.v., Weizsäcker, C.C.v. (1981), Marktstruktur und Marktverhalten bei Qualitätsunsicherheit, *Zeitschrift für Wirtschafts- und Sozialwissenschaften*, 101, 607–626.

Vany, A.S. de, Saving, T.R. (1983), The Economics of Quality, *Journal of Political Economy*, 91, 979–1000.

Wieland, K. (1984), Quality and Competition on the Market of Physician Services – A Theoretical Investigation, in: Eimeren, W.v., Engelbrecht, R., Flagle C.D., (Hrsg.), *System Science in Health Care*, Heidelberg, New York, Tokyo: Springer, 1111–1114.

Wiggins, S.N, Lane, W.J. (1983), Quality Uncertainty, Search and Advertising, *American Economic Review*, 73, 881–894.

CONTROLLING INSIDER TRADING IN EUROPE AND AMERICA: THE ECONOMICS OF THE POLITICS*

David D. Haddock and Jonathan R. Macey

1. INTRODUCTION

The purchase or sale of corporate stock by employees or other closely associated individuals, when done on the basis of information that is not publicly available, is called insider trading. Insider trading is illegal in the United States, and the Securities and Exchange Commission (SEC) vigorously enforces the laws with both civil and criminal penalties. By contrast, insider trading is legal in most European countries. A few other European countries have mild rules constraining insider trading, but those rules have not been enforced actively.

There are two kinds of laws in Europe that affect insider trading, and they work in opposite directions. First are outright statutory proscriptions against the practice. Only France, Denmark and Britain have such statutory proscriptions.[1] France and Denmark provide only mild sanctions, and the total number of lawsuits and administrative actions brought in those countries is nearly nil.[2]

Germany, like most European countries, has no laws against insider trading. In 1970, however, the German Commission on Stock Exchange Organization adopted a set of "recommendations" that condemned insider trading by staff members of German corporations. These recommendations do not have the force of law, but simply "invite" German corporations to insert provisions in their corporate charters prohibiting certain sorts of transactions by insiders.[3] On July 1, 1985, Britain became the first European country to adopt criminal penalties as punishment for insider trading.[4] It is too early to analyze how extensively these sanctions will be enforced.

A second and perhaps more important set of rules are the bank secrecy laws of several European nations. These laws have significance across national borders because they can be used by non-residents to avoid the insider trading regulations of their own countries.[5] For example, in Switzerland not only are there no rules against insider trading, but local bank secrecy laws and customs almost invite insider trading.[6] In Switzerland insider trading through bank secrecy is constrained only by Convention 16, a bilateral agreement between the United States and Switzerland. Convention 16 provides that any person under U.S. jurisdiction who uses a Swiss bank to intermediate a transaction on a U.S. security exchange automatically releases that bank from normal secrecy laws as they apply to that transaction.[7] Nevertheless, the Swiss Bankers Association, an independent Swiss organization, must approve the disclosure of any information to U.S. authorities. More importantly, Convention 16 applies only to commercial banks, not to brokerage firms or merchant banks. The strictest Swiss secrecy laws still apply to these latter firms, and it is these firms that presumably do most of the trading by insiders trying to evade the tough U.S. laws.

Switzerland is not even the European country whose secrecy laws are most conductive to insider trading. In Liechtenstein, insiders may trade in stock through "nominee corporations," which are companies in which the actual indentities of the owners are hidden.[9] Thus, regardless of how the local laws of U.S. or European countries may restrict insiders from trading, such insiders can set up nominee corporations in Liechtenstein and trade through them.

In a series of moves that have strained relations between nations, the United States persistently had pressured European governments, particularly the Swiss, to adopt rules making insider trading illegal. The *Wall Street Journal* has predicted that the Swiss soon will consider a Parliamentary bill to comply with the requests, although the effective date will not be until 1987.[10] Ironically, this legislation seems likely to result in even more insider trading through Swiss banks than there is at present, because Convention 16 is effective only until the Swiss adopt a law of their own proscribing insider trading. After such a new Swiss law is adopted, U.S. officials will have to rely on conventional, multilateral reciprocity agreements to obtain information about illegal insider trading. If the past is any guide, such information is likely to be difficult to obtain.

This paper takes a fresh look at the legal proscriptions against insider trading in the United States, since those rules seem likely to serve as a model for those adopted in Europe. We examine the nature of the rules against insider trading and argue that, if permitted to choose, the shareholders of some corporations would benefit if insiders in these corporations were allowed to trade freely, and shareholders in other corporations would be worse off. As such, the argument that *all* firms should be compelled to ban the practice is suspect. In addition, we offer a new thesis based on the theory of regulation and the efficient capital market hypothesis to explain the political motivation for the harsh U.S. laws that seem likely to extend to much of Europe shortly.

2. LESSONS FROM THE EFFICIENT MARKET HYPOTHESIS

Acceptance of the efficient capital market hypothesis now is virtually universal within the academic community.[11] That hypothesis asserts that at any time securities prices will fully reflect all relevant available information about the underlying corporation.[12] A basic implication of the hypothesis is that it is not possible to profit beyond a so-called normal return from stock market purchases based on historical information about a stock's price, because such historical information will already be reflected in the price of the stock.[13] Consequently, to profit from information about a particular firm one must obtain information that relates to a firm's future prospects, but which has not already become reflected in a firm's share price.

The more efficient the stock market becomes, the more rapidly information becomes reflected in a firm's share price, and hence the more difficult it will be to profit on the basis of information discovery. Indeed, if the market were perfectly efficient it would not be possible to profit at all from searches; relevant new information would alter share prices instantaneously, so those who are holding the shares at that moment, not the searchers, would capture the value of the new information. Therefore, those who are particularly adept at obtaining information about a firm's prospects are better off if the market is *not* perfectly efficient.

The pursuit of trading profits in a market that is efficient (but not perfectly so) is akin to a foot race. Just as the footrace is won by the swiftest runner, the trader who will profit from stock trading will be the one who first is able both to obtain a valuable piece of information not already reflected in stock prices and then transmit this information to the market by buying or selling. To see who profits from the rules against insider trading we must identify the winners of the trading race and the way that the insider trading rules affect the race's outcome.

For our purposes the contestants in the trading race can be placed in three categories representing three major groups involved in stock market trading, (1) true insiders, (2) quasi-insiders, and (3) outsiders:

(1) True insiders are corporate officers, directors, other employees, and closely associated parties, such as legal counsel and employees of audit-

ing firms, who have immediate access via their employment duties to new firm specific information about a firm's present value of future income stream. In the absence of any rules against insider trading such inside "contestants" may well be expected to win every race. The rules against insider trading are intended to disqualify this group from competing. To the extent that this group is disqualified (that is, to the extent the legal rules are effective) the next fastest group that can legally trade will be expected to win.

(2) The next best information processors competing for trading profits in the stock market includes those we call "quasi-insiders" or "market professionals." Most of the members of this group work for investment banks and stock brokerage firms as arbitrageurs, researchers, brokers, and portfolio managers, and they devote their careers to acquiring information about a firm, an industry, or a group of firms or industries. Simultaneously, these market professionals develop skills for evaluating the information they obtain. Unlike true insiders, these people owe no "fiduciary duty" to the firms they study, meaning that they take no implied responsibility to look after the firm's interests as a consequence of their chosen field of employment. Because they actually work in the exchanges or in closely alllied firms, quasi-insiders can *execute* trades of a firm's stock more promptly even than a firm's true insiders, and can be beaten by a true insider only because of the latter's quicker acquisition of relevant information about the firm. Market professionals invest large amounts of resources in developing an ability to obtain early information about firms, to quickly assimilate that information, and to execute speedy stock market transactions before other traders have drained the information of its value.[14] True insiders, in contrast, have less need to make such investments in seeking and using information because they have the advantage of holding jobs where their attention is directed to the valuable information by their duties to the employing firm.

(3) The least likely group of contestants to profit from valuable new information are the ordinary shareholders and other complete "informational outsiders". In a large corporation with widely dispersed share ownership, these informational outsiders will include most of the firm's shareholders, although a few shareholders will usually be true insiders or quasi-insiders. Courts and scholastics have distinguished the public at large from the group that includes a firm's shareholders, but for our purposes the differences between these groups are immaterial.[15] Both are at a hopeless trading disadvantage if they want to compete for informational profits against either true insiders or quasi-insiders because the outsiders can neither observe, grasp, nor act on new information as quickly as their competitors can.

Absent legal restraints, true insiders consistently beat both market professionals and outsiders because of superior access to useful information. The insider is the quickest starter of the three. Market professionals, our quasi-insiders, have a similar information acquisition advantage over outsiders to that that true insiders have over them; they are able to discover valuable information more rapidly than are outsiders. Moreover, once they have the relevant information, market professionals are quicker to execute transactions than anyone else, even the true insiders. So market professionals consistently beat outsiders.

The ability of any of the three groups to profit from new firm specific information is affected by the legal system. As we show below where we describe the insider trading rules, those rules now cover *only* true insiders.[16] They do not much constrain the behavior of the market professsionals even though such market professionals have a distinct advantage over ordinary shareholders and other outsiders, allowing the quasi-insiders more promptly to learn of, execute on, and hence profit from new information. Because the legal system eliminates true insiders but leaves quasi-insiders free to trade, the rules against insider trading benefit not the outsiders, but the quasi-insiders, and at the expense of true insiders.

A plausible explanation for the rules affecting insider trading is found in the economic theory of regulation, which applies principles of microeconomics to the supply of and demand for governmental regulation.[17] Directly or indirectly, interest groups affected by regulation purchase from regulators the set of legal rules that maximize their net wealth. Regulation is thus parcelled out in response to private demands.[18] The theory predicts that the group that most highly values control over the form of a particular regulation will usually be the highest bidder, and thus will be the winner of the implicit regulatory auction. Market professionals benefit most from the compulsory form of the rules constraining insider trading, for the rules leave them unimpeded by true insiders, but still enable them to use the informational and executory advantages they hold over outsiders to capitalize on firm specific investments.[19] Unless there are restraints on trading, true insiders capture much of the gain that goes to market professionals otherwise. Particularly well-informed shareholders in some firms will likely be harmed by insider trading. Such shareholders also will seek to prevent their true insiders from trading on the basis of inside information. These shareholders will join with market professionals in preferring SEC enforced rules against insider trading, because that transfers much of the enforcement cost to taxpayers generally.

It is reasonable to ask why true insiders do not better defend their interest in retaining the ability to trade on inside information. Why didn't *they* capture the SEC, rather than the market professionals? The answer is that there are more true insiders than market professionals, each of whom realizes smaller and much more variable gains from trading than do professionals, and the insiders' opportunity cost of monitoring the SEC is higher as well. True insiders control the operations of firms. Good ones are highly rewarded for running firms well, which means developing popular new products, reacting appropriately to changes in relative prices and new competition, reacting to personnel changes, and so on. Only rarely do most individual insiders have an opportunity to capture insider trading profits. If insiders are going to lobby for regulation, they will try to obtain tariffs or cartels for their industry, to restrict competition for their own jobs, and so forth. Market professionals, in contrast, do nothing else but manipulate securities portfolios. It is their full-time job, and so it will be the primary target of any rent-seeking regulation they propose and support through friendly legislators.[20]

Many of the shocks that any given insider can profit from originate within the insider's firm, either through the insider's own efforts or through the efforts of others within the firm. Henry Manne has argued forcefully that insiders should be permitted to trade on such information.[21] We do not intend to inform that particular debate beyond noting that no one has explained why firms ought not be permitted voluntarily to opt out of a ban on insider trading if shareholders believe that insider trading opportunities are the best incentive in the corporation's particular case. Our goals here are to expand the Manne scenario on one boundary, but to limit it on another.

3. INSIDER TRADING RULES IN THE UNITED STATES

Although insider trading is prohibited in the United States neither at common law,[22] nor by state statute,[23] three separate provisions of the national Securities Exchange Act of 1934[24] impose prohibitions on the practice. Section 16(b) compels officers, directors, and certain statutorily defined insiders to disgorge any profit made from the sale and purchase, or purchase and sale, of an equity security of their firm within a period of less than six months.[25] The reach of Section 16(b) can be avoided by holding securities for longer than six months,[26] and so even the drafters of the provision recognized that the rule would have little effect in curbing insider trading.[27]

SEC Rule 10b-5,[28] on the other hand, is as broad as Section 16(b) is narrow. Rule 10b-5 requires those in possession of material inside information to refrain from trading in the stock to which that information pertains, or else to disclose the nature of that information to the public well before trading.[29] The jurisprudence that surrounds this rule emphasizes "the necessity of preventing insiders from exploiting their informational advantage" over others.[30] Because of the broad scope of the statutory language, the rule is subject to varying interpretations, and, as described below, its effective meaning has evolved over time.[31]

Nothing in the terms of Section 10(b) or Rule 10b-5 limits the scope of enforcement to corporate insiders.[32] Market professionals, and indeed the general public, seem to be covered by the language of the rule.[33] The Supreme Court's recent decisions in *Chiarella v. U.S.*[34] and *Dirks v. SEC*,[35] which we discuss below, have done much to clarify and to narrow the scope of Rule 10b-5. After these cases, Rule 10b-5 imposes an affirmative duty to disclose only upon true insiders.[36] There now is no obligation to "disclose where the person who has traded on inside information was not [the corporation's] agent . . . was not a fiduciary, [or] was not a person in whom the sellers [of the securities] had placed their trust and confidence."[37] The Court expressly rejected the previously widely held view that Rule 10b-5 requires equal information among all traders.[38] Significantly, those who acquire information on the basis of a special access due to a position on the market, as opposed to a position in the firm, are expressly exempted by the Court from any duty to disclose. Thus, the Court in Chiarella drew the line between the permitted and the prohibited precisely where this paper predicts, in other words, precisely between true insiders and quasi-insiders. True insiders are barred by their so-called "fiduciary duties" from engaging in insider trading, while quasi-insiders usually are left free to engage in unfettered trading on the basis of whatever privileged inside information they are able to gather.[39]

The holding in Chiarella, reaffirmed in Dirks, represented an important change in the legal ability of quasi-insiders to engage in inside trading. Prior to Chiarella Rule 10b-5 had been interpreted to mean that:

> all members of the investing public should be subject to identical market risks, – which market risks include, of course, the risk that one's capital available to put at risk may exceed another's capacity or capital . . . inequalities based upon unequal access to knowledge should not be shrugged off as inevitable in our way of life . . .[40]

This "equal access to information" interpretation of Rule 10b-5 was the dominant approach to the Rule from 1968, the date of the *Texas Gulf Sulphur*[41] decision, until 1980 when *Chiarella* was decided.

3.1. SEC v. Texas Gulf Sulphur

In *Texas Gulf Sulphur*, company insiders had knowledge that the firm had located a mammoth ore discovery in western Ontario. The discovery could be expected to increase the value of the firm's shares greatly, but it was inadvisable for Texas Gulf Sulphur to announce the discovery before concluding mineral leases on the ore-bearing sites. Premature announcement would increase the price at which those leases could be concluded. But when insiders were found to have purchased Texas Gulf Sulphur stock in advance of public announcement of the mineral discovery, the SEC brought suit to force these insiders to disgorge their profits. The court's decision provided the well known "disclose or abstain" doctrine which requires that:

> anyone in possession of material inside information must either disclose it to the investing public, or, if he is disabled from disclosing it in order to protect a public confidence, or he chooses not to do so, must abstain from trading in or recommending the securities concerned while such information remains undisclosed.[42]

Under the doctrine developed in *Texas Gulf Sulphur* it seemed irrelevant whether the defendants were true insiders or quasi-insiders, because the word that begins the quotation is "anyone", not "any employee of the firm to which the inside information relates." The court's sweeping interpretation implies complete indifference to the *source* of the informational advantage, so the rule seemed to encompass both true insiders and market professionals.[43]

During the period between *Texas Gulf Sulphur* and *Chiarella*, the extent to which Rule 10b-5 extended beyond true insiders was unclear, and the application of the rule to quasi-insiders in possession of informational advantages was unsystematic.[44] The dominant view seems to have been that the function of the rules against insider trading was to deny any informational advantage that any person may have had over his or her trading partner.[45] This interpretation was of no particular value to the brokerage community. To the extent that the rule was enforced, it simply transferred wealth from whoever invested resources in developing valuable information, whether true insiders or quasi-insiders, to that person's partner.

While the basic holding in *Texas Gulf Sulphur* was of no particular value to market professionals, another, somewhat less notorious aspect of that decision had important implications for this group. This aspect relates to the Court's method of interpreting the "disclose or abstain" doctrine. If Rule 10b-5 were truly intended to benefit present shareholders or the investing public in general, then the disclosure of material, nonpublic information required by the rule would have to be made to the public or, alternatively, to the shareholders on whose behalf the rule ostensibly was enacted. Disclosure to any other group largely would benefit only that group, and not the public or the shareholders. As we show below, however, the test the court actually formulated in *Texas Gulf Sulphur* implicitly requires that disclosure be made only to those market insiders that this article argues Rule 10b-5 was intended to benefit.[46]

Some of the trading by *Texas Gulf Sulphur* insiders took place shortly after company officials issued a news release that disclosed the relevant information about the mineral discovery the company had made. The insiders were held liable for their trades despite this release. The court held that the insiders should have waited until the information was "disseminated."[47] The court then concluded that material inside information will be deemed to have been disseminated as soon as it appears on the Dow Jones broad tape.[48]

The Dow Jones broad tape is a *subscription* news service that provides detailed financial information *to the financial community*.[49] Information disseminated over the tape is likely to reach the financial community first, since the financial community continuously monitors the tape. But even in the unlikely event the news on the tape reaches the public and the market professionals simultaneously, the professionals are able to *execute* trades on the basis of that information more quickly than the public generally.[50] Thus, contrary to the statements by the court, the legal standard for determining whether information has been disclosed sufficiently for insiders to trade legally does not benefit the public, but only market professionals.

3.2. U.S. v. Chiarella and Dirks v. SEC

Vincent Chiarella was a financial printer employed by Pandick Press in New York. Chiarella made purchases in the stocks of Pandick's client firms based on confidential information he acquired about those firms in his capacity as a printer.[51] Chiarella was prosecuted for a criminal violation of section 10(b) of the Securities Exchange Act of 1934. The alleged violation of section 10(b) resulted from Chiarella's contravention of SEC Rule 10b-5.

The Court's opinion in *Chiarella* established a new limitation on liability under Rule 10b-5. The Court held for the first time that violation required that a defendant owe a fiduciary duty to the corporation to which the information pertains.[52] Absent a fiduciary duty arising from a contractual or quasi-contractual obligation, there is no liability under Rule 10b-5. True insiders owe a fiduciary obligation to the firms for which they work, but quasi-insiders do not. The holding in *Chiarella* was of great benefit to quasi-insiders, because it eliminated most potential restrictions on trades made on the basis of any superior knowledge they possess.

The value to quasi-insiders of the Supreme Court's new interpretation of Rule 10b-5 was made still more apparent in *Dirks v. SEC.*[53] The Supreme Court held that Raymond Dirks, an investment analyst, and so a quasi-insider, did not violate Rule 10b-5 when he sold to his investment banking clients valuable information about the Equity Funding Corporation. Dirks received from Equity Funding insiders tips about a massive fraud by the firm's officers, and Dirks then advised clients to sell Equity Funding shares on the basis of those tips.[54] But, following the reasoning in *Chiarella,* the Court held that Dirks, who had no connection with Equity Funding, could not owe a fiduciary duty to that firm or its shareholders.[55] Absent any fiduciary duty, Dirks could not be guilty of violating Rule 10b-5.

In sum, the formulation of the rules of fiduciary duty developed in *Chiarella* and *Dirks*, enhanced the value of Rule 10b-5 to the investment banking community. The earlier case of *SEC v. Texas Gulf Sulphur* prohibited true insiders from trading, but it was the "fiduciary duty" requirement developed in *Dirks* and *Chiarella* that clearly established the immunity from prosecution of quasi-insiders.

4. THE ARTICULATED JUSTIFICATIONS FOR THE RULES AGAINST INSIDER TRADING

4.1. Insider trading and the public

It has been said that the Rule 10b-5 is justified on the basis that stock trades are inherently unfair unless both sides of the transaction share equal information,[56] or alternatively, equal access to all available information relevant to the transaction.[57] Such a formulation of the rule assigns half the property rights in valuable information to whoever possesses an informational *dis*advantage. Anyone in possession of valuable information is required to donate the information to his less informed trading partner or else abstain from trading. This equal access conception of Rule 10b-5 extends the reach of the rule to both true insiders and quasi-insiders, because it covers anyone with an informational advantage. Thus, under either the "equal access" or the "complete equality" version of Rule 10b-5, the property rights in valuable information are shifted from *both* insiders and market professionals to complete outsiders. Interestingly the SEC, joined by several influential commentators, argued for many years that some version of the equal access theory should underlie Rule 10b-5.[58]

The Supreme Court's holding in *Chiarella* finally ended speculation about whether or not the equal access theory would prevail in the Supreme Court. As noted above, the Court categorically rejected such a theory in favor of a fiduciary duty theory.[59]

Those in possession of valuable information about a firm invest resources to acquire such information and assume risk when acting upon it. Adoption of the equal access theory would lead to an under production of information by reducing the return without reducing cost or risk. Thus formal adoption of an equal access theory would have made both insiders and market professionals worse off without making outsiders better off. Alternatively, if the valuable information is casually rather than deliberately acquired, the case for disclosure to those with an informational disadvantage may seem somewhat stronger.[60] But securities markets allocate capital efficiently only if information is rapidly reflected in stock prices. If some investors believe one industry is relatively more profitable than it actually is, capital formation will be diverted toward the less profitable industry instead of to alternative opportunities. Regardless of whether the information is casually or deliberately acquired, there is a strong reason, based on concerns for efficiency, to hurry new information regarding stock prices to the market. Where the information about a corporation has been casually acquired, there will be no incentive to disseminate the information rapidly if the acquiror is not permitted to profit from it.

Thus, justification for a rule that would turn the property rights in valuable information over to the public requires justification even as it concerns casually acquired information. The classic justification for such a rule has been that to do otherwise would be "unfair."[61] In fact, Manne demonstrated that outsiders will be *better* off if insiders are allowed to trade.[62] A wise holder of a perfectly diversified portfolio will never buy or sell stock based on public information about a particular firm. Purchases and sales will be made only to maintain portfolio diversification, and to redistribute consumption over the life-cycle. If an insider is selling stock on the basis of negative inside information about his firm, an outsider who happens to be buying at that time will be better off. As Scholes argues, the sales by the insider will drive the price of the firm's stock down by conveying negative information about the firm to the market.[63] Since the holder of the diversified portfolio was going to purchase the stock anyway, he clearly will prefer the lower price he gets as a result of the insider trading.[64] By parity of reasoning, if the insider information is positive, the purchasing insider will drive the price of his firm's stock up. Now those outsiders who sell are better off selling to the insider at a higher price than selling to another uninformed outsider at the previous lower price. Insider trading makes stock prices adjust more quickly than they would otherwise. This prompt adjustment aids outsiders, but harms market professionals both by dimininishing their ability to profit from their own stock trading, and, perhaps more importantly, by lowering the public's demand for their advice.

Thus, there is no justification for assigning the property rights in inside information to complete outsiders. But suppose all of this is wrong, and for some as yet undiscovered reason all new corporate information should be turned over to the public. As shown in the preceding section, the current formulation of Rule 10b-5 would not accomplish this result.[65] If the rule was designed to benefit the public, as its proponents indicate, then the Court was in error in *Dirks* and in *Chiarella*.

4.2. Rule 10b-5 and shareholders

We do not assert here that insider trading never harms shareholders. Our assertions, rather are that insider trading never harms the public in general, and that the interests of the shareholders and the interests of the public must be distinguished in this regard. Indeed we are willing to concede that insider trading may harm shareholders in certain contexts. For example, inside trading may create a moral hazard by allowing insiders to profit on bad news.[66] In addition, allowing insiders to trade may also give insiders a "perverse incentive" to choose unduly risky (high variance) projects to maximize expected trading profits.[67] Finally, it has been argued that insider trading may harm shareholders by causing the timing of disclosure to be delayed.[68] These are dubious arguments, and their valdity has never been shown empirically. Furthermore, even if insider trading does sometimes impose agency costs on a firm's shareholders, the benefits to the shareholders on other occasions may exceed these costs. If so shareholders would be willing to sell to managers the right to engage in insider trading.

Coase has shown that, absent transaction costs, property rights will be allocated to their highest valued use.[69] Coase's observation, however, is contingent upon the parties being able to "contract around" the initial allocation. Thus, from the standpoint of shareholders, *so long as the parties are free to contract around the initial rule*, it is irrelevant whether the property right in inside information is assigned in the first instance to a firm's managers or its shareholders because in either case the parties can engage in a value-maximizing exchange by allocating the property right in information to its highest valued user.[70]

If transactions costs are low, firms can be expected to specify their preferred inside trading rule in their articles of incorporation and in their managers' employment contracts. The cost to shareholders of inserting such provisions in manager's contracts is insignificant. On the other hand, it also seems clear that the cost of enforcing such contracts is high.[71] But even if we assume a high cost of enforcement for firms, is there any reason to expect the SEC's enforcement costs to be low? In any event, it does not follow that there is a need for a *per se* ban on insider trading, or that the SEC is the efficient authority to enforce such a ban.

Given that there are differences among firms, shareholders in some firms may prefer a ban on insider trading while shareholders in other firms prefer to permit the practice. Consequently, any costs associated with insider trading largely can be eliminated by replacing the current prohibition on insider trading with a default rule that acts as a standard form contract banning insider trading. Firms that would be better off if insiders were allowed to trade could then contract around the rule.

5. CONCLUSION

In this paper we observe that legal rules prohibiting insiders from trading on non-public information do not benefit the "public" as the proponents of such rules claim. While the rules against trading by insiders make it possible for non-insiders to reap gains that the insiders would have enjoyed in the absence of such prohibitions, these gains annure to a discrete special interest group we have dubbed market professionals and not to the public generally. Market professionals gain disproportionately from bans on insider trading because they are in a position to act on information that insiders cannot use, and can do so more quickly than any other group, including shareholders. Thus we disagree with recent arguments made both by the U.S. State Department and Securities and Exchange Commissions that Europeans would benefit if the widespread prohibition on insider trading that exists in the U.S. were exported outside of that country's boarders.

We have also posited that insider trading rules do not merely transfer wealth from insiders to market professionals. Because insiders have a contractual relationship with the shareholders of the firms for which they work, the Coase Theorem suggests that, absent legal constraints, these parties will decide for themselves what sort of rules on insider trading will benefit them most. Since the shareholders ordinarily do not stand to benefit from a prohibition on trading by insiders, we predict that they will prefer a legal system that permits them, if they wish, to sell this right to insiders in exchange for lower direct wages. Because the rules against insider trading prohibit shareholders from doing this, such rules harm rather than help shareholders. The rules against insider trading can best be explained with reference to the economic theory of regulation. The rules benefit a discrete highly organized interest group – market professionals – at the expense of diffuse poorly organized groups – insiders and ordinary shareholders. The SEC, a U.S. government agency highly responsive to its constituency of market professionals, has lately been pressing increasingly hard to enforce the rules that prevent insiders from competing with market professionals for the trading profits available to those in possession of privileged firm specific information. Such activity reduces the options available in structuring intrafirm relationships, consequently decreasing the efficiency of corporations, which is hardly the situation informed Europeans, as a body, should aspire to recreate.

NOTES

* We have received helpful comments on earlier versions of this paper from Michael Dooley, Jens Fejo, Barbara Klose-Ullmann, Roberta Romano, Cliff Smith and Peter Zweifel. We have also benefited from other comments received in presentations at the Law and Economics Conference of the Wissenschaftszentrum Berlin, at the Liberty Fund Conference on Insider Trading, and at the University of Munich. A more detailed version of the theoretical arguments presented here and its empirical underpinnings may be found in our forthcoming papers in the Journal of Law and Economics and the Northwestern University Law Review.

1. *See generally* Centre d'études Juridiques Europeenes, Institut Für Europäisches und Internationales Wirtschaftsund Sozialrecht, St. Gallen, Etudes Suisses de Droit Europeen Schweizerische Beitrage Zum Europarecht, Bank 28, Hirsh, Forstmoser, & Mundheim, L'Avant-Projet de loi Fédérale Sur Les Opérations D'Inities (Genève, Georg & Cie S.A., 1984).
2. Loss, *Multinational Approaches – Corporate Insiders*, New York, Matthew Bender (1975) at 111; Rider & Ffrench, *The Regulation of Insider Trading* (1979) at 238.
3. *See* Loss *supra* note 2 at 60–63 (referencing untitled paper by Helmut Coing).
4. Company Securities (Insider Dealing) Act 1985, Chapter 8, Sections 8–18; *See also* Yoran, Insider Trading in Israel and England, Alpha Press, Jerusalem, 1972, pp. 59–126.
5. The Stone Wall of Swiss Secrecy, Business Week, April 29, 1985 at 92.
6. *Id.*
7. *Id.*
8. *Id.*
9. *Id.*

10. Swiss Likely to Propose Bill on Insider Trading Ban, Wall Street Journal, May 1, 1985 at 38, col. 1.
11. *See* Gilson & Kraakman, *The Mechanisms of Market Efficiency*, 70 *Va. L. Rev*. 549, 549–50 (1984) (efficient capital markets hypothesis has achieved the widest acceptance of all recent developments in financial economics); Jensen, *Some Anomolous Evidence Regarding Market Efficiency* 6 *J. Fin. Econ*. 95 (1978) (there is no other proposition in economics which has more empirical evidence supporting it than the efficient market hypothesis).
12. Fama, *Efficient Capital Markets: A Review of Theory and Empirical Work*, 25 *J. Fin*. 383 (1970); *See also* Sharpe, Discussion, 25 *J. Fin*. 418, 418 (1970); "Simply put, the thesis is this: in a well-functioning market, the prices of . . . securities will reflect predictions based on all relevant information. This seems almost trivially self-evident to most professional economists" *Id.*
13. This is commonly known as the weak form of the efficient market hypothesis. *See* Fama *supra* note 12 at 383. *See also* Lorie & Hamilton, The Stock Market: Theories and Evidence 75–82 (1973).
14. *See* Gilson & Kraakman, *supra* note 11 at 571-72.
15. *See infra* text accompanying notes (TAN) 56–71.
16. *See infra* TAN 22–55.
17. Stigler, *The Theory of Economic Regulation* 2 *Bell Journal of Economics* 3 (1971); Peltzman, *Toward a More General Theory of Regulation*, 19 *Journal of Law and Economics* 211 (1976); Posner, *Economics, Politics, and the Reading of Statutes and the Constitution*, 49 *U. Chi. L. Rev*. 263 (1982).
18. *Id. See also* Landes & Posner, *The Independent Judiciary in an Interest-Group Perspective* 18 *J. Law & Econ*. 875, 877 (1975) ("legislation is supplied to groups or coalitions that outbid rival seekers of favorable legislation").
19. Bjerring, Lakonishok, & Vermaelen, *Stock Prices and Financial Analysts' Recommendations*, 38 *J. Fin*. 187 (1983) (abnormal returns possible from following analysts recommendations); Givoly & Lakonishok, *The Information Content of Financial Analysts' Forecasts of Earnings: Some Evidence on Semi-Strong Form Efficiency*, 1 *J. Acctng & Econ*. 165 (1979); Grossman, *On the Efficiency of Competitive Stock Markets Where Traders Have Diverse Information*, 31 *J. Fin*. 573 (1976); Grossman & Stiglitz, *Information and Competitive Price Systems*, 66 *Am. Econ. Rev. Papers and Proceedings*. 246 (1976); *but see* Jensen, *Risk, The Pricing of Capital Assets, and the Evluation of Investment Portfolios*, 42 *J. Bus*. 167 (1969).
20. The above discussion is a lengthy way of saying that the market professionals win the regulatory auction because the benefits to them of obtaining favorable legislation are higher than the benefits to rival groups. Looking at the other side of the equation, market professionals are likely to be successful in obtaining favorable insider trading legislation because the costs to them of organizing effective political action are lower. *See* Posner, *supra* note 17 at 265–66 (important determinant of the net benefit of legislative protection is the cost of organizing political action).

    Market professionals are already well organized into effective political groups such as the Association of Investment Analysts, the Securities Industry Association, the National Association of Securities Dealers, the New York Stock Exchange, and so forth. True insiders are not organized, nor are their interests as homogeneous. The more homogeneous the interests of a particular group, the less costly effective political action will be. Posner, *Theories of Economic Regulation*, 5 *Bell J. Econ* 335, 345 (1974), and Haddock and Macey, *Regulation on Demand*, forthcoming in 29 *J. Law & Econ*. (April 1987). Moreover, some insiders will oppose permissive insider trading rules because they *want* to be prohibited from insider trading in exchange for higher salaries, and will want others to bear the cost of monitoring and enforcing this restriction. *See* Macey and Haddock, *A Simple Model of Insider Trading*, forthcoming in 81 *Northwestern L.R.* (1986).

21. Manne, *Insider Trading and the Stock Market at 166* (1966).
22. *See* Goodwin v. Agassiz, 283 Mass. 358, 186 N.E. 659 (1933); *see also* Freeman v. Decio, 584 F.2d 186, 191–95 (discussing common law rules on insider trading); Carlton & Fischel, *The Regulation of Insider Trading*, 35 *Stan. L. Rev.* 857 (1983) at 883.
23. *Id.*
24. 15 U.S.C. Section 78 *et seq.* (1984).
25. 15 U.S.C. Section 78p(b) (1982).
26. Jennings & Marsh, Securities Regulation: Cases and Materials, (fifth ed. 1982) at 1315–16 ("any moderately bright manipulator should be able . . . to string out his activities . . . and thus escape any penalty").
27. *See* Hearings before the Committee of Banking and Currency on S. 84, 72d Cong., 2d Sess., and S.56 and S.97, 73d Cong., 1st and 2d Sess., 1934, 6557 (describing 16(b) as "crude rule of thumb"); *See also* Jennings & Marsh, *supra* note 26 at 1315 (16(b) imposes unjust liability upon entirely innocent persons).
28. 17 C.F.R. Section 240.10b-5 (1984).
29. SEC v. Texas Gulf Sulphur Co., 401 F.2d 833, 848, 856—57 (1968), *cert. denied*, 394 U.S. 976 (1969).
30. Dooley, *Enforcement of Insider Trading Restrictions* 66 *Va. L. Rev.*, 1, 56 (1980).
31. *See infra* TAN 44–65.
32. Brudney, *Insiders, Outsiders, and Informational Advantages Under the Federal Securities Laws* 93 *Harv. L. Rev.* 322, 329 (1979).
33. *See id.* at 339; Fifth Annual Institute On Securities Regulation 287–304 (Mundheim, Fleischer, & Schupper, eds. (1974) PLI Conference (discussion by Lipton)).
34. 445 U.S. 222 (1980). In *Chiarella*, Vincent Chiarella, a financial printer, used confidential information from disclosure documents he was preparing to reap gains in stock trading. *See infra* TAN 51–52.
35. 463 U.S. 646 (1983). In *Dirks*, Raymond Dirks, a financial analyst, received inside information from officials at Equity Funding, an insurance firm. The information enabled Dirks to give advanced notice to his clients concerning an impending disastrous announcement pertaining to the firm's earnings. *See infra* TAN 53–55.
36. So-called "tippees," those to whom insiders give information may also be liable. *See infra* TAN 51–59; *Dirks v. SEC* 463 U.S. at 657.
37. *Chiarella v. U.S.* 445 U.S. at 232; quoted with approval in *Dirks v. SEC* 464 at part III.
38. 445 U.S. at 232–33; quoted with approval in *Dirks.*
39. *See* Fischel, *Insider Trading and Investment Analysts: An Economic Analysis of Dirks v. SEC*, 13 *Hofstra L. Rev.* 127 (1984).
40. SEC v. Texas Gulf Sulphur Co. 401 F.2d 833, 852 (1968).
41. *Id.*
42. *Id.* at 848.
43. *See* Brudney, *supra* note 32 at 339; 343–49; Prentice, *The Impact of Dirks on Outsider Trading* 13 *Sec. Reg. L.J.* 38, 41–42 (1985).
44. *See* Brudney, *supra* note 32 at 332.
45. *Id.*
46. *See infra* TAN 47–50.

47. 401 F.2d at 854.
48. *Id.*
49. Pessin & Ross, Words of Wall Street 31 (1983) (describing Broad Tape).
50. Market professionals are able to execute trades more quickly than the public generally because they are, or have more immediate access to, the specialists and market makers who physically execute the transactions. *See supra* TAN 13–14.
51. 445 U.S. at 224.
52. 445 U.S. at 228. A fiduciary duty is an implied contractual term in an agency agreement. *See* Fischel, *supra* note 39. For example, trustees owe a fiduciary duty to the beneficiaries of the trusts they administer and corporate officers and directors owe a fiduciary duty to the shareholders of the firms for which they work.
53. 463 U.S. 646 (1983).
54. *Id.*
55. *Id.* at Part III.
56. Ferber, *The Case Against Insider Trading: A Response to Professor Manne*, 23 *Vand. L. Rev.* 621 (1970); Painter, *Rule 10b-5: The Recodification Thicket*, 45 *St. John's L. Rev.* 669, 714 (1971); Schotland, *Unsafe at Any Price: A Reply to Professor Manne*, 53 *Va. L. Rev.* 1425 (1967); Kaplan, *Wolf* v. *Weinstein: Another Chapter on Insider Trading*, 1963 *Sup. Ct. Rev.* 273; Loss, *The Fiduciary Concept as Applied to Trading by Corporate 'Insiders' in the United States*, 33 *Mod. L. Rev.* 34 (1970); *See also* Easterbrook, *Insider Trading, Secret Agents, Evidentiary Privileges, and the Production of Information* 1981 *Sup. Ct. Rev.* 309, 323–30 (articulating and rejecting various arguments against insider trading).
57. *See* Brudney *supra* note 32 at 322.
58. This was the position taken by the SEC before the U.S. Supreme Court in Dirks v. SEC, *see* 463 U.S. 646 at Part IIIA.
59. *See supra* TAN 36–39.
60. Kronman, *Mistake, Disclosure, Information and the Law of Contracts* 7 *Journal of Legal Studies* 1, (1978).
61. *See supra* note 56.
62. Manne, *supra* note 21 at 102–04.
63. Scholes, *The Market for Securities: Substitution Versus Price Pressure and the Effects of Information on Share Prices*, 45 *J. Bus.* 179, 182–84 (1973).
64. *See* Manne *supra* note 21 at 100–04.
65. *See supra* TAN 22–55.
66. Carlton & Fischel, *supra* note 22.
67. Leftwich & Verrecchia, *Insider Trading and Managers' Choices Among Risky Projects*, CRSP Working Paper 63 (1981).
68. Haft, *The Effect of Insider Trading Rules on the Internal Efficiency of the Large Corporation*, 80 *Mich. L. Rev.* 1051 (1982)
69. Coase, *The Problem of Social Cost*, 3 *J. Law & Econ.* 1 (1960).
70. Carlton & Fischel, *supra* note 22 at 873.
71. Carlton & Fischel, *supra* note 22, at 863; Easterbrook, *supra* note 56 at 334.

REFERENCES

Bjerring, James, Josef Lakonishok, and Theo Vermaelen, "Stock Prices and Financial Analysts' Recommendations," *Journal of Finance* (March, 1983), **38**, 187–204.

Brudney, Victor, "Insiders, Outsiders, and Informational Advantages Under the Federal Securities Laws," *Harvard Law Review* (December, 1979), **93**, 322–76.

Carlton, Dennis, and Daniel Fischel, "The Regulation of Insider Trading," *Stanford Law Review* (May, 1983), **35**, 857–95.

Coase, Ronald, "The Problem of Social Cost," *Journal of Law and Economics* (October, 1960), **3**, 1–44.

Dooley, Michael, "Enforcement of Insider Trading Restrictions," *Virginia Law Review* (February, 1980), **66**, 1–83.

Easterbrook, Frank, "Insider Trading, Secret Agents, Evidentiary Privileges, and the Production of Information," *Supreme Court Review* (1981), **1981**, 309–65.

Fama, Eugene, "Efficient Capital Markets: A Review of Theory and Empirical Work," *Journal of Finance* (May, 1970), **25**, 383–417.

Ferber, David, "The Case Against Insider Trading: A Response to Professor Manne," *Vanderbilt Law Review* (April, 1970), **23**, 6–27.

Fischel, Daniel, "Insider Trading and Investment Analysts: An Economic Analysis of *Dirks v. SEC*," *Hofstra Law Review* (Fall 1984), **13**, 127–46.

Gilson, Ronald, and Reiner Kraakman, "The Mechanisms of Market Efficiency," *Virginia Law Review* (May, 1984), **70**, 549–644.

Givoly, Dan, and Josef Lakonishok, "The Information Content to Financial Analysts' Forecasts of Earnings: Some Evidence for Semi-Strong Form Efficiency," *Journal of Accounting and Economics* (1979), **1**, 165–85.

Grossman, Sanford, "On the Efficiency of Competitive Stock Markets Where Traders Have Diverse Information," *Journal of Finance* (May, 1976), **31**, 573–85.

Grossman, Sanford, and Joseph Stiglitz, "Information and Competitive Price Systems," *American Economic Review: Papers and Proceedings* (May, 1976), **66**, 246–53.

Haddock, David, and Jonathan Macey, "Regulation on Demand: Special Interest Groups and Insider Trading Law," forthcoming in 29 *Journal of Law and Economics* (April 1987).

Haddock, David, and Jonathan Macey, "A Simple Model of Insider Trading," forthcoming in 81 *Northwestern Law Review* (1986).

Haft, Robert, "The Effect of Insider Trading Rules on the Internal Efficiency of the Large Corporation," *Michigan Law Review* (April, 1982), **80**, 1051–71.

Hirsh, Alain, Peter Forstmoser, and Robert Mundheim (eds.), *L'Avant-Projet de loi Fédérale sur les opérations d'initiés*, Geneve: Georg & Cie S.A. (1984).

Jennings, Richard, and Harold Marsh, *Securities Regulation: Cases and Materials* (fifth edition), Mineola, NY: Foundation Press (1982).

Jensen, Michael, "Risk, the Pricing of Capital Assets, and the Evaluation of Investment Portforlios," *Journal of Business* (April, 1969), **42**, 167–247.

Jensen, Michael, "Some Anomolous Evidence Regarding Market Efficiency," *Journal of Financial Economics* (June, 1978), **6**, 95–101.

Kaplan, Stanley, "*Wolf v. Weinstein*: Another Chapter on Insider Trading," *Supreme Court Review* (1963), **1963**, 273–324.

Kronman, Anthony, "Mistake, Disclosure, Information and the Law of Contracts," *Journal of Legal Studies* (June, 1978), **7**, 1–34.

Landes, William, and Richard Posner, "The Independent Judiciary in an Interest-Group Perspective," *Journal of Law and Economics* (December, 1975), **18**, 875–901.

Leftwich, Richard W., and Robert Verrecchia, "Insider Trading and Managers' Choice Among Risky Projects," CRSP Working Paper 63, University of Chicago Graduate School of Business (August, 1981).

Lorie, James, and Mary Hamilton, *The Stock Market: Theories and Evidence*, Homewood, IL: Richard D. Irwin (1973).

Loss, Louis, "The Fiduciary Concept as Applied to Trading by Corporate 'Insiders' in the United States," *Modern Law Review* (January, 1970), **33**, 34–52.

Loss, Louis, *Multinational Approaches – Corporate Insiders*, New York City: Matthew Bender (1975).

Manne, Henry, *Insider Trading and the Stock Market*, New York City: The Free Press (1966).

Mundheim, Robert Arthur Fleischer, Jr., and Jerome Schupper (eds.), *Fifth Annual Institute on Securities Regulation*, Practising Law Intitute (1974).

Painter, William, "Rule 10b-5: The Recodification Thicket," *St. John's Law Review* (May, 1971), **45**, 699–732.

Peltzman, Sam, "Toward a More General Theory of Regulation," *Journal of Law and Economics* (August, 1976), **19**, 211–40.

Pessin, Alan, and Joseph Ross, *Words of Wall Street: 2,000 Investment Terms Defined*, Homewood, IL: Dow Jones-Richard D. Irwin (1983)

Posner, Richard, "Economics, Politics, and the Reading of Statutes and the Constitution," *University of Chicago Law Review* (Spring, 1982), **49**, 263–91.

Posner, Richard, "Theories of Economic Regulation," *Bell Journal of Economics* (Autumn, 1974), **5**, 335–58.

Prentice, Robert, "The Impact of *Dirks* on Outsider Trading," *Securities Regulation Law Journal* (Spring, 1985), **13**, 38–71.

Rider, Barry, and H. Leigh Ffrench, *The Regulation of Insider Trading*, Dobbs Ferry, NY: Oceana (1979).

Scholes, Myron, "The Market for Securities: Substitution Versus Price Pressure and the Effects of Information on Share Prices," *Journal of Business* (April, 1972), **45**, 179–211.

Schotland, Roy, "Unsafe at Any Price: A Reply to Professor Manne," *Virginia Law Review* (November, 1967), **53**, 1425 78.

Sharpe, William, "Discussion," *Journal of Finance* (May, 1970), **25**, 418–20.

Stigler, George, "The Theory of Economic Regulation," *Bell Journal of Economics* (Spring, 1971), **2**, 3–21.

Yoran, Aaron, *Insider Trading in Israel and England*, Jerusalem: Alpha Press (1972).

Business Week, "The Stone Wall of Swiss Secrecy" (29 April 1985) 92.

Wall Street Journal, "Swiss Likely to Propose Bill on Insider Trading Ban" (1 May 1985) 38.

THE REGULATION OF SHOP OPENING HOURS IN THE UNITED KINGDOM

Susan M. Jaffer and John A. Kay

1. INTRODUCTION

The trading hours of UK retailers are restricted by law. This is true not only in Britain, but in most European countries. The most important exception is Sweden, where legal restrictions were removed in 1972 and this change was finally confirmed as permanent in 1984. In the USA, some states have "blue laws" limiting Sunday trading; others do not, and Massachusetts greatly relaxed its legislation in 1983.

Legislation of this kind is often justified by reference to alleged economic detriments of unrestricted trading. However the issues involved have received little academic attention. Some discussion of the theoretical rationale of restriction is to be found in de Meza (1984) and empirical analysis by Morrison and Newman (1983). The purpose of this paper is to review more broadly the economic issues involved. We do not examine social or religious arguments, and concentrate on the issue of what effect such regulations have on the level of costs and prices in *retailing*. Section 2 describes the present legislation, and section 3 explains the recent British debate on the subject, centred round the activities of a Committee of Inquiry established by the government in 1983. In section 4 we describe the structure of costs in U.K. retailing, and how that structure might be affected by extensions to trading hours, while section 5 examines the likely demand for Sunday trading. In section 6 we bring these supply and demand factors together and assess the overall impact of deregulation on costs and prices in British retailing.

2. THE PRESENT LAW

Current restrictions on shop opening hours are of two kinds. Sunday trading is limited by reference to the goods which may be sold. It is illegal to sell an item which is not specifically exempted from restrictions. The list of exemptions is long (see Appendix A) and appears to be motivated either by the perishable nature of the commodity (fresh food, newspapers) or by the possibility of urgent need (petrol, bandages, whisky). The exemption list generates anomalies which are the subject of frequent ridicule. It is legal to sell Playboy on Sunday, but not to sell the Bible: to sell plants but not the pot in which they are contained; to sell fresh carrots but not tinned; to sell gin but not dried babies' milk; to sell fish and chips from a hamburger bar, or hamburgers from a fish and chip shop, but not to sell fish and chips from a fish and chip shop. These anomalies are partly the inevitable product of arbitrary borderlines between commodities, and partly the inability of any list to evolve quickly in response to changing consumer tastes: thus the treatment of video films (a commodity not envisaged when the 1950 Act was drawn up) has been the subject of recent litigation.

The second group of regulations limit *evening opening*. In general, shops must close by 8 pm (9 pm one evening per week) and must have an early closing day, although this latter requirement may be removed by agreement between traders and the local authority and such agreements have been widely reached. Shops may re-open at midnight, but this is not common.

The history of legislation to limit retail trading hours dates from as early as 1448, with the Fairs and Markets Act 1448. General Sunday legislation began before the Reformation, of which the most important was the Sunday Observance Act of 1677. Modern legislation restricting Sunday trading had two concerns: the protection of shop-workers and small traders, and to maintain the traditional character of Sundays. In 1936 two Acts were introduced, the Shops (Sunday Trading Restriction) Act 1936 and the Retail Meat Dealers' Shops (Sunday Closing) Act 1936.

The interest groups promoting this legislation were unusally heterogeneous. Small traders supported it, partly seeing it as a device for the statutory promotion of a cartel, and also visualising extended opening hours as a weapon which larger retailers would be able to deploy against them. Other interests were concerned to limit the noise and congestion in residential areas. With most retailers small, and specialist, the hours of work of retail employees were generally defined by the opening hours of the shop; thus legislation to restrict opening hours was seen as part of a general move to protect employees in unorganised industries. *Sunday closing* was strongly urged by religious groups.

All exsisting legislation was consolidated into the Shops Act 1950. Although this presented the law in a more convenient form, it did little to overcome the obscurities, anomalies and enforcement problems already recognised. The law now differs in *Scotland*, where the ancient legislation is deemed to have lapsed, and the only modern legislation relates to barbers and hairdressers.

The period since the passage of the shop hours legislation has seen major changes in the structure of retailing (see Bamfield (1980)). The size of retail outlets has increased, as has the concentration of their ownership. Self-service has become widespread, and the skill and knowledge expected of, or possessed by, retail employees, has declined. Many large stores are now built on out-of-town sites, and are primarily accessible by car. New types of retail outlet have developed, closely associated with other leisure activities, such as do-it-yourself (DIY) stores and garden centres. Many of these latter shops do open on Sunday, and generally find it their busiest trading day. There are are almost no DIY items which can legally be sold on Sunday, although some of the stock of a garden centre falls within the exceptions.

Enforcement of the Act is the responsibility of local authorities. The shopkeeper (not the customer) commits a criminal offence. In recent years the law has not been generally upheld. Some local authorities do not enforce it at all, some act only in response to complaints and very few prosecute all offenders. Some large traders – including subsidiaries of major public companies – are willing to treat regular fines for breach of the Shops Act as an acceptable price for the profits of regular Sunday opening. Available remedies for those local authorities that do seek to enforce the law are not confined to prosecution however; an injunction to restrain illegal trading can be used in cases of deliberate flouting of the law and this is effective in restraining Sunday trade because continued defiance of the law will lead to proceedings for contempt of court. This patchy enforcement of the law has come about for a number of reasons: many local authorities are out of sympathy with the law, and are reluctant to devote resources to its support.

3. PRESSURE FOR REFORM

Since 1950 numerous committees have examined the possibilities for extending permitted trading hours, and no less than 13 private members bills have been presented to Parliament – all of which were defeated by a large majority. In August 1983 the Home Office appointed a Committee of Inquiry to consider what changes were needed in the Shops Act.

The Committee invited evidence from affected parties, and received a total of over 7,000 expressions of opinion. These were diverse. Religious groups remained against Sunday opening. The most vociferous opposition came from the principal union representing shop workers, the Union of Shop, Distributive and Allied Workers. Retailing is poorly unionised, and USDAW members are only about one-sixth of all retailing employees. The rationale of USDAW's opposition is not altogether clear, even after studying their evidence. Although when legislation restricting opening hours was introduced there was a close relationship between the trading hours of shops and the working hours of employees, this has now almost entirely disappeared. Shops are, on average, open for around 60 hours per week, while the standard working weeek is 39 hours. Since approximately half of all retail employees work part-time, the average working week is a good deal shorter than this. It is therefore unlikely that extended opening would now lead to longer hours and this was not often suggested.

An opposite trend might be evident, in that longer opening hours would lead to the more extensive use of part-time labour and hence the substitution of part-time for full-time jobs. Full time employees are more likely to be union members and it is apparent that USDAW sees itself as representing principally the interests of these kinds of workers. USDAW membership is also particularly strong in co-operative shops, which have lost market shares very substantially in the last 25 years, and hence may feel at risk from more rapid change in retailing structures. USDAW also claimed that extended opening hours would lead to substantial reductions in employment in retailing with up to 200,000 of an existing 1.6 million full-time equivalent jobs disappearing. It is not apparent how this would come about and the economic analysis below does not suggest that this is remotely possible.

Although many individuals submitted their opinion to the Committee, there are many more organised pressure groups reflecting producer interests than those which represent consumers. The National Consumer Council – a government sponsored body charged with this latter function – favoured liberalisation and commissioned opinion polls which showed that a majority of consumers supported this recommendation. The Consumers Association – a private non-profit body which publishes reports on consumers tests – took a similar view.

Opinion among retailers themselves was sharply divided. Organisations representing small traders were, in the main opposed to extensions to opening hours, although it is most frequently small shops which open in defiance of the present law. Among larger retailers, some of the more innovative chains were strong supporters of Sunday trading. Asda, who undertook no significant retailing activities until 20 years ago and are now a leading hypermarket chain, favoured Sunday trading while most other major food retailers were opposed. Habitat-Mothercare, again a relatively new company which has pioneered new retailing styles, were leading advocates of extended trading hours from the consumer and household goods sectors. Although it is true that traders experiencing slow growth were less likely to favour Sunday opening, successful retailers with a relatively conservative trading style, such as Marks and Spencer, Sainsbury and John Lewis, were also opposed.

Thus the divisions within retailing did not relate in any simple way to objective characteristics of the retailers concerned, in terms of size, sector or growth rate. One important, but hardly surprising, exception is that most retailers in trades where illegal Sunday opening is already widespread, particularly DIY and garden centres, favoured liberalisation. Most evidence, and particularly those submissions from the retail trade itself, was concerned with alleged economic benefits and detriments from extended opening. Those who favoured deregulation claimed that prices would be reduced and employment in retailing increased. Opponents suggested that costs and prices would rise. No substantive evidence was produced in support of either group of assertions.

4. SHORT TERM EFFECTS ON COSTS

It is apparent that longer hours of opening would, immediately, increase retail costs. The size of the increase depends on the extent of opening which, in turn, depends on the extra costs involved. Analysis therefore requires a detailed study of retailing costs. Information was derived from special analyses undertaken for us by retailers; from a questionnaire sent to a larger sample of retailers; and from the published accounts of companies principally engaged in retailing. As a result, cost structures were obtained for about 150 different types of retail outlet, cross-classified by turnover and by commodity group. These structures were weighted using the similar classification employed by the annual retailing enquiry. A detailed description of the data base employed is contained in Jaffer and Morris (1984).

The information obtained is summarised in Table 1. The gross margin earned by a retailer is the difference between his purchasing and selling price, expressed as a total of his sales proceeds net of tax. This gross margin averages just over 20% for groceries and just under 40% for clothing; other commodities generally have margins in between these extremes.

Labour costs account for nearly half of all retailing costs; an average of 43% of gross margin is absorbed in labour costs. The next most important element of costs is premises. This figure is considerably higher than that reported in company accounts since we attempted a full imputation of the current rental value of retailing premises. For retailers who occupy freehold sites this involves a considerable reduction in

Table 1. Average retail costs and margins in the IFS sample

Type of Outlet	Gross Margin	Costs as % of gross margin					Implied Net Margins
		Labour	Premises	Energy	Services & Transport	Other	
Food	20.7	47.7	28.6	4.3	20.3	0.7	0.04
Clothing and footwear	39.8	45.7	35.4	5.1	20.4	1.3	−3.3
Drink confectionery & tobacco	25.7	39.9	25.0	3.0	22.8	0.8	2.1
Household goods	32.2	39.2	29.8	4.9	19.6	1.4	1.9
Mixed retail	31.8	41.0	27.1	4.3	16.3	0.9	3.0
All	27.6	42.7	28.1	4.4	19.1	0.9	1.3

Source: IFS retail cost model (see Jaffer and Morris (1984)).

reported profits but one which more accurately reflects the opportunity costs of particular retail activities. With this correction, the costs of retailing total just over 95% of gross margins obtained. The balance is net margin, or economic profit of retailers reflecting, presumably, rents accruing to established trading reputations and other factors. This net margin amounts to 1.3% of the price of goods sold. The implied net margin for clothing and footwear is negative, suggesting that there is excess capacity in this retailing sector.

We then sought to identify the likely changes in cost for each type of retailer should trading hours be extended on Sunday by a uniform eight hours. Information on opening hours was obtained from our questionnaire and from evidence provided by retailers to the Committee of Inquiry. Current opening hours are around 60 hours per week, although this varies across different types of retailers. Some mixed retailers open for less than 50 hours, while some food outlets open for more than 70 hours a week. On average Sunday opening of eight hours would add around 13% to the length of the working week.

Labour costs are by far the most important component of the increased variable costs which would accompany longer trading hours. Retailing employees are covered in the United Kingdom by Wages Council agreements which stipulate that double wages should be paid for an eight-hour spell on Sunday and that spells between four and a half and eight hours should be charged as eight hours. Although there is some doubt that a wage premium as high as this would persist following more widespread Sunday trading, we assume that these current rules would be adhered to.

However, the increase in labour costs would not be directly proportional to the number of working hours. We interviewed retailers with current experience of Sunday opening, obtained either from Scotland (where there are few legal restrictions) or from illegal trading in England and Wales. They explained that only a proportion of their normal work force was in fact employed on Sunday, and non-essential functions deferred until during the week. Because of the higher costs of Sundqy labour, activities such as shelf replenishment may be postponed, and little managerial activity takes place on Sunday. On the basis of their experience we estimated the likely increase in both Sunday labour costs and labour costs on other days of the week. Similar evidence was used to estimate effects on other costs, but labour costs predominate.[1]

Table 2 summarises the results of our short-run analysis. It shows that, on average, an increase of eight hours (in an average trading week of 60 hours) is predicted to add around 10 % to overall costs, with over 9 % of this generated by increased labour costs. Cost increases are greater for

Table 2. Predicted short-run cost increases from Sunday trading

	(Changes expressed as % of existing gross margin)		
	Food	Non-Food	All Retail Outlets
Labour	9.18	9.66	9.46
Services and Transport	0.49	0.55	0.52
Energy	0.31	0.38	0.35
	9.98	10.59	10.33

Source: IFS retail cost model.

those retailers with higher gross margins, so that food retailers would on average face lower cost increases than say clothing and footwear outlets.

5. THE DEMAND FOR SUNDAY TRADING

Whether cost increases of this magnitude can be compensated by trading advantages, and therefore whether retailers would be likely to open on Sunday clearly depends on how much demand there is for Sunday shopping opportunities. To answer this question, we commissioned a special survey from Market and Opinion Research International (MORI) of some 2,000 respondents, interviewed at 172 sampling points across the U.K. The questionnaire and its results are described in Morris and Jaffer (1984). We were concerned principally to investigate two subjects: the strength of demand for Sunday trading and the extent to which those who might shop on Sundays currently do so at peak rather than off-peak times during the week.

Table 3 shows our estimates of the likely demand for Sunday trading for different kinds of goods, should all shops open on Sundays.[2] It is

Table 3.

	Demand for Sunday trading % of weekly trade
Food	9
Clothing and footwear	16
Drink, confectionery and tobacco	15
Household goods	20
Mixed	10
Other	10

Source: Estimates based on MORI questionnaire.

interesting that the responses to the consumer survey indicated the greatest demand for Sunday shopping to be for goods which are currently traded, legally or illegally, on Sundays. It is difficult to know whether this would persist following more extensive Sunday trading or whether it reflects respondents inability to envisage behaviour outside their immediate experience. Our estimates of the likely demand for Sunday trading indicate that 16% of clothing and footwear sales would be made on Sundays. The popularity of Sunday clothes shopping reflects the desire of consumers to have more time available for comparison shopping (which has many of the attributes of a leisure activity). This contrasts with food, for which only 9% of shopping would be done on Sundays. Food shopping is generally regarded as something of a chore, and is often done on a Thursday or a Friday rather than at the weekend.

The proportion of all trade which could occur on Sundays if all shops are open will not, however, correspond to the experience of any particular retailer. There are two other factors at work, each operating in opposite directions. First, not all shops will open on Sundays, and those which do will therefore attract more custom than they would obtain if Sunday opening were universal and will enjoy a higher market share on Sunday than on other trading days. Second, shops which shut will not lose all their potential Sunday customers. Some will come back on a different day of the week. Estimation of the degree of customer loyalty is a speculative matter. We suppose it might be high in clothing – where particular outlets have strong identities – and low in drink, confectionery and tobacco. We undertook a range of simulations based on the whole range of extreme assumptions. At 100% loyalty, it does not pay anyone to open; at zero loyalty, the extent of Sunday trade depends only on overall demand and the number of other shops which are open. Table 4 shows our central assumptions for sales losses from Sunday closing. We compare these figures with break-even estimates of sales requirements derived from our cost analysis. This is done for each of the 150 retailing types considered: Table 4 shows averages for the main commodity sectors.

Thus by comparing the assumed sales loss from not opening with the cost penalty involved with Sunday trading, we can determine whether Sunday opening would be profitable for each individual retailer. We can then estimate the likely extent of opening by weighting each individual decision by the proportion of total retail sales currently occurring in outlets of that type. The results show that food shops accounting for 46% of present sales might be expected to open. The possible extent of opening by clothing shops is much lower at 23% of current sales, as for most retailers the potential loss from remaining closed is not as great as

Table 4. Estimating the Pattern of Sunday Opening

	Average Break-Even Sales	Assumed Sales Loss from opening on Sunday	Estimated % Opening	Resulting % of Trade on Sunday
Food	10.6	10	46	5
Clothing and Footwear	12.5	12	23	3
Drink, Confectionery and Tobacco	10.0	15	100	15
Household goods	13.0	20	100	20
Mixed retail	12.4	10	15	2
Other	13.3	10	0	0
All		12	48	7

Source: IFS retail cost model.

Table 5. Estimated Effects on Weekday Trade of Sunday Opening

	Expected Sunday Sales	Extent of Existing Sales Peak	Estimated reduction in peak sales	Medium term impact on costs	Likely reduction in capacity
	%	%		(% of gross margin)	%
Food	10	20	30	2.03	5.8
Clothing and footwear	12	40	60	3.04	3.4
Drink, confectionery and tobacco	15	15	20	1.18	17.6
Household goods	20	35	70	4.18	30.0
Mixed retail	10	30	50	0.50	2.0

Source: IFS retail cost model.

the cost penalties imposed by opening. On the other hand, almost all household goods and drink, confectionery and tobacco outlets would be likely to open.

6. LONGER TERM EFFECTS

The pattern of Sunday trading we have described will affect sales on other days of the week. This will in turn alter retailing costs. The extent of these changes will be particularly influenced by the degree to which Sunday trading diminishes peak rather than off-peak weekday sales. Our consumer survey indicated strongly that it would; people who would take advantage of Sunday opening are, in large measure, those who have little time to shop during normal working (and opening) hours.

In Table 5 we show the implication of these two effects for costs in the medium term. Column 1 shows the reduction in weekday trade, as reported in Table 4. Columns 2 and 3 show estimates derived from the MORI survey of the existing peak demand for each retail sector, and how much of this peak demand would transfer to Sundays.[3] The reduction varies from 20% for drink, confectionery and tobacco, to 70% for household goods. In column 4 we show the net effects on costs, allowing for savings due to the lessening of peak demand. For example, staffing would be easier to manage, stores would be less crowded and scheduling would become easier.

However, larger long run savings will occur through a reduction in the capacity of the industry. With less demand during the week, new supermarkets and shops are likely to be smaller, and existing shops will be re-modelled (for example) to include fewer checkouts. The cost increase we have described above will put pressure on the margins of those who do not find it profitable to open on Sunday and on the weaker traders; those who are currently, in our terms, making zero or negative profits will be accelerated in their departure from the industry.

To analyse this, we developed a simple general equilibrium model of the retailing sector. The least profitable of our 150 retailing types is eliminated from the industry. The model then reassigns the sales of those outlets which disappear across other traders in the same commodity group, and recalculates profitability. The next least profitable outlet is eliminated and the process continues until space utilisation returns to the levels prevailing before the change.

The final column of Table 5 shows the likely reduction in capacity implied. (Capacity in this sense includes the fixed components of all cost items). The table shows that the most dramatic change is predicted to

Table 6. Simulating the Effects of Sunday Trading: Summary of Results

	Food	Non-food Compromising Clothing	Drink, Confectionery and Tobacco	Household Goods	Mixed Retail	Other	All
1. Short run cost increase (% gross margin)	9.98	10.59				–	10.33
2. Estimated Sunday trade (% weekly turnover)	5.00	3.00	15.00	20.00	2.00	–	7.00
3. Overall variable cost increases in medium term (% existing gross margin)	2.03	3.04	1.18	4.18	0.50	–	2.00
4. Estimated reduction in capacity (%)	5.8	3.4	17.6	30.0	2.0	–	9.00
5. Consequent saving in fixed costs (% existing gross margin)	2.6	7.5	1.8	13.8	0.8	–	3.9
6. Equal profit change in prices (%)	−0.12	−0.23	−1.18	−3.24	−0.10	–	−0.64

occur in household goods retailing, where the effect of Sunday trading is large. Capacity reductions are smaller in food and clothing, which have a more homogeneous trading pattern and likewise lower predicted opening.

The central conclusions of our analysis are summarised in Table 6. If all retailers were to open on Sundays, costs are estimated to rise by some 10% of gross margin. However, in fact not all retailers will open, and this cost rise will be offset almost immediately by cost savings from a lower and more homogeneous level of weekday demand. Our estimates of the medium-term cost increase imply an overall cost increase of some 2% of gross margin. In the longer run, a smaller level of both average and peak demand on weekdays (including Saturday) will lead to capacity reductions. Column 4 presents our estimates of the shrinkage in capacity which would restore retailing profitability and capacity to utilisation to current levels. This varies from 30.0% for household goods to 2.0% for mixed retail. The fifth column of the table then shows the consequent saving in final costs which we predict would occur. With the newer, smaller, industry, those retailers who remain will, according to our model, be trading at lower cost per unit turnover. Assuming this trend in capacity reduction does occur, then retailers will on average be able to make the same level of profit as at present, at slightly lower prices. Column 6 of Table 6 presents our estimates of the reduction in price which might be expected to occur. This is around 0.12% for food, 0.23% for clothing, and 3.24% for household goods.

7. CONCLUSIONS

If Sunday trading were to lead to an increase in costs and prices, it would be necessary to consider whether the benefits to consumers of additional choice of shopping hours and times was sufficient to offset the additional costs involved. However, the economic case for regulation fails at this first hurdle. Restriction of trading hours raised prices, by reducing the efficiency with which retailing capacity is used. Deregulation offers both lower prices and wider choice.

A version of results described above (Kay et al, 1984) was presented to the Committee of Inquiry, which recommended the complete removal of all restrictions on trading hours of shops in the U.K. The government accepted this recommendation, and in November 1985 introduced a bill to give effect to it. Opposition to liberalisation from the retailing industry has largely disappeared. Several major retailers who expressed support for continued regulation in evidence to the Committee have now changed their views, and most others appear to have accepted the inevitability of the change. USDAW remains vigorously opposed to liberalisation, but it is on religious groups that the principal burden of conducting a campaign to retain restrictions on trading hours has now fallen.

APPENDIX

Exempted Transactions for Sunday Trading

Schedule 5 of part IV of the 1940 Act "transactions for the purposes of which a shop may be open in England and Wales for the serving of customers on Sunday"

1. The sale of:
   (a) intoxicating liquors;
   (b) meals or refreshments whether or not for consumption at the shop at which they are sold, but not including the sale of fried fish and chips at a fried fish and chip shop;
   (c) newly cooked provisions and cooked or partly cooked tripe;
   (d) table waters, sweets, chocolates, sugar confectionery and ice cream (including wafers and edible containers);
   (e) flowers, fruit and vegetables (including mushrooms) other than tinned or bottled fruit or vegetables;
   (f) milk and cream, not including tinned or dried milk or cream, but including clotted cream whether sold in tins or otherwise;
   (g) medicines and medical and surgical appliances:
      (i) at any premises registered under Section 75 of the Medicines Act 1968, or
      (ii) by any person who has entered into a contract with an Area or District Health Authority for the supply of drugs or appliances;
   (h) aircraft, motor, or cycle supplies or accessories;
   (i) tobacco and smokers' requisites;
   (j) newspapers, periodicals and magazines;
   (k) books and stationery from the bookstalls of such terminal and main line railway or omnibus stations, or at such aerodromes as may be approved of by the Secretary of State;
   (l) guide books, postcards, photographs, reproductions, photographic films, and plates and souvenirs
      (i) at any gallery, museum, garden, park or ancient monument under the control of a public authority or university; or
      (ii) at any other gallery or museum, or any place of natural beauty or historic interest, or any zoological, botanical or horticultural gardens, or aquarium, if and to the extent that the local authority certify that such sale is desirable in the interests of the public; or
      (iii) in any passenger vessel within the meaning of Part II of the Finance (1909–1910) Act 1910, while engaged in carrying passengers;
   (m) photographs for passports;
   (n) requisites for any game or sport at any premises or place where that game or sport is played or carried on;

(o) fodder for horses, mules, ponies and donkeys at any farm, stables, hotel or inn.
2. The transaction of:
(a) post office business
(b) the business carried on by a funeral undertaker".

NOTES

1. Labour costs are based on opening hours, with costs adjusted for the prescribed Sunday premium. Premises and transport costs are unchanged: energy costs rise in line with opening hours. Similar adjustments are made for other, minor, cost items.
2. These estimates are based on consumers' estimates of the proportion of their shopping which they wish to do on Sunday, weighted by their current exependiture.
3. Respondents were asked when they currently did shopping for various commodities: this information was then related to prospective Sunday Shopping habits.

REFERENCES

J.A.N. Bamfield, "The changing face of British retailing", *National Westminster Quarterly Review*, May 1980, pp. 33–45.

Business Statistics Office, *Business Monitor SDA 25*, pre-publication estimates, May 1985.

S.M. Jaffer and C.N. Morris, "A Simulation Model of Retailing Costs", *IFS Working Paper No 53*, 1984.

J.A. Kay and C.N. Morris, "Sunday Trading Inefficient Equilibria and Probable Outcomes of Liberalisation in the United Kingdom", Journal of Industrial Economics, forthcoming.

J.A. Kay, C.N. Morris, S.M. Jaffer, and S.A. Meadowcroft. "The Regulation of Retail Trading Hours", Appendix 6 to the Report of the Committee of Inquiry into Proposals to Amend the Shops Act, *The Shops Act: Late-Night and Sunday Opening*, October 1984.

Market and Opinion Research International Ltd, "Sunday Trading Tables for 1984", Research study conducted for the Institute of Fiscal Studies, 1984.

S.A. Morrison and J. Newman, "Hours of operation restriction and competition among retail prices", *Economic Inquiry*, 21, 1983.

D. de Meza, "The Fourth Commandment – is it Pareto efficient?" *Economic Journal*, 94, 1984.

BELGIAN PUBLIC POLICY TOWARDS THE RETAILING TRADE

Roger Van den Bergh

1. INTRODUCTION

Public interest arguments are often advanced to justify existing regulations. Regulation is said to be supplied in response to market imperfections (e.g. monopoly, externalities, imperfect consumer information) or inequitable market practices (e.g. dishonesty in trading). The pronounced public interest goals may, however, not be really present. A distinction must be made between the public pronouncements of the regulator and the real nature of the regulations. Legislatures may for instance couch special interest statutes in public interest terms for political reasons.

The economic theory of regulation seeks an explanation for the existence of legal rules which cannot be explained by the public interest approach. The theory claims that economic regulation often serves the private interests of politically effective groups. Legislation transfers wealth from society as a whole to well-organized groups; societal wealth and economic efficiency are reduced to benefit these groups (1). Regulation is seen as a product whose allocation is governed by laws of supply and demand. On the demand side of the market interest groups outbid competing interest groups. On the supply side of the market politicians sell legislation in order to maximize own profits consisting in economic or political support.

This paper examines whether the Belgian legal regulation of the retailing trade provides support for the economic theory of regulation. From the various aspects with which the study of the retailing trade and of public policy towards it deals, particularly those with respect to entry will retain our attention. The paper is set up as follows. Section 2 contains a brief description of existing Belgian regulations affecting entry into the retailing trade. Section 3 demonstrates that the public interest theory of regulation cannot explain this legal situation. In section 4 the economic theory of regulation is advanced as a promising alternative for explaining the present Belgian regulations affecting the retailing trade. Section 5 summarizes the results and calls for further analytical and empirical investigation.

2. BARRIERS TO ENTRY AND (LACK OF) MARKET TRANSPARENCY

2.1. History

Limitation of entry into the retailing trade has its origins in the economic crisis of the thirties. Around 1930 Belgium had one retail store per 32–37 inhabitants, at the time probably the highest ratio among industrialized countries (Boddewyn, 1971, 35). The overcrowding of the retailing trade could probably have been corrected by the market itself because new types of modern retailers pressurized prices in such a way that a thinning out of retailing ranks seemed inevitable. However, this expected market result was not welcomed by those concerned with the social implications of a quantitative decline of small, traditional retailers. These were even seen as a factor of stability and fluidity of the social order, otherwise polarized between capital and labor. When the first "padlock law" was proposed to Parliament, special reference to this view was made and in that perspective it was declared that "measures to let middle class retailers survive must even be taken when they are economically criticizeable" (2). Economic liberals, rejecting interventionism and corporatism, largely lost their case.

The complaint about the excessive number of retailers led to the Royal Decree Nr. 82 of November 28, 1939 (hereinafter referred to as the Itinerant Trade Act) restricting itinerant trade, and to the padlock laws, restricting the opening and enlarging of diversified stores above a certain size.

2.2. Itinerant trade

Itinerant trade is defined under Belgian law as the sale of or the offer to sell commodities to the consumer from door-to-door, on the street and on markets and at places accessible to the public and not specifically devised for sale activities. When a licensing system was introduced in 1935, various categories of people were denied the privilege of itinerant trade and an increasingly long list of products, for which no licenses could be granted, became part of the Belgian restrictive regulation (3).

Among the various places outside the premises of the seller mentioned in the definition of itinerant trade, especially the last one, referring to the accessibility of the place and its destination caused difficult problems of interpretation. For example, sales take place in stations, theaters, cinemas, ballrooms, hotels and homes. How does one assess the accessibility of these places and their destination? Of course at the time of the sale these places are all accessible for the public and appropriate for sale activities. But must the required accessibility not be understood in an objective sense; must the place not be accessible at *any* time and not only during the selling operations? The last question mobilized much attention and energy of judges and commentators for more than forty years (Swennen and Van den Bergh, 1983, 90–93). Until the outlawing of travelling sales by the Trade Practices Act (4) the legal terms "accessible for the public" were often interpreted in a broad sense, to make the legality of the sales challenged contingent on the possession by the vendor of a license. After the promulgation of the Trade Practices Act an inverse tendency became apparent. In order to limit the applicability of the Itinerant Trade Act and the connected permissibility of itinerant sales by license holders the terms "accessible for the public" were interpreted in a restrictive way. This interpretation was ultimately approved by the Cour de Cassation (5).

2.3. Establishment restrictions for large retail outlets

Apart from the regulation of itinerant trade, further protectionist measures were taken against "big" retailers. From January 1937 until December 1960 expansion of large stores was restricted. After the expiration of the padlock laws shopping centers and large commercial facilities, such as supermarkets and hypermarkets, were built in the suburbs. New branches were opened, usually by large stores. In 1975 a licensing system was introduced whereby not only country planning and urban renewal play a part but into which the criterion of need is also explicitly introduced (6).

According to the Royal Decree of August 8, 1975 every project to open a retail outlet of a certain size (7) must be submitted to an examination on so-called socio-economic grounds. The following criteria for evaluation are mentioned:

- Is the projected retail outlet of a size and type that fits into the community where it is to be established? Does it contribute to the realization of a functional balance between the suburbs and the city center?

- Consumer interests: the influence on consumer's choices, on prices and the danger of monopolization must be examined; the royal decree also refers to the accessibility of the commercial facilities by public transport (8).
- Influence on employment: the quality of the offered jobs (stable work, working-hours and facilities, career-perspectives) is also to be taken into consideration.
- Finally the impact of the projected large retail outlet on the established retailers must be examined. A new entrant may not endanger the existence of previously established retailers when there are already enough commercial facilities to satisfy consumer needs properly. A functional balance must be achieved between the commercial center in the city and the suburbs while the establishment of a new shop in the city center must favor urban renewal.

2.4. Professional licensing

Under the motto "Quality rather than quantity" a law was enacted in 1958 to improve the performance of small and medium-size retailers. The present Belgian licensing law of December 15, 1970 which has replaced the previous one and has been revised by the law of August 4, 1978, does not regulate any single profession but makes this avenue available for small and medium crafts and trades. When a request of a representative professional federation is endorsed by the High Council of the Tradespeople and the Liberal Professions (9) and accepted by the Minister a Royal Decree is published in the *Moniteur belge* (Official Gazette). After publication, anyone (physical person or corporation) exercising such a licensed profession must obtain a certification from his provincial Chamber of Crafts and Trades. Proof that the requirements are satisfied must be given. Violation of the Professional Licensing Act is punished by penal sanctions and can lead to cease-and-desist orders on the basis of the Fair Trade Practices Act.

2.5. Consumer information

Sections 2–4 Trade Practices Act provide for the obligation to indicate prices of goods and services to the consumer, the manner in which this is to be done and special rules concerning price-comparisons. Section 2 requires the nonequivocal and written indication of prices of all goods and services offered. The prices displayed must be netprices, including all taxes and services to be paid by the consumer. Whoever posts slashed prices must explicitly refer to the prices he previously and usually charged for identical products during a period of at least one month (the last condition does not apply to deteriorating products). According to Sec. 4 Trade Practices Act it is permissible to reduce prices without making any reference to previous prices but in that case reference must be made to a regulated price. Referring to fixed or recommended prices and comparing one's prices to those of someone else is forbidden. Violation of these rules may lead to criminal prosecution.

With respect to advertising (10) the law contains a general provision against comparative advertisements. Comparisons are forbidden even when they inform the consumer correctly. The only exception to this stringent rule is the situation where the businessman can show the necessity of the comparison. This exception however validates only correct comparative advertising and not misleading or disparaging (11) advertisements. At the beginning the criterion of necessity was interpreted very narrowly: for a time only publicity for replacement parts, which must of necessity explain into which brand named products they fit, seemed to be a valid exception to the prohibition of mentioning the name of competitors. In recent cases involving pharmaceutical products judges went further: when new products are launched it is permissible to make comparisons with the older substitutes in the market, for instance to explain a different method of fabrication (12).

2.6. Sales at loss prices

Sales at loss prices are forbidden by Sec. 22 Trade Practices Act. The law distinguishes between sales at loss prices in the narrow sense, that is a sale below purchase or replacement cost, and sales at loss prices in a broader sense, referring to sales with exceptionally reduced profit margins, taking into account the purchase price and the general costs. Exceptions to the prohibition are mentioned in Sec. 23: they apply (a) to cases of liquidation and clearance sales, (b) when the profitless sales are necessary in order to dispose of obsolete or deteriorating products and (3) when the loss price is set to meet competition. The latter exception is very narrowly construed by the courts. A businessman may meet but not beat competition; the price which is met must be generally applied (not only by a few competitors) and when the competitor's price infringes the legal rules a cease-and-desist action must be brought before the courts. Businessmen may thus not prevent or reduce the damage by responding to a competitor's challenging price but must initiate a legal action, the outcome of which is far from certain because of the interpretation problems caused by almost undefinable legal terms such as "exceptionally low" and "general costs".

The prohibition of Sec. 22 only pertains to sales of products by retailers to consumers. However, as far as the previous distribution level (producers-retailers) is concerned the catch-all rule of Sec. 54 (13) may be applied. In its judgment of February 21, 1984 the Brussels Court of Appeals held that "it is unfair to grant certain selected retailers without a justifiable economic reason abnormally profitable purchasing conditions with the purpose or the expectation of creating market distortions and inhibiting a normal competition on the merits". This statement was made in a case on the lawfulness of the fuel price-war initiated or pursued by some oil companies in Belgium during the last week of September and the first two weeks of October 1983. With the purpose of enlarging its rather small market share (2–3%) Mobil Oil, a company which operates mainly full automatic service stations, launched the slogan that profits of 0.30 or even 0.50 BF per litre fuel could be made by choosing a Mobil station (0.30 BF profit in comparison with the price charged by self-service stations and 0.50 BF profit compared to the price asked by licensees or proprietors of traditional filling stations). The price reductions of Mobil were followed by competitors and a process of constant undercutting of prices was initiated. In the heat of the battle Seca, one of the other smaller oil companies, started to "give away" the fuel: consumers only had to pay the taxes. A professional association of the sector of garages and filling stations brought a cease-and-desist action; one of the arguments was the "discrimination" against owners of traditional filling stations who did not get price reductions high enough to participate in the price-war. The Court ruled that freedom of commerce allows every economic operator to offer the lowest possible price, taking into account the situation of the market, his costs and his purchase price. Nevertheless this freedom does not authorize an entrepreneur to drive out competitors by charging "artificially low prices". The Court held that a price differentiation at the producer-retailer level, which is only practised to follow "a spiral of sinking prices" in order to maintain, whatever it may cost, the lowest prices on the market without bearing the consequences of a general price reduction and with the effect that own agents or agents of a competitor are driven out of the market, is a means to achieve an illegitimate goal (14).

3. THE PUBLIC INTEREST THEORY OF REGULATION

This section argues that the public interest theory of regulation cannot explain the existence of the Belgian regulations with respect to the retailing trade. The pronounced public interest goals of the legal rules are either not really present or not achieved.

3.1. Professional licensing

As far as the professional licensing law is concerned the articulated purpose has been the promotion of small and medium-size retailers and craftsmen by improving their professional skills. A first reading of the Act already points in the opposite direction. Since established traders and craftsmen, as the law itself states, are not required to undergo any subsequent test of competence, it is clear that licensing is not a means of maintaining standards.

In 1958 the Government was granted no right to initiate or modify any licensing regulation. This exclusion of state initiative causes ineffectiveness from the perspective of reaching the goals of quality improvement. A request that access to a designated profession be regulated must be formulated by a representative professional federation. In general the Government cannot take any initiative in this respect (15) but the Minister of the Tradespeople and the Liberal Professions has the final say (16) in accepting a request for licensing after the petition has been scrutinized and seconded by the High Council of the Tradespeople and the Liberal Professions. Evidence of managerial skills (general and commercial) always must be presented in the request; furthermore requirements of specific professional skills can be requested by the professional federation. The law hampered the establishment of certification requirements in non-craft retailing. (A full list of regulated professions, indicating the date at which the regulation has been issued and modified, is added as an appendix to this paper). This vast sector (for example grocery and clothing stores) remained largely unaffected by licensing regulations. The new law of December 15, 1970 has authorized the Government to impose requirements of "managerial knowledge" on all or part of the small and medium size retailing and wholesaling trade, even if no professional federation requests it, but only after consulting with the High Council of the Tradespeople and Liberal Professions whose advice, however, is not binding. Until now the Minister did not use this possibility. Such an interference would probably be interpreted by the interested groups as violating the rules of political decency.

A generally advanced rationale based on public welfare arguments as to why certain occupations should be licensed is lack of information and misinformation. Consumers are said to have the knowledge necessary to make a wise decision when buying the complicated goods and services offered for sale today (Moore, 1961, 104). In that view professional licensing could be seen as a means of reducing the transaction cost and contributing to more open communication lines between producers and consumers.

Looking at the existing regulations, however, we find that the law also applies to services, the quality or safety of which can be easily evaluated by the consuming public without substantial cost. Do choice difficulties justify a licensing system for hairdressers, dry-cleaning stores, photographers or restaurants to guarantee the safety or quality of the offered services? Perhaps there is more reason to regulate the entry into professions where the professionals themselves sell second-hand cars, install central heating systems or manufacture a tooth prosthesis. The informational asymmetry increases as quality becomes more difficult to control. But also in the last mentioned cases quality and safety can be guaranteed by means which do not impair the entry to the market.

In general, information remedies are a better solution than the direct regulation of production or trade processes whenever inefficient outcomes are the result of inadequate consumer information (Beales, Craswell and Salop, 1981). Uncertainty over quality can be remedied by mandatory information disclosure, quality certification and comparative tests by consumer organizations. These information remedies allow consumers to protect themselves according to their own personal preferences and do not place the difficult task on regulators to combine diverse preferences into a common standard. Neither will the consumer have to pay for knowledge and services in which he is not really interested (17). One should indeed not forget that, whenever professional licensing is used as a tool, the legislative intervention will go further than an appropriate information remedy: the consumer will be confronted with a common standard of offered products and services. In contrast, information remedies will not endanger the ability of the market to react upon evolutions, entry not being restricted. Such remedies leave the market free to respond to changing consumer demands and do not cause serious harm if the regulator turns out to have been mistaken. For example, if consumers are not really interested in increasing the quality of certain professional services or if they do not value some of the professional skills prescribed by the regulator, a licensing system will force the market to inefficiency. Likewise the setting of legal rules imposing almost necessarily a simple choice on all consumers does not allow consumers to strike different balances between price and quality.

Assuming that the informational asymmetry cannot be eliminated by information remedies (which is a rather weak argument for most of the professions mentioned in the appendix), regulation of performance and quality might be considered. These regulations too will result in entry barriers but, in comparison with professional licensing, will not have to recognize vested interests. All established tradesmen and craftsmen, and not only new entrants will have to fulfill the required conditions.

Other public interest rationales (see Moore, 1961, 106–110) are not considered here. For instance, the argument that society knows best what is good for the individual, raises philosophical problems. In the case of the retailing trade it cannot be argued that social costs (those borne by others than the buyers of the products and services) are greater than private costs. None of these rationales may justify any licensing of occupations in the retailing trade.

3.2. Limiting the entry of itinerant traders and the establishment of large retail locations

The regulation of itinerant trade is clearly not promulgated in a public interest-perspective of ensuring the competitive process. Shops may have some degree of monopoly power arising from locational advantages and differentiation of product (e.g. by service, quality). In the absence of regulations itinerant traders can enter into and exit very easily from a small local market. Hence they have an important role in keeping retail markets contestable.

The Large Retail Locations Act hinders the entry and the growth of large retail firms. It clearly conflicts with the need to maintain entry barriers as low as possible to improve market performance.

3.3. Comparative advertising

Comparative advertising, as forbidden by Belgian Law, may function as a means of lowering the entry barriers put up by brand loyalty. In our view the monopolistic effects of advertising are not such that they are no longer acceptable within a theory of competition as a dynamic process. The scope of this paper does not allow us to go into the debate with regard to advertising as a barrier to entry. Exponents of the Harvard School regard "non-informative" advertising as an important cause of the evolution of competitive markets into oligopolies. The exponents of the Chicago School oppose this view. As far as access to the retailing trade is concerned, there certainly is a certain threshold in the market for newcomers which they have to overcome in their initial advertising efforts. However, the initial losses caused by intensive advertising and low opening prices can probably be recouped in the long run (18). Nevertheless, manufacturers may succeed through heavy promotion of brand names in creating a situation where there is a strong brand loyalty. Entry for competitors becomes very difficult when a general prohibition of correct comparative advertising stabilizes the barriers to entry. In such circumstances the existence of market dominating enterprises with large market shares will make entry costly. Comparative advertising giving competitors the possibility to use the goodwill created through advertising for the product involved seems to be a cheap way of entering the market (the new entrant can use the generic portion of the advertising efforts) and the surest way of undermining the monopoly power based upon consumer loyalty through advertising. A recent more lenient interpretation by judges of the necessity-criterion is therefore of importance.

A quite audacious judgment was delivered by the Court of Appeals of Brussels on June 7, 1983. The Pepsi-Cola-Company had started a promotional campaign consisting essentially in taste-tests proposed to consumers. These were invited to express their preferecne with regard to three unidentified cola-drinks. The results of the drinks in favor of Pepsi-Cola were filmed in shopping centers and showed in cinemas. The Court held that the public could easily suppose that from the tested drinks one was the famous Coca-Cola, because this last product has a share of no less than 80 % of the Belgian market. Nevertheless the prohibition of comparative advertising was not enforced because the Court believed that this was an instance of necessity, as provided for by the law. If a commercial contains the probability of a comparison with an enterprise in a dominant position, it would be contrary to the stringent rules of competition not to grant the enterprise which occupies only a weak position on the market the right of disseminating publicity permitting to enter the market in a significant way (19).

In a product differentiated market advertising plays a crucial role in ensuring a good mass communication between both sides of the market. Advertising reduces consumers' search costs and, as a result, the transaction cost of the economics of information for society at large (Kaufmann, 1984, 34–37). More than other forms of advertising, comparative advertising improves the cross-elasticities of products and strengthens price competition. In any case of rivalry remarks about the rival will influence the person who has to make a choice more directly than the description of the own qualities. Likewise, if every competitor must stick to advertising his own product, more efficient forms of market information are prohibited. The function of comparative advertising as an efficient means of information in the competitive process should generally be recognized. A public interest oriented legal regulation of advertising stands only one restriction: that the consumer not be deceived.

It has already been mentioned above that Belgian law contains, apart from the general outlawing of comparative advertising, specific prohibitions on price comparisons (see 2.5). These prohibitions contrast sharply with the comprehensive price indication provisions. Inconsistency is one of the weaknesses of Belgian economic public policy. Here we have a striking example: in the same Act full disclosure about prices is combined with prohibitions on price comparisons which, because market transparency is weakened, hinder the consumer in his role of allocator of production.

3.4. Sales at loss prices

Unless the protection of small and medium-size retailers were to be seen as benefiting the general public, as was the case in the thirties (see 2.1.), no public interest rationale can be readily advanced to justify the prohibition of sales at loss prices. As far as the prohibition has been conceived as an instrument of consumer protection, it was quite superfluous. Misleading price offers giving the consumers a wrong impression of the overall price level of a retail outlet can be stopped by a cease-and-desist order, based on Sec. 20, 1°, Trade Practices Act (prohibition of misleading advertising). When the prohibition of profitless sales was introduced, the distinction between correct offers (exceptional prices advertised and practised for specific, named products) and misleading ones implying assumptions about the general price level of a certain store was not made clear.

The applicability of the proviso does not depend on the strength of the firm practising the forbidden sales, nor on the frequency or intensity of the sales at prices without a "normal" profit margin. Neither the circumstance that the profitless sale affects only one single product, nor the benefit for the consumer may be considered in the assessment. This inevitably leads to the prohibition of practices having no significance for the preservation of a competitive market structure or even of practices which are necessary for the functioning of the competitive process.

When products are offered at a reduced price, the judge is confronted with the problem of determining whether the profit margin is too low or not. In this respect the judge must take into account, as Sec. 22 Trade Practices Act indicates, "the general costs". The law does not refer to measuring the cost in the economic sense. In practice judges often make rough estimates: the price to the consumer is compared with the purchase price paid by the reseller; in function thereof the profit margin is proportionally determined. Relevant for the application of Sec. 22 Trade Practices Act seems to be average cost and not marginal cost. Insofar as Sec.

22 Trade Practices Act is not only an instrument to prevent loss leader selling but also a device to prevent predatory pricing practices, it requires to charge prices which are above average cost or that at least cover it. Prices equal to or greater than marginal cost but less than average cost and a fortiori prices less than marginal cost seem to be generally forbidden. The same goes for prices above average variable cost but less than total average cost. If a monopolist produces to a point where price is less than average cost but equal to marginal cost, only less efficient firms will suffer larger losses per unit of output; more efficient firms will lose less or even operate more profitably (Areeda/Turner, 1975, 711). Section 22 Trade Practices Act affects not only the monopolist but even the smallest firm which has no power at all to drive out or exclude rivals by selling at unremunerative prices. Furthermore, it is also applicable when the market structure is atomistic and when, if concentration exists, there are no significant barriers to entry. Finally the proposed price level (average total cost) is such that it also ensures existence of less efficient rivals.

It has already been mentioned above (see 2.6.) that the prohibition on sales at loss prices does not apply to sales from producer to wholesaler/ retailer. Such discounts can, however, fall within the prohibition of Sec. 54 Trade Practices Act. In the case of the fuel price-war the Court used the loaded word "discrimination" to stress the dishonesty required by law. In fact the concern was directed at the consequences of a deteriorating price structure (the Court named it "a spiral of sinking prices") not for the oil companies involved (no one, not even the Court believed that the price war could have driven oil companies out of the market), but for some of the filling stations in which Belgium abounds. The Court ruled that price differentiations with the only purpose to follow a spiral of sinking prices constitutes a means to achieve an illegitimate goal when the effect of the practice can be reasonably (without need of actual proof) believed to be the elimination of distributors. Restrictions on price competition will, if they do not foreclose competition at all, stimulate non-price competition. In the case of fuel retailing the result may be a high density of filling stations without any substantial performance improvement, the quality of the different brands being equal. In Belgium there are other examples of sectors where non price-competition is accompanied by a proliferation of retail locations (20).

4. THE ECONOMIC THEORY OF REGULATION

In practice public interest cannot be upheld as the rationale for the Belgian regulations with respect to the retailing trade described above.

The present legal situation can be better explained as the result of effective self-serving behaviour by politically well organized groups. Belgian public policy thus supports the basic hypothesis of the economic theory of regulation. The existing regulations also provide useful material for testing the common assumptions of this theory. This section is devoted to the evidence which the Belgian experiment can bring. The creation of rents for the benefit of the traders and the effectiveness of the political market in regulation will be successively examined.

4.1. The explanations given by the theory

George Stigler's hypothesis that "every industry or occupation that has enough political power to utilize the state will seek to control entry (. . .) or retard the rate of growth of new firms" (Stigler, 1971, 5) gets substantial support from the case of the Belgian retailing trade.

Professional licensing is used to increase the profitability of occupations. Through licensing requirements entry becomes difficult, the income of established professionals is protected and the consumer pays for the entire operation by loosing possibilities of choice and paying higher prices (21). The creation of rents is apparent from the exception of existing traders from new regulations. The legislation is very generous in recognizing vested interests. The law grants blanket dispensations to established practitioners; these can comply with the law by simply registering themselves in the Trade Registry before the publication of the Royal Decree. Such "grandfather-clauses" are typical of regulation designed to benefit traders rather than to protect consumers. The Large Retail Locations Act resulted from demands of small independent retailers fearing to be squeezed out of the new shopping centers. They asked for more "orderly growth". From the above mentioned criteria (see 2.3.) the first and the fourth are usually read together. The interest of consumers and employees seem of minor importance in the overall assessment. In the case of an application for an establishment in the suburbs a license is usually given only when the projected retail outlet is "autonomous", i.e. when it does not need the neighborhood of other retail outlets to "survive" (22). The protection of small and medium-size retailers also guides judges in their ruling against marginal retailers. Otherwise the final solution given to the dispute about the accessibility of a place to sell (see 2.2.) can hardly be explained. The prohibitions of comparative advertising and sales at loss prices hinder the entering and the growth of competitors.

To a large extent the retailing trade is able to exploit the political machinery to its own ends. Especially forms of economic corporatism, where professional associations exercise self-regulatory powers, should be considered here. Although professional licensing must be implemented under the watchful eye of the High Council of the Tradespeople and the Liberal Professions and the Minister, the Government is still too dependent on the initiative of the particular profession. Apart from economic corporatism, consultative corporatism also exists in the same consultative body and political corporatism, while not existing formally, is indirectly present since some M.P.s are associated with certain interest groups of the retailing trade.

The economic theory of regulation suggests that small and single-issue oriented groups will be the most effective in gaining transfers at the expense of the general polity. There is some support for this suggestion in the Belgian retailing cases. The definitions of regulated professions are often very narrow; in most cases they are the outcome of the bargaining process between related professions, defending their own territory, in the High Council of the Tradespeople and the Liberal Professions. Due to these narrow definitions, the cost of the wealth transfer will be widely spread among the population.

If the groups are looking for benefits comparable to those of successful cartelization, the large numbers and the asymmetry of interests (factors which discourage cartelization) will encourage the demand for alternative protective regulation. The larger the occupation, the more votes it has; the free-rider problem will also be easier to overcome if the asymmetry condition is fulfilled (Posner, 1974, 347). This might explain why the small and medium-size retailing trade as a whole provided support for the issuance of the prohibitions on comparative advertising and sales at loss prices. Both remedies can be qualified as surrogates for hardly feasible private cartelization agreements.

The financing of regulation (political support, resources) raises the well known problem of the free-rider. This problem exists both between professional groups, who all benefit from regulations with broad possibilities of application and within them, because all members of a trade benefit when a group applies for restrictions on entry. It has been suggested that the lobbying organization avoids the problem by selling useful services (Moore, 1961, 114, Olson, 1971). It cannot be denied that the professional associations who were most successful in obtaining anti-competitive regulations furnish many services to their members (information about new developments in law, journals, meetings, advertisements). These services cannot be purchased at a competitive price elsewhere, so that the association can exploit its monopoly position to raise funds necessary for lobbying.

The wealth transfers from society to the interest groups remain largely unquestioned because of the high information and transaction costs associated with the legislative process. Individuals are seldom aware of the impact of the regulations on their personal wealth, especially in cases where they are disguised in public interest measures. Even if the consumer were to become aware of the inefficiency after the promulgation of the regulations, he would not be able to take revenge on the politicians as a voter because of the nature of the election process. Pluralism of preferences does not exist in the election process: elections take place with great time-intervals and the citizen cannot individualize his choice regarding a specific item such as professional licensing of a specific sector. Moreover, the voting has only a neglectable influence on the results of the election and on personal welfare (Stigler, 1971, 10–13, Daems and De Grauwe, 1981, 34–37). Nevertheless, if there were no transaction costs, economic theory of regulation suggests that a rational public could be able to block corporatist regulations. Hence legislators and judges, who interpret the legal rules, have the important task of unmasking the wealth transfers involved and to reduce the information costs to the electors.

4.2. The limitations of the theory

Despite its strengths, the economic theory of regulation still has a number of weaknesses. The theory is not precise enough to predict which professions will become regulated at which time and what form the regulation will take. The theory explains who receives the benefits and the burdens of regulation and describes the effect of regulation upon the allocation of resources. It needs, however, further development and refinement to gain predictive content. Secondly, the theory cannot explain why more than once inappropriate means are chosen to achieve the protectionist ends.

With respect to the latter, the Belgian experience offers interesting examples. We will discuss two of these ineffective measures to protect small and medium-size retailers. The prohibition of sales at loss prices (see 2.6.) failed because large retailers can use their buying power in order to obtain better purchasing conditions, so that they do not have to sell with low profits to undercut the prices of their smaller competitors. Thus, the negative impact of the low prices on the survival chances of small retailers is the same in these circumstances as in the case the prices are forbidden by the Trade Practices Act. Professsional licensing too might have dysfunctional results. In the long run, since new entrants will have to overcome regulatory imposed entry barriers by buying premises from existing traders or acquiring qualifications, all members of the regulated trade will only be earning a normal return. They will thus tend to press for greater entry restriction. A continual raising of entry barriers might, however, no longer be politically feasible. In 1978, in the middle of the economic crisis, the Professional Licensing Act was modified. The Government has received the power to adapt previously enacted licensing requirements in order to eliminate establishment difficulties in a specified profession (Swennen, 1979). Politicians will rarely regulate a trade entirely in the interest of a single group. They will balance the marginal benefits to themselves from adjusting regulations. The wishes of any one interest group will not be pursued to the exclusion of all others when this might cause political damage. In 1978 employment was clearly a reference point of higher importance in the making of the policy. The same reason might explain why the padlock laws repealed in 1960 were replaced in 1975 with size related restrictions and a granting procedure, in which different interests must be taken into account. The belief in the function of the middle class retailers as a third alternative, between capitalism and socialism, was definitely no longer present in 1975.

5. CONCLUSION

The study of the Belgian public policy towards the retailing trade supports the view that economic regulation is better explained as a product supplied to interest groups (economic theory of regulation) than as an expression of the social interest in efficiency (public interest theory of regulation). Barriers to entry are erected by the laws on itinerant trade, professional licensing and establishment restrictions for large retail outlets. Wealth transfers are especially involved in professional licensing, which increases the profitability of established retailers in the short run. The use of government power for erecting barriers to entry causes harmful resource misallocations. If the improvement of market performance were the aim of the regulations, entry barriers should be kept as low as possible. The economic theory of regulation can also be used to explain the protective legislation in the area of the retailing trade, where private cartelization would hardly be feasible. The prohibitions of the Fair Trade Practices Act (comparative advertising, sales at loss prices) discussed above seriously hamper price competition and do not deserve the denomination "competition law".

The hypotheses of the economic theory of regulation need, however, further refinement to make them empirically testable. The Belgian case offers some useful material for this purpose.

APPENDIX

Regulations issued under the Professional Licensing Act

This appendix provides a list of regulated professions in alphabetical order. The year of issuance of the professional licensing regulation is indicated between brackets. Detailed references are given by Van den Bergh and Van de Velde, 1985.

Bicycle mechanic (1964)
Brickwork- and concrete contractor (1964)
Butcher – wholesaler (1963)
Central heating contractor (1961)
Coach-work – repairer (1982)
Dry cleaner – dyer (1978)
Electro-technical electrician (1968)
Forage and straw (wholesaler) (1967)
Garagist – repairer (1974)
Gas heating with individual appliances contractor (1975)
Glazing contractor (1974)
Hairdresser (1962)
Illuminated advertising contractor (1983)
Insurance broker (1961)
Joiner – carpenter (1960)
Liquid fuel retailer (1974)
Marble contractor (1966)
Miller (1962)
Motor-cycle mechanic/Moped mechanic (1964)
Native cereals retailer (1963)
Non-metal roofing contractor (1975)
Optician (1964)
Painting contractor (1963)
Photographer (1966)
Plasterer (1961)
Refrigerator electrician (1974)
Restaurants (1984)
Sanitary installations contractor – plumber (1975)
Second-hand cars retailer (1974)
Solid fuel retailer (1966)
Stone-cutting contractor (1965)
Technician in dental prostheses (1973).
Tile mason (1968)
Undertaker (1982)
Wallpaper, wall- and floor-covering contractor (1969)
Washer (laundry) (1978)
Watch-maker – repairer (1970)
Zinc and metal roofing contractor (1975)

NOTES

*The author thanks Hugh S.E. Gravelle, Göran Skogh and two anonymous referees for useful comments and suggestions on a previous draft. He remains, however, solely responsible for the content of the paper.

1. The economic theory of regulation is also referred to as "rent-seeking". Rent-seeking is the process of seeking wealth transfers from government. (An economic rent is the payment for the use of an economic asset that is greater than the opportunity cost of the asset). In this formulation the theory reminds of the "capture theory": political scientists hold that the regulator is often dominated by the industries he is supposed to regulate.
2. Report presented by Vindevogel, *Parliamentary Documents of the Chamber of Representatives*, Special session 1936, Nr. 117.
3. Royal Decree Nr. 82 of November 28, 1939 on itinerant trade; Royal Decree Nr. 71 of November 30, 1939; Royal Decree of December 18, 1939; Royal Decree of October 16, 1951; Ministerial Decree of October 20, 1951; Royal Decree of November 3, 1952; Ministerial Decree of November 5, 1952; Ministerial Decree of April 15, 1953; Ministerial Decree of June 15, 1953; Ministerial Decree of September 11, 1953; Royal Decree of December 12, 1955; Ministerial Decree of April 22, 1965; Ministerial Decree of June 12, 1968; Ministerial Decree of March 10, 1970. Texts are published in *Tweetalige wetboeken Story*, edited by Ronse/Van Gerven, Gent, s.d.
4. Travelling sales, as opposed to itinerant sales are sales, offers to sell or even displays in view of sale outside normal trade premises (trade houses and affiliates registered in the Trade Registry) which are not covered by a license issued under the 1939 Act. These sales are prohibited by Sec. 53 Trade Practices Act 1971. A Royal Decree of April 22, 1974 limited the prohibition of Sec. 53 to sales in *private* places but this provision has been annulled by the Conseil d'Etat on March 30, 1978 because it was taken *ultra vires* (text published in *Arresten van de Raad van State*, 1978, Nr. 18.848 and *Rechtskundig Weekblad*, 1977–78, 2455 with a comment by J. Stuyck).
5. The Court stated "that accessibility is an objective qualification of the place where one sells that does not depend on the intent of the itinerant trader who, as in the case under jurisdiction, hires a place to sell his merchandise to the public during two afternoons and opens the place to that end (Cour de Cassation, March 19, 1982, *Rechtskundig Weekblad*, 1982–83, 628, with a comment by P. De Vroede).
6. Large Retail Locations Act of June 29, 1975, *Moniteur belge* of July 1, 1975; Royal Decree of August 8, 1975 relating to the criteria that must be taken into account when applications to establish a large retail outlet are examined, *Moniteur belge* of August 30, 1975.
7. In cities: a gross built surface superior to 3.000 m^2 or a net commercial surface superior to 1.500 m^2; outside cities: a gross built surface superior to 1.000 m^2 or a net commercial surface superior to 750 m^2. When these sizes are reached, the law does not only apply to new openings but also to (1) extensions of existing constructions, (2) projects to exploit one or more commercial outlets in an existing building which was not destined to commercial activities and (3) projects to modify the nature of the commercial activity of a building already affected to commercial ends (e.g. wholesale).
8. In practice this criterion leads to a requirement of proper access roads and car parking facilities! Belgian retailing depends on highly mobile customers.

9. The High Council of the Tradespeople and the Liberal Professions acts as a consultative body for the government. It is the only official representative organ of the tradespeople and the liberal professions. Members are designated by professional and interprofessional associations; there is no direct election. The Council has no regulatory powers but plays a crucial role in professional licensing (and regulation of weekly closing times): a negative advice of the Council is sufficient to make the issuance of a professional licensing regulation impossible. On some matters (for example, the dates of clearance sales) the Council must be consulted.
10. Commercial advertising is defined in Belgian law as "any information which is disseminated by any means with the direct or indirect purpose of promoting the selling of a product or a service to the public". (Sec. 19 Trade Practices Act). Section 20 Trade Practices Act prohibits (1) publicity likely to mislead the public as to the identity, the nature, the composition, the origin, the quality or the characteristics of a product; (2) comparative publicity which is misleading, disparaging or simply identifying one or more businessmen without necessity; (3) publicity which causes confusion with another businessman or craftsman, his products or his activities and; (4) publicity favoring forbidden practices.
11. In practice judges conclude too easily that the advertisement is of a disparaging nature. For example the slogan "not 7.777 BF but 6.666 BF" was forbidden on that ground (President of the Commercial Court of Bruges, April 20, 1979, *Ingénieur-Conseil*, 1979, 302). A judge delivered the same opinion with regard to the Pepsi Cola-slogan "one and a half litre cola at the price of one litre" (President of the Commercial Court of Brussels, April 16, 1980, *Ingénieur-Conseil*. 1980, 1951). For other examples see: Swennen and Van den Bergh, 1983, 49–50. In our opinion there is no disparagement in a price comparison; by so doing no deficiency or shortcoming of the competitor's product is accentuated.
12. President of the Commercial Court of Brussels, January 9, 1979, *Ingénieur-Conseil*, 1979, 40; President of the Commercial Court of Brussels, November 15, 1982, *Rechtskundig Weekblad*, 1983–84, 717, with a comment by J. Stuyck. On the basis of Sec. 13 A2 Benelux Trademark Act the last opinion (even) accepted the mentioning of a trade-mark when it is necessary to explain the qualities of the introduced substitute and thus to enter the market.
13. This rule prohibits every act contrary to honest business practices whereby a businessman damages or attempts to damage the professional interests of one or more other businessmen.
14. Court of Appeals Brussels, February 22, 1984, *Revue de droit commercial belge*, 1984, 622, see the criticism by Van den Bergh, 1984.
15. There are three exceptions to this rule. The Government can, after consulting the High Council of the Tradespeople and the Liberal Professions unilaterally impose requirements of managerial knowledge on small and medium-size enterprises exercising retailing or wholesaling activities (Sec. 4 Professional Licensing Act of December 15, 1970). It can also modify an existing regulation to remedy entry difficulties into a specific profession. In that case the modification may however not enlarge the definition of the profession or make the entry requirements more severe. (Sec. 3 §8 Professional Licensing Act of December 15, 1970 as modified by the Act of August 4, 1978). Finally the Government may at any time modify existing regulations in order to ensure the coordination imposed by international treaties (Sec. 3 §7 Professional Licensing Act of December 15, 1970).
16. The Minister, however, only exceptionally formulates a veto.
17. For example, the professional knowledge of restaurant holders should, according to

the applicable licensing regulation, also incorporate: "elementary notions of the different physical, chemical and biochemical phenomena, their influence during the fabrication, the cooking and the conservation of products. Elementary notions as to the nutritive needs of the human organism". Furthermore all useful information concerning public transport, entertainment and local tourism has to be available on request: this is also named "professional knowledge". The regulation further requires the elementary knowledge of the law applicable to the exercised profession *and* to e.g. "brewery contracts" (whether the professional exploits a pub or not).

18. Compare Monopolkommission, 1985, 74, citing figures of 100.000 to 200.000 DM. Thus, entry barriers seem too low to preclude entry.
19. Court of Appeals Brussels, June 7, 1983, *Ingénieur-Conseil*, 1983, 205.
20. Sec. 58 of the V.A.T. Laws provides for the obligation to sell cigarettes at the price mentioned on the tax strip and thus outlaws price competition at the retail level. Belgium abounds in cigarette shops. In most of these assortments are larger than in supermarkets. We do however not believe that greater choice possibilities outweigh the costs of the absence of price competition.
21. The licensing of restaurants, for example, was clearly an effort to protect Belgian businessmen from foreign competition. The Belgian legislator even excluded the popular "fritures" (itinerant traders who sell chips on the street) from the scope of the regulation. If quality improvement were the aim of the professional licensing, stricter rules for Chinese lumpias than for own Belgian chips would not be justifiable.
22. Results of research performed at the University of Antwerp Law School (working papers in Dutch are available).

6. REFERENCES

Areeda, Phillip and Turner, Donald T., "Predatory Pricing and Related Practices under Section 2 of the Sherman Act", *Harvard Law Review*, February 1975, 88, 697–733.

Beales, Howard, Craswell, Richard and Salop, Steven C., "The Efficient Regulation of Consumer Information", *Journal of Law and Economics*, December 1981, 24, 491–539.

Boddewyn, J.J., *Belgian Public Policy toward Retailing since 1789*, Michigan State University, 1971.

Daems, Herman and De Grauwe, Paul, "Determinanten van de overheidsreglementering", in *Overheidsinterventies. Effectiviteit en efficiëntie*, Leuven, Departement Toegepaste Economische Wetenschappen, 1981, 25–41.

Kaufmann, Pieter Joachim, *Passing Off and Misappropriation in the Law of Unfair Competition*, Rotterdam, 1984.

Monopolkommission, *Die Konzentration im Lebensmittelhandel*, Baden-Baden: Nomos Verlagsgesellschaft. 1985.

Moore, Thomas G., "The Purpose of Licensing", *Journal of Law and Economics*, October 1961, 93–117.

Olson, Mancur, *The Logic of Collective Action*, Cambridge: Harvard University Press, 1971.

Peltzman, Sam, "Toward a More General Theory of Regulation", *Journal of Law and Economics*, August 1976, 19, 211–240.

Posner, Richard A., "Theories of Economic Regulation", *Bell Journal of Economics*, Autumn 1974, 5, 335–358.

Stigler, George J., "The Theory of Economic Regulation", *Bell Journal of Economics*, Spring 1971, 2, 3–21.

Swennen, Henri. "De vestigingswetgeving", *Tijdschrift voor Privaatrecht*, 1979, N ° 3–4, 16, 439–454.

Swennen, Henri and Van den Bergh, Roger, *Overzicht van rechtspraak Wet Handelspraktijken (1976–1982)*, Antwerpen: Kluwer Rechtswetenschappen, 1983.

Van den Bergh, Roger, "Stop concurrentie in uw tank", *Tijdschrift voor Belgisch Handelsrecht*, October 1984, 17, 585–613.

Van den Bergh, Roger and Van de Velde, Jacqueline, "Belgisch Vestigingsrecht", in Dillemans Roger, ed., *Rechtsgids*, Gent, 1985.

ASSESSING THE EFFECTIVENESS AND ECONOMIC EFFICIENCY OF AN E.E.C. POLLUTION CONTROL DIRECTIVE: THE CONTROL OF DISCHARGES OF MERCURY TO THE AQUATIC ENVIRONMENT

John Ashworth, Ivy Papps and David J. Storey

1. INTRODUCTION

In an earlier paper (Guruswamy et al. (1983)) we traced the development of an EEC Directive designed to reduce discharges of mercury to the aquatic environment. This paper extends that work by conducting an economic appraisal of the efficiency and effectiveness of the Directive.

To conduct this essentially ex-post appraisal several questions must be answered. First, to what extent can changes in the discharges of mercury to the aquatic environment be attributed to the Directive, and, conversely, how much is attributable to other factors such as changes in demand for the final product (chlorine and caustic soda), technical change, price of inputs etc.? Second, once the impact of the Directive is isolated, to what extent has the improvement in environmental quality obtained through discharge reduction been achieved in an economically efficient manner? In short did the Commission impose a control mechanism designed to achieve value for money in environmental improvement? Finally it is important to understand the base and assumptions on which the Commission formulated its policy. Did it collect relevant information? Did it use the information which it collected in a way which would achieve "best" results?

The importance of this appraisal is not simply for *ex-post* purposes. Instead, since the Mercury Directive was the first of the so-called "black-listed" substances, it is designed to inform policy debate on other substances where controls are currently being debated or where controls are expected to be imposed in the future.

2. BACKGROUND

In November 1973 as part of its first Environmental Action Programme, the Council of Ministers of the European Economic Community required the Commission officials to develop a Directive controlling the discharges of dangerous substances to European waterways. This requirement was fulfilled by the so-called "Parent" Directive[1] (proposed in October 1974 and adopted in May 1976) which required the development of further Directives on specific substances (including mercury). These "Offspring" Directives were to provide for the control of discharges by means either of "limit values" placed directly on discharges (that is, the definition of a maximum allowable discharge from each plant) or by the use of "environmental quality objectives" (EQOs) which defined the minimum quality of the receiving waters. Member states were to be allowed to use whichever of these two methods of control seemed appropriate. In March 1982, after protracted negotiations, the European Council of Ministers agreed the first important offspring Directive[2] (the Mercury Directive) which was intended to control discharges of mercury from the chlor-alkali industry.[3]

The chlor-alkali industry produces chlorine, caustic soda and an economically insignificant amount of hydrogen by a process of electrolysis in a brine solution using a mercury cathode and a graphite anode during which mercury is discharged into neighbouring waterways. During the 1970s, there were approximately 9 million tonnes of chlorine capacity located in the countries of the European Community, most of it in Germany, Italy, France and the UK. There are two types of mercury cell plant: waste-brine and recirculating-brine. For given levels of capacity, output and expenditure on pollution control, waste-brine plants are thought to discharge more mercury than the recirculating-brine plants.[4] Less than 20% of total EEC capacity is of the waste-brine type. However, of the UK's 1.3 million tonnes of capacity, over 70% consisted of waste-brine plants.

During the period between the agreement of the Parent Directive and the proposal for the Mercury Directive, the Commission undertook research both into the dangers of mercury and conditions in the chlor-alkali industry and on the impact of controls upon the European industry.[5] From this it concluded that waste-brine and recirculating-brine plants were, in fact, different and the proposed Mercury Directive took this difference into account by allowing greater discharges from waste-brine plants.[6] The Commission was also convinced that discharges depended only on the capacity of the plant and not on its actual output and, accordingly, framed the limit values in terms of plant capacity.

3. THE ISSUES

It is clear that the development of the Directive was underpinned by the Commission's belief in these two propositions about the nature of the discharge function: (a) the difference between waste-brine and recirculating-brine plants and (b) the belief that discharges depend on capacity rather than output. If these propositions were not correct, the outcome of the Directive may be quite different from that intended.

If both types of plants face the same discharge function, the differential treatment accorded by the Directive offers an artificial advantage to waste-brine plants which will be able to operate with lower marginal abatement costs than will the recirculating-brine plants. Such a difference in marginal abatement costs is clearly inefficient. The outcome may also offend against some notion of fairness since the waste-brine plants have been given an "undeserved" comparative advantage.

The implications of the importance of capacity rather than output as a determinant of discharges are somewhat more complex. Clearly capacity and output are related to some extent and if all plants are operated at full capacity (or if all have the same degree of capacity utilisation) then, even if the Commission were wrong and output were important, the Directive would have the same effect as it would have if it were framed "correctly". Consider, however, the situation where capacity utilisation is, for some reason,[7] inversely related to capacity. If output were – as the firm believed – an important determinant of discharges, the larger plant would find it relatively easier to achieve its discharge target as set by the Directive in terms of capacity. Again this difference in treatment of the two plants has implications for both the efficiency and equity effects of the Directive. Moreover, if both plants are owned by the same firm, a Directive framed in terms of capacity provides an incentive to shift some production from the small to the large plant, thus introducing a further source of inefficiency by persuading the firm to undertake production with levels of capacity utilisation which they would otherwise not have chosen. Thus, although the distinction between capacity and output may not matter in some cases, there are situations in which it is of some importance and it is, therefore, necessary for policymakers to identify the discharge function correctly.

We may, therefore, assess policy-making by the Commission in this area by asking four empirically testable questions:

- was the Commission correct in its assumption that waste-brine and recirculating-brine plants face different discharge functions?
- was the Commission correct in its crucial assumption that *capacity*, rather than *output*, was the main determinant of variations in quantities of mercury discharged?
- was the Mercury Directive efficient in achieving specified reductions in discharges at lowest *aggregate* cost to the industry?
- to what extent can any observed reductions in discharges be attributed to the Directive?

4. THE DISCHARGE FUNCTION

To determine the extent to which output/capacity determines discharges of effluent it is necessary to specify a discharge function, constructed from data provided by firms in the industry. It is, however, far from clear what exactly the Commission believed this relationship to be. There was general agreement that abatement equipment reduced discharges of effluent. However, members of the Commission told us emphatically that, given abatement expenditures, discharges depended only on capacity and this view conflicts with that of the largest UK producer which told us that *output* was an important determinant of discharges. The belief that the discharge function was different for waste-brine and recirculating-brine plants but the same for all plants of the same type was embodied in the Directive but with no explicit discussion of the nature of this difference. Indeed, during the long debate on the Mercury Directive, there was never any discussion of the exact formulation of the discharge function. Unlike the Commission we have set out to estimate this important function.

During the period 1972–80 there were eight chlor-alkali plants operating within the UK. Of these, four were waste-brine plants operated by a single large chemical producer and four were recirculating- brine plants operated by three different firms. All eight plants provided us with annual data[8] on discharges, capacity, output and expenditure (on capital and current account) for abatement.

Since it seems likely that there is a flow of information between plants (particularly between those operated by the same firm), the operation of one plant will depend to some extent on the operation of others and there will, therefore, be contemporaneous correlation. We do not know the precise nature of this interdependence so we require an estimating procedure which will take it into account in a fairly general way. We decided, therefore, to use the technique of seemingly unrelated regression (SUR) as developed by Zellner (1962)[9] to estimate the discharge function for the UK chlor-alkali industry.

In its most general form, the beliefs of the various parties about the discharge function may be written as:

$$D_{it} = f(Q_{it}, E_{it}, C_{it}) \tag{1}$$

where D_{it} = discharges of mercury from plant i in year t (Kg of mercury)
Q_{it} = output of plant i in year t (1000 tonnes of chlorine)
E_{it} = *accumulated* annualised expenditure on abatement equipment by plant i at year t (£1000)[10]
C_{it} = capacity of plant i at time t (measured in 1000 tonnes p.a. of chlorine capacity)

We have few *a priori* expectations about the functional form to be examined but given the nature of the data it was felt that only simple formulations should be examined. Given this the specification

$$\ln D_{it} = \alpha_i + \beta_i \ln Q_{it} + \gamma_i \ln E_{it} + \delta_i \ln C_{it} + u_{it} \quad (2)$$

would seem appropriate.[11] Using this equation the first of the four questions of Section III can be examined.

Unfortunately, problems arise in estimating the equations (or more precisely, given the interrelationship between plants, the system) in an unpooled form. The capacity of each plant is unchanged over the whole estimating period thus giving perfect multicollinearity with the constant term for each plant. While there is obviously no problem if pooling of plants is appropriate it is necessary to test whether coefficients are indeed equal before pooling is imposed. This leaves a choice of estimating either:

$$\ln D_{it} = \alpha_i + \beta_i \ln Q_{it} + \gamma_i \ln E_{it} + u_{it} \quad (3)$$

or:

$$\ln D_{it} = \beta_i \ln Q_{it} + \gamma_i \ln E_{it} + \delta_i \ln C_{it} + u_{it} \quad (4)$$

and then running a series of statistical tests to see whether restrictions (i.e. pooling) are possible. An example of the type of restriction possible would be that $\beta_i = \beta\ \forall_i$; that is, the effect of output on discharges is the same no matter which plant we are observing. Thus, if the Commission were correct in their beliefs, β_i would be equal to zero and γ_i would be negative and the same for all plants of the same type. The case of α_i and δ_i are clearly different. If the Commission were correct then δ_i would be the same for each plant while α_i would be different since capacities differed.[12] The weight of the argument might suggest that (4) is the preferred specification. However, estimation of equation (4) revealed that, while β_i and γ_i could be pooled and, therefore, could be treated as the same for all waste-brine plants, it was not possible to pool for capacity and δ_i should be considered as different for each plant. Since the Commission's hypothesis regarding capacity is rejected from the estimation of equation (4) the specification of equation (3) was examined.

The estimated equation for the four waste-brine plants was found to be

$$\ln D_{it} = \underset{(0.15)}{4.09} + \underset{(0.04)}{0.98} \ln Q_{it} - \underset{(0.03)}{0.28} \ln E_{it} \quad (5)$$

(Estimated standard errors in parentheses)

$R^2 = 0.86 \qquad \chi^2_8 = 10.91$

Although the calculation of some of these statistics differs from that used in OLS, their interpretation is the usual one. The χ^2 statistic is a test of pooling; that is, it tests the hypothesis that data from different plants should be treated as though they came from the same plant. The critical value for the statistic in this case is 15.5 and, therefore, the hypothesis is accepted. In other words, all four waste-brine plants appear to face the same discharge function.

It will be seen that equation (5) is incompatible with the Commission's beliefs for the waste-brine plants which dominate the UK industry. This result supports the firm's hypothesis that output does, in fact, affect discharges since the coefficient on output is significantly different from zero while the constant is significant and the same for all plants suggesting that capacity has no independent effect. Finally the sign of the abatement expenditure coefficient is significantly negative as predicted.[13]

The results for the four recirculating-brine plants are more ambiguous. Using equation (3) as for the waste-brine plants, we found that pooling was not possible. This suggests that for recirculating-brine plants the Commission may have been correct in their belief that capacity is a determinant of discharges. Hence the estimated equations for the four UK recirculating brine plants were found to be

$$\begin{aligned}
\ln D_{1t} &= \underset{(0.51)}{1.22} \ln C_{1t} + \underset{(0.29)}{0.70} \ln Q_{1t} - \underset{(0.36)}{0.72} \ln E_{1t} \\
\ln D_{2t} &= \underset{(0.66)}{1.34} \ln C_{2t} + \underset{(0.29)}{0.70} \ln Q_{2t} - \underset{(0.36)}{0.72} \ln E_{2t} \\
\ln D_{3t} &= \underset{(0.48)}{1.04} \ln C_{3t} + \underset{(0.29)}{0.70} \ln Q_{3t} - \underset{(0.36)}{0.72} \ln E_{3t} \qquad (6) \\
\ln D_{4t} &= \underset{(0.48)}{0.93} \ln C_{4t} + \underset{(0.29)}{0.70} \ln Q_{4t} - \underset{(0.36)}{0.72} \ln E_{4t} \\
R^2 &= 0.76 \qquad \chi^2_6 = 6.78
\end{aligned}$$

The coefficients on output and expenditure can be constrained to be the same for all plants as indicated by the χ^2 statistic for pooling but pooling is not possible for capacity. The results are presented in the above manner to emphasise that the four equations were treated simultaneously.[14]

It can be seen[15] that there is a significant positive coefficient on output and a negative coefficient on expenditure, which is significant at the 10% significance level. It also can be seen that the results are unclear regarding capacity but that pooling is rejected. This means that the implications are different for each plant. Further implications are rather more difficult given the number of observations and the possible multicollinearity between capacity and output. All the equations are jointly significant in the two variables but examination of the individual plants is interesting in that in one of the cases capacity is clearly significant, in two of the cases it hovers on the borderline of significance and in the fourth case it is insignificant. While this must be treated with caution, it does suggest that the Commission may have acted on incorrect information to regard capacity as overwhelmingly more important than output.

In spite of the difficulties, however, the results do appear to make a number of points. Firstly, it would appear that the Commission were correct in treating the different production processes separately and hence the firms were correct in lobbying to be treated differently.[16] The elasticity with respect to output is less for recirculating-brine plants. However, this coefficient is significant, which is in contradiction to the Commission. The disappointment for the Commission must be with regard to capacity which appears to have no consistent influence. The expenditure variable is on the borderline of significance. One further issue to note is that given pooling on expenditure is permissible it appears that the Commission was correct in assuming that all firms would use the abatement equipment, purchased from a single supplier in the case of the recirculating-brine plants, equally efficiently.

One way of interpreting the Commission's beliefs in the light of the relevance of both output and capacity for recirculating-brine plants is that the elasticity of discharges with respect to capacity is much larger than that with respect to output. We may estimate these elasticities directly from equation (6). The elasticity with respect to output is 0.70 which is lower than for the waste-brine plants where it is 0.98 and with respect to capacity is 1.22, 1.34, 1.04 and 0.93 for the four plants respectively. It can be seen that, although the elasticities are higher for all four plants, that these values are calculated at the point estimates and some of these have large estimated standard errors attached. Further, the elasticities are not so much higher that capacity can be thought to dominate output.

Although we have a limited set of data and the quality of that from the recirculating-brine is not uniformly satisfactory, the empirical information available to us is at least as good, to our knowledge, as that used by the Commission. Our conclusion must be that, on this point, the Commission did not do very well and failed to identify correctly the relevant discharge functions, most notably with respect to output. It remains to be seen what effect this failure had on the Commission's ability to formulate an efficient and effective policy.

5. THE EFFICIENCY OF THE MERCURY DIRECTIVE

In this context efficiency is defined as obtaining the maximum possible reduction in effluent discharged for any given sum of expenditure by the

Table 1. Maximum allowable discharges of mercury and marginal costs of abatement for plants of the UK chlor-alkali industry implied by the mercury directive

	Plant	Maximum allowable discharges of mercury (Kg p.a.)	Marginal cost of abatement (£ per Kg reduction of mercury p.a.)
Waste-brine	1	300	22,000
	2	285	25,250
	3	445	28,370
	4	3750	1,298
Recirculating-brine	5	70	3,926
	6	30	5,108
	7	85	889
	8	150	437

industry as a whole. The condition for this efficiency is that the marginal abatement cost of each discharge should in the most simple case be equal (see, for example Baumol and Oates (1975)). Hence, where the marginal costs of each discharger differ, then requiring the low marginal cost abaters to reduce their discharges by a single unit of effluent and relaxing the controls upon high cost abaters to allow an increase in discharges by one unit will achieve the same level of total discharges at lower *aggregate* cost.

Unfortunately we have no information about the relationship between discharges and the quality of the receiving waters.[17] Therefore, our analysis of the efficiency of the Directive must concentrate on the implications of the quantities discharged at the limit values for each plant. Table 1 shows the maximum allowable discharges of mercury and the implied marginal costs for each plant calculated on the basis of our estimated equations (5) and (6) for waste-brine and recirculating-brine plants respectively. Equations (5) and (6) show that the firm may incur abatement costs either by reducing output – thus reducing revenue – or by installing abatement equipment – thus increasing capital and operating costs. However, both the firm and the Commission believe that the only feasible – i.e. the lowest cost – method of abatement is the installation of abatement equipment. Preliminary analysis reported in Ashworth et al. (1986) suggests that this belief is correct for the discharge levels specified by the Mercury Directive for all sensible outputs. Thus, the relevant marginal abatement costs (MAC) are given by:

$$MAC_{iw} = -\frac{\delta E}{\delta D} = \frac{1000 \times \hat{E}_{it}}{0.28 \times D_{it}} \qquad (7)$$

for the ith waste-brine plant and

$$MAC_{ir} = -\frac{\delta E}{\delta D} = \frac{1000 \times \hat{E}_{it}}{0.72 \times D_{it}} \tag{8}$$

for the ith recirculating-brine plant where D_{it} is the maximum permitted discharge from plant i and $\hat{E}_{it}$ is the value of expenditure required by plant i to achieve D_{it} while producing at its average level of output. MAC is, therefore, measured in £s per Kg reduction in mercury discharged.

These marginal costs must necessarily be examined in the same light as other results calculated using point estimates but it is hoped that they can give an indication of the possible efficiency of the Directive. As can be seen from Table 1, the results are quite marked. It would appear that the effect of the Directive on waste-brine operators may be to close a small plant or in the case of one firm operating a number of plants to close some of these.[18]

As far as recirculating-brine plants are concerned, these are clearly affected in the calculation by the coefficient on expenditure and this cannot be considered very reliable. However, the same figure, given that pooling is possible on expenditure, is used in all cases so some conclusions may be drawn. Here it would appear that small plants seem to have been penalised more heavily than larger plants. Further, in comparison with the recirculating-brine producers the small waste-brine plants have been harder hit by the Directive. The implication is that economies of scale exist in the industry in terms of mercury discharges, even if they appear very slight in the chemical production process. The Directive may have had wider-ranging effects than possibly was imagined.

Overall, it would appear that the Directive has not achieved an efficient solution regarding the allowable discharges. Moreover, it appears that the imposition of uniform emission standards, by taking no account of the lower marginal costs enjoyed by larger plants, have given a cost advantage to these plants.

In reaching this conclusion, however, there are several qualifications which have to be borne in mind. First, we are only examining discharges and not damage. Thus it could be argued that the major waste-brine plant is discharging at a location where the damage effect of its discharge is minimal in comparison to the location of other plants. In fact, there may be some validity in this argument but as can be seen from the above discussion the result is achieved more by chance (and perhaps powerful lobbying) than by the Commission being fully aware of the decisions which it was taking. Secondly, the marginal abatement costs are estimated on the basis of capacity and output in 1980. Since that date there has been a major reduction in output with the closure of three plants. Bearing in mind the importance of output, at least for the waste-brine plants, it is unclear whether these relationships continue in today's conditions. In our opinion the results of our study suggest that a re-examination of these issues is imperative to avoid resources being frittered away.

6. THE EFFECTIVENESS OF THE MERCURY DIRECTIVE

Between 1972 and 1980, discharges of mercury from the UK chlor-alkali industry fell from a high of about 36,000 Kg in 1973 to approximately 13,000 Kg in 1980 and as a result, by 1980 most of UK plants could meet – or were close to meeting – the emission standards set in the Directive. One might be tempted to conclude that the Directive, therefore, had little effect in the UK since no further reductions of discharges were required when the Directive was implemented. Such an interpretation would, however, ignore the long debate leading up to the final Directive. Indeed, a proposal for the Mercury Directive was published in 1979 containing similar limit values while the debate after the acceptance of the Parent Directive in 1976 made it quite clear that the chlor-alkali industry was likely to be an early target. Thus, during much of the decade, there were expectations on the part of the chlor-alkali industry that they were going to be subject to control. It may be argued, therefore, that the industry reacted to these expectations by installing abatement equipment in anticipation of such control, and this reaction may be considered as the effect of the Directive. However, the industry could not have held such expectations before the end of 1974 when the proposal for the Parent Directive was published. Moreover, firms may be expected to respond to such expectations with a substantial lag. For such reasons,[19] we think it likely that the chlor-alkali industry would have been able to respond to expectations of a Directive some time between 1975 and 1978.

We define the impact of the Directive, I, as the average proportion of the fall in discharges which can be attributed to the Directive. The measure is

$$I = \frac{1}{n} \sum_{t=1}^{n} \frac{(ED_t - AD_t)}{(AD_0 - AD_t)} \qquad (9)$$

where AD_t and ED_t are respectively actual and expected discharges in year t and AD_0 is the maximum discharges for each plant, at whatever time period. The sum of these gives the maximum discharges that were

Table 2. Values of I for waste-brine and recirculating-brine plants, 1975–8

	Waste-brine		Recirculating-brine	
	Point Estimate	95% Confidence Interval	Point Estimate	95% Confidence Interval
1975	0.141	+0.005, +0.317	0.219	−0.324, +1.281
1976	0.049	−0.068, +0.203	0.180	−0.276, +1.087
1977	0.041	−0.070, +0.189	0.163	−0.222, +0.932
1978	0.007	−0.108, +0.159	0.158	−0.258, +0.993

observed in the sub-industry, although not necessarily in the same time period. While it is aesthetically more pleasing to use discharges in 1972 as AD_o, this is not really feasible in this case due to missing data from one of the recirculating-brine plants. It should be noted that all the maximum figures relate to either 1972, 1973 or 1974.[20] Year 1 is the impact date – that is, the year in which the firm began to react to expectations of a Directive. Year n is 1980 – the last year for which we have data.[21] Expected discharges are measured as the discharges predicted on the assumption that abatement expenditure after the impact date would have been zero in the absence of the Directive.[22] In other words we attribute all expenditure on abatement after the impact date to the Directive[23] and, therefore, set $K_n = 0$ for all years after the impact date. Expected discharges are calculated on the basis of equations (5) and (6) for waste-brine and recirculating-brine plants respectively. The results are presented in Table 2. Since we are unsure of the exact impact date, we have calculated I for the years 1975–8 inclusive.

The confidence interval was found by calculating the confidence interval for the estimated value of $\ln D_{it}$ and thus obtaining the corresponding estimates for the range of D_{it} for each plant. We then aggregated these estimates over all plants to form ED_t and, thus, calculated the corresponding values of I. This interval cannot be described as the "best" for I (although it is the best for $\ln D_{it}$) but the "best" interval cannot be calculated since we have standard errors only for the estimating equation, that is, for $\ln D_{it}$. However, it is *a* 95% confidence interval and we believe that it provides a better indicator than does a point estimate alone. Clearly, if the extreme value is taken, then the impact of the Directive is probably overstated.

It can be seen that the maximum effect of the Directive under the most generous interpretation is 0.317 for waste-brine plants, that is, at most 32% of the fall in discharges can be attributed to the Directive. However, this would imply that the firm realised at the end of 1974 that they would be the subject of controls and responded by introducing abatement techniques less than fifteen months later. Such rapidity of reaction seems unlikely although we report the results in order to be as generous as possible to the policy makers. For the reasons outlined above, we, ourselves, believe that 1977 or 1978 are more likely impact dates and, in this case, the maximum impact appears between 0.16 and 0.19 for waste-brine plants.

The case of the recirculating-brine plants is much less clear. Primarily, this is because the estimated relationship is less good and hence large standard errors are present. In this case, the most generous interpretation would be that all of the discharge reduction was due to the Directive, again assuming a very fast reaction on the part of the firms.[24] Taking our preferred dates then the maximum appears to be between 0.93 and 0.99. However, this result should be treated with some caution. Had the point estimate been used the reduction would be between 0.158 and 0.219 and for all years the intervals include zero. Further, the nature of the data available is less than ideal as only two of the plants undertook any expenditure on abatement activities in the period and very little of this expenditure occurred after 1979. One other issue is to consider the average annual discharges for recirculating-brine plants for the period 1972–1975 against the average annual discharges for 1976–1980. In the first period these were 4242 kg of mercury per year, while in the second period these were 3817 and so it can be seen that the fall in discharges is only around 10% of the total at the beginning of the period.[25]

7. SUMMARY AND CONCLUSIONS

This examination of the Mercury Directive suggests that the EEC made two major decisions; first to distinguish between waste-brine plants and recirculating-brine plants, and secondly to frame the Directive by assuming that capacity, rather than output, determined discharges.

This paper has examined these decisions *using data for the UK*, and perhaps the results may not be relevant to other Community countries to which the legislation applied. Nevertheless it appears that the Commission was correct in distinguishing between waste-brine and recirculating-brine plants since the groups have (statistically) significantly different characteristics. Our results, however, suggest that the Commission was significantly in error in framing the Directive in terms of capacity rather than output. It was pointed out[26] by the chemical giant operating the waste-brine plants that output did affect discharges and this assertion appears justified from our data. More disconcertingly, perhaps, the results for the recirculating-brine plants show that the independent effect of capacity is no stronger than that of output. Bearing in mind that the majority of European industry (excluding the UK) used the recirculating-brine process this is a potentially serious error.

Given these errors it should not be surprising that, in terms of economic efficiency, the Directive performs poorly. In particular, we note the major variations in the marginal abatement costs incurred by different UK plants when meeting the terms of the Directive and in particular the presence of major scale economies. A fully convincing case that the Commission policy was inefficient could only be made by examining the locations at which the discharges were made but it seems unlikely that differences in damage varied inversely in proportion to the major variations in marginal abatement costs. But even if they did vary in this way, such a result would only have been achieved by chance and provides no measure of confidence that an efficient allocation of water space is likely to be achieved by future Directives. To some degree our final result that a relatively small proportion of the reduction in discharges of effluent was attributable to the Directive prevented poorly informed EEC policy from adversely affecting the industry. However, the lessons of mercury need to be understood more fully in Brussels.

In our view policies which will cost European industry hundreds of millions of pounds have to be preceded by fully adequate economic studies. Those studies undertaken on behalf of the Commission could never have proved to be satisfactory since they failed to address themselves to the crucial question of the estimation of the discharge function. Such a function for the industry, or sub-industry, *must* be constructed so that the marginal abatement costs of differing combinations of discharge reductions may be formulated. This enables the efficiency considerations to be specially identified and any potential equity judgements incorporated and assessed. In the case of mercury, we believe the additional costs to the chlor-alkali industry have not been excessive since the Directive itself had had relatively little impact. The same may not be true for other industries in future.

NOTES

*We are grateful to Jill Peters for computing assistance and to the firms of the UK chlor-alkali industry for providing the data for this paper. The data collection was financed by a Special Research Grant from the University of Durham. Goran Skogh and two anonymous referees provided helpful comments on earlier drafts. Any mistakes which may remain after all this help are our responsibility.

1. EEC (1976).
2. EEC (1982).
3. Guruswamy et al. (1983) for further details of the development of the Directive.
4. This implies a belief that the average costs of abatement are higher for water-brine plants than for recirculating-brine but *not* necessarily that marginal costs differ to the same degree. Within the text of the Mercury Directive, however, there was no evidence that the Commission were aware of this distinction.
5. Economist Intelligence Unit (1977), Schubert (n.d.) and Steiner (n.d.).
6. The Mercury Directive sets limit values of 5 grams per tonne of chlorine capacity for waste-brine and 1 gram per tonne of chlorine capacity for recirculating-brine plants. The EQOs are 1 μg per litre of water affected by discharges for both waste-brine and recirculating-brine plants. Both limit values and EQOs to be achieved by 1 July 1986. Less stringent limit values (8 grams per tonne) applied during the early 1980s.

7. Perhaps the small plant has a more effective marketing department or, in the case of a multi-plant firm, the firm find this pattern of capacity utilisation to be most efficient. This is not an artificial example. Such a pattern was observed for the British plants.
8. One of the recirculating-brine plants could provide data only from 1974.
9. Ashworth et al. (1984) provide further details of the difficulties of estimation and the use of this technique. Although it is discussed quite frequently in econometrics textbooks and is therefore, theoretically, a common technique, it is not generally available on standard computer packages with suitable testing of pooling or incorporating in the possibility of serially correlated errors. In the course of this investigation both of these possibilities had to be considered. Before applying SUR we naturally considered a standard F test for total pooling and for pooling of particular variables, which includes the least-squares with dummy variables method, to see whether pooling was possible without recourse to SUR but found it was necessary to take the contemporaneous correlation into account if any pooling was to be possible. (No attempts were made to use variance-components methods as it was believed that the correlation was across plants rather than over time. Given that serial correlation could be accommodated with SUR following Parks (1967) this gave further benefit to following this approach). Ashworth et al. (1984) discuss this point in more detail, and also ran tests suggested by Coniffe (1982) to test whether SUR is a correct procedure. Given our initial belief that contemporaneous correlation probably existed, SUR looks appropriate and it is not surprising that simple tests of pooling were rejected while tests using SUR were accepted.
10. E_t was calculated as:

$$E_t = \sum_{n=0}^{t-1} \frac{r_n K_n}{P_n} + \frac{X_t}{P_t}$$

where P_n is the value of the RPI in year n, r_n is the nominal rate of interest measured by the Local Authority bond rate, K_n is expenditure on abatement equipment in year n and X_t is expenditure on abatement activities on current account. For further details of the suitability of this variable as an index of abatement activities see Ashworth et al. (1984).
11. Clearly a Box-Cox (1964) examination would be the way to examine the functional form. For all the results given, a grid search (over 0.1 intervals for λ) was done and relative to this it was found that the specification chosen was not significantly different from the best result: the test being the likelihood ratio test (see Maddala (1977): p. 317)) at 10% significance level. These results suggest the specification chosen was reasonable. For further comments see Ashworth et al. (1984).
12. While it is true that the constant, α_i, can encompass more than just the capacity effect, it must be remembered that, since capacity is the same in each period, it would have the same effect in explaining variation in discharges *in an unpooled version.* Moreover, although testing for α_i identical for all plants cannot *prove* that the Commission's beliefs were correct since differences in the α_i could be due to variations in omitted variables, a finding that α_i was the same for all plants would give us some confidence that the Commission was incorrect because it would be unlikely that omitted variables would nullify the capacity effect.
13. Using the equation (4) with capacity included gives estimated elasticities of discharges on capacity of between 2.8 and 4.1 while that on output is only 0.97. It may be that the Commission misinterpreted the information in the light of perceiving greater

possible effects from capacity. It should be noted that although it would be anticipated that output and capacity are correlated, multicollinearity did not appear to be a problem as individual 't' tests proved to be significant. As would be anticipated $\delta_i \ln C_{it}$ for each plant is almost identical to α and hence predictions using a functional form which includes capacity and without pooling this variable would give very similar implications regarding the effect of the Directive. This gives further support for the answers given to the question posed in later sections. It would clearly be possible to specify an equation which included capacity and excluded output. It would appear that this is the type of specification which the Commission had in mind. The authors' view is that the only way in which this would be feasible would be if output proved to be insignificant in the original equation (2). As stated in the text, our view is that if adjustments had to be made via output then in the long run these would be reflected in capacity changes but it would appear that legislation framed in output terms would encompass capacity whereas the reverse is not true hence the initial test using output. Given that output appears to matter there seems to be no gain in pursuing capacity separately.

14. These results are estimated assuming a first-order autoregressive error, in addition to the contemporaneous correlation imposed by using Zellner's approach. Results without this assumption are of broadly the same order and the reason for choosing these results are that, although the need to use AR(1) can be rejected at 5% significance level, it cannot be rejected at 10 %. Two of the calculated $\hat{\varrho}$ are significant and rather than using just these two values and imposing zero values elsewhere it was decided to allow $\hat{\varrho}$ to be calculated. The philosophy followed is that suggested by Judge et al. (1980) '. . . little is known about the relative powers of such test procedures or the relative efficiencies of the resulting preliminary test estimators. If single-equation results are any guide, the cost of assuming zero autocorrelation when it is present is likely to be much greater than the cost of assuming nonzero autocorrelation when it is zero'. The estimated values of $\hat{\varrho}$, calculated following the method of Parks (1967) are:

$$\hat{\varrho}_1 = 0.05$$

$$\hat{\varrho}_2 = 0.52$$

$$\hat{\varrho}_3 = 0.43$$

$$\hat{\varrho}_4 = 0.04$$

Results using the more sophisticated method of Guilkey and Schmidt (1973) are almost identical.

15. It should be noted that these results must be treated with caution. While the results given for the waste-brine plants give the same indication whatever considerations are made with regard to the presence of serial correlation or the inclusion of capacity, the results for the recirculating-brine plants are a little more volatile. The issue is further clouded by the data available. Here, again, comparisons with the position of the waste-brine plants is worth making. In the recirculating-brine case the abatement equipment was built into one of the plants and hence the plant had to be treated identically to another plant with no abatement expenditure. If the evidence of the waste-brine plants can be used then this should not be a serious problem. In so far as it is possible to tell over such a short period there appears to be no significant change in the relationship between output and discharges when expenditure on abatement activity is made. This is evidenced by the stability of the coefficient on

Table 3. Values of I_1 for waste-brine and recirculating-brine plants 1975–8

	Waste-brine		Recirculating-brine	
	Point Estimate	95% Confidence Interval	Point Estimate	95% Confidence Interval
1975	0.094	+0.004, +0.211	0.125	−0.144, +0.652
1976	0.034	−0.045, +0.139	0.106	−0.138, +0.591
1977	0.030	−0.047, +0.132	0.100	−0.126, +0.549
1978	0.004	−0.073, +0.107	0.095	−0.140, +0.566

output when a test was run but there are very few degrees of freedom. The additional problem of one of the plants only operating for seven of the nine years can be accommodated in estimation using the technique of Schmidt (1977). It was felt that we could not just ignore observations which were not from common time periods given the already small data set.

16. Estimating the whole industry together is a possibility but seems unduly sophisticated given the data. If this is done the results for the individual components stay much as reported. The problem is that Coniffe's test is very close to rejecting use of SUR as an appropriate technique for the whole industry.
17. To our knowledge, a systematic relationship is unknown at present. The Directive was formulated in the absence of such information. It must, however, be emphasised that this *is* a significant limitation since the damage caused by a unit of discharge varied according to what is discharged. The most sophisticated cost abatement models explicitly take location into account through a weighting system whereby discharges at location i where damages are reaching a threshold are weighted more heavily than at j where the river/estuary may be faster flowing and its diffusion/dilution effects greater. Examples of such models include those reviewed in Ackerman et al. (1974) or Rowley et al. (1979).
18. This is indeed what has occurred with two small waste-brine plants.
19. See Ashworth et al. (1987) for more detailed justification.
20. The results for waste-brine plant are unchanged whether $AD_o = AD\ 1972$ is used or the suggestion in the main script. The distinction is only needed for the recirculating-brine plants. It should be emphasised that whatever measure is used for AD_o that the large standard error gives the same implied results.
21. It is worth noting that this is not the only way of defining impact. An alternative specification would be:

$$I_1 = \frac{1}{n}\sum_{t=1}^{n}\frac{(ED_t - AD_t)}{AD_o}$$

which would measure the amount by which the Directive reduced discharges. However, since the reduction in discharges is so large in the waste-brine plants, it is interesting to know how much of the reduction can be attributed to the Directive. The values for I_1 are given in Table 3.

22. The estimation of expected discharges is an attempt to estimate what would have happened without the Directive. "Expected discharges" is *not*, therefore, the predicted values of the regression equation since the expected values of E_{it} are not equal to the actual values.
23. This extreme assumption clearly overestimates the impact of the Directive.
24. The presence of negative values is just a hazard of using statistics. We would not suggest that the Directive had a detrimental effect. Similarly, it is possible that the upper limits could give values above 100 %, again because of the use of intervals.
25. The figures for the first period are only approximate because of the missing data. The highest figure for discharges for this plant was used for both these two periods to arrive at the figure quoted.
26. In private discussion with the authors.

REFERENCES

Ackerman, B.R., Ackerman, S.R., Henderson, D. and Sawyer, J.W. *The Uncertain Search for Environmental Quality*. New York: Free Press, 1974.

Ashworth, J.S., Papps, I. and Peters, J. "The Estimation of the Costs of Reducing Mercury Discharges by a Chlor-Alkali Producer". Working Paper No. 70. Department of Economics, University of Durham, 1984. Revised, January 1986.

Ashworth, J.S., Papps, I. and Storey, D.J. 'Assessing the Impact upon the British Chlor-Alkali Industry of the EEC Directive on Discharges of Mercury into Waterways". *Land Economics*, (1987). Forthcoming.

Baumol, W.J. and Oates, W.E. *The Theory of Environmental Policy*. Englewood Cliffs: Prentice-Hall, 1975.

Box, G.E.P. and Cox, D.R. 'An Analysis of Transformations'. *Journal of Royal Statistical Society*, Series B, 26 (1964): 211–252.

Coniffe, D. "Testing the Assumptions of Seemingly Unrelated Regressions". *Review of Economics and Statistics*. 65 (1983):172–4.

Economist Intelligence Unit "The Economic Effects of Pollution Control Measures on Defined Industrial Sectors, Mercury Discharging Indistries". Report prepared for the Environmental and Consumer Protection Service Commission of the European Communities. Brussels, 1977.

EEC "Council Directive of 4 May 1976 on pollution caused by certain dangerous substances discharged into the aquatic environment of the community" (76/464/EEC). *Official Journal of the European Communities*. L81 (May 1976): 23–9.

EEC "Council Directive of 22 March 1982 on limit values and quality objectives for mercury discharges by the chlor-alkali electrolysis industry". *Official Journal of the European Communities*. L81 (March 1982): 29–33.

Guilkey, D.K. and Schmidt, P. "Estimation of Seemingly Unrelated Regressions with Vector Autoregressive Errors". *Journal of American Statistical Association*. 68 (1973): 642–7.

Guruswamy, L.D., Papps, I. and Storey, D.J. "The Development and Impact of an EEC Directive: The Control of Discharges of Mercury to the Aquatic Environment". *Journal of Common Market Studies*. XXII.1 (September 1983): 71–100.

Judge, G.G., Griffiths, W.E., Hill, R.C. and Lee, T.S. *The Theory and Practice of Econometrics*. London: Wiley, 1980.

Maddala, G.S. *Econometrics*. London: McGraw-Hill, 1977.

Rowley, C.K. et al. "A Study of Effluent Discharges to the River Tees". Department of Environment and Transport, Research Report No. 31. London: HMSO, 1979.

Parks, R.W. "Efficient Estimation of a System of Regression Equations When Disturbances are Both Serially and Contemporaneously Correlated". *Journal of the American Statistical Association*. 62 (1967): 500–509.

Schmidt, P. "Estimation of Seemingly Unrelated Regressions with Unequal Numbers of Observations". *Journal of Econometrics*. 5 (1977): 365–377.

Schubert, R.H.W. "Appraisal of the ecological consequences (ecotoxicity) of mercury discharges for the aquatic environment". Report submitted to the Environment and Consumer Protection Service, Commission of the European Communities, Brussels.

Steiner, C. J-P. "Abatement Techniques in the Control of Mercury Pollution". Report submitted to the Environment and Consumer Protection Service, Commission of the European Communities, by BNF Metal Technology Centre.

Zellner, A. "An Efficient Method of Estimating Seemingly Unrelated Regressions and Tests of Aggregation Bias". *Journal of the American Statistical Association*. 57 (1962): 348–368.

PARTICIPANTS OF THE CONFERENCE ON LAW AND ECONOMICS, BERLIN

Bruce Ackermann, Columbia University in the City of New York
Susan Rose-Ackermann, Columbia University in the City of New York
Michael Adams, Volkwirtschaftliches Institut, University of Bern
Peter H. Aranson, Dep. of Economics Emory University Atlanta
John Ashworth, Dep. of Economics, Durham University
Alexander van der Bellen, Institut f. Wirtschaftswissenschaften, University of Vienna
R. van den Berg, Dep. of Economics, University of Antwerpen
Charles B. Blankart, Dep. of Economics, Technical University Berlin
Catherine Montgomery Blight, School of Agriculture, University of Edinburgh
Jan C. Bongaerts, International Institute for Environment and Society, Wissenschaftszentrum Berlin
Roger Bowles, School of H. +S.S University of Bath
Nikolaus Bremer, FB Rechtswissenschaft, University of Hannover
Francisco Cabrillo Rodriguez, Catedratico de la Universidad, Madrid
Charles M. Cameron, Woodrow Wilson School of Public and International Affairs, Princeton University
William S. Comanor, Department of Economics, University of California, Santa Barbara
Barry D.D. Denyer-Green, Sussex, U.K.
Roland Eisen, FB Wirtschaftswissenschaften, Johann-Wolfgang-Goethe University, Frankfurt
Christina Gades, FG Rechtswissenschaft, University of Hamburg
Jens Fejo, Institute of European Market Law, University of Copenhagen
Jürgen Frank, University of Hannover
Jürgen Gotthold, FB Rechtswissenschaft, University of Bremen
Hugh S.E. Gravelle, Queen Mary College, Economics Department, University of London
David D. Haddock, Yale Law School
Dirk Heinrichs, International Institute for Environment and Society, Wissenschaftszentrum Berlin
Manfred J. Holler, Institute of Economics, University of Munich
Michael Hutter, Dep. of Economics, University of Munich

Gerhard Illing, Dep. of Economics, University of Munich
John A. Kay, Institute for Fiscal Studies, London
Otto Keck, International Institute for Environment and Society Wissenschaftszentrum Berlin
Guy Kirsch, Seminar für Finanzwissenschaft, University of Fribourg
Eckhard Knappe, FB Volkswirtschaftslehre und Sozialpolitik, University of Trier
Kornelius Kraft, International Institute of Management, Wissenschaftszentrum Berlin
Jean Dominique Lafay, Faculté Sciences Economiques, Université de Poitiers
Michael Lehmann, Max Planck Institut, Munich
Ulrich van Lith, University of Köln
Jonathan R. Macey, Emory University, School of Law, Atlanta
Dolores Tremewan Martin, School for Advanced Urban Studies, University of Bristol
Leonhard Männer, Volkswirtschaftliches Seminar, University of Göttingen
Ingolf Metze, Institut f. Wirtschafts- und Sozialwissenschaften, University of Münster
Dennis C. Mueller, Department of Economics, University of Maryland
J.M. Oliver, School of Business and Social Sciences, The Hatfield Polytechnic, Hertford
Ivy Papps, Dep. of Economics, University of Durham
Santos Pastor, Dep. de Economiy y Hacienda, Facultad de Dereche, Madrid University
Mark Pauly, Leonard Davis Institute of Health Economics, Philadelphia
Werner W. Pommerehne, Institut f. empirische Wirtschaftsforschung University of Zürich
William M. Rees, Lecturer in Law, Law Faculty, Durham University
Matthias Ruete, School of Law, University of Warwick
Markus Sailer, International Institute of Management, Wissenschaftszentrum Berlin
Hans-Bernd Schäfer, FB Rechtswissenschaft II, University of Hamburg
Ingo Schmidt, Institut f. Volkswirtschaftslehre, Hohenheim University Stuttgart
Dieter Schmidtchen, Department of Economics, University of the Saarland
Hermann Schnabl, Institut f. Sozialforschung, University of Stuttgart
Fritz Schneider, Institute of Economics, University of Linz
Klaus Schrüfer, Dep. of Economics, Johann-Wolfgang-Goethe-Universität Frankfurt
J.-Matthias Graf v.d. Schulenburg, International Institute of Management, Wissenschaftszentrum Berlin
Joachim Schwalbach, International Institute of Management, Wissenschaftszentrum Berlin
Petra Seidel, Universität-Gesamthochschule Siegen
Christian Seidl, Karl-Franzens-Universität, Graz
Göran Skogh, Dep. of Economics, University of Lund
Anne Staines, The School of Law, Newcastle upon Tyne Polytechnic
Ian Staines, Wessyngtech Software Engineering Ltd., Washington Tyne and Wear
R. Barry Thomas, Law Faculty, Durham University
Manfred Tietzel, FB Wirtschaftswissenschaft, University of Duisburg
Gordon Tullock, Center for Study of Public Choice, George Mason University, Fairfax
Michael Utton, Dep. of Economics, University of Reading
Cento Veljanovski, Faculty of Laws, University College London
Haary A.A. Verbon, Dep. of Economics, University of Amsterdam
Wolfgang Weigel, Institut f. Wirtschaftswissenschaften, University of Vienna
Bernhard Wilpert, Psychological Institute, Technical University of Berlin
Frans van Winden, Dep. of Economics, University of Amsterdam
Ulrich Witt, Dep. of Economics, University of Mannheim
Edward Ch. Zimmermann, Wissenschaftszentrum Berlin
Peter Zweifel, Institut für empirische Wirtschaftsforschung, University of Zürich

SUBJECT INDEX

GPSR Compliance

The European Union's (EU) General Product Safety Regulation (GPSR) is a set of rules that requires consumer products to be safe and our obligations to ensure this.

If you have any concerns about our products, you can contact us on ProductSafety@springernature.com

In case Publisher is established outside the EU, the EU authorized representative is:

Springer Nature Customer Service Center GmbH
Europaplatz 3
69115 Heidelberg, Germany

Batch number: 10824484

Printed by Printforce, the Netherlands